CHANGING JAPAN

CHANGING JAPAN

OPPORTUNITIES AND CHALLENGES FOR INDIA

Sanjana Joshi

Maulana Abul Kalam Azad Institute of Asian Studies, Kolkata

SHIPRA

Views expressed are those of author and not necessarily of the Institute.

ISBN: 978-81-7541-234-7

First Published in India in 2008

Changing Japan: Opportunities and Challenges for India

Published by :

SHIPRA PUBLICATIONS

115-A, Vikas Marg, Shakarpur, Delhi-110092 (India)
Tel. : 91-11-65277210, 22500954, Fax : 91-11-22458662
Email : info@shiprapublications.com
www.shiprapublications.com

Contents

Introduction

Why Study Japan?

- Japan was the first Asian economy to have miracle growth. In 1952, Japan was considered a "less-developed country," with per capita consumption roughly one fifth that of the United States. But over the following two decades, Japan averaged an annual growth rate of 8 per cent, enabling it to become the first country to move from "less-developed" to "developed" status in the post-war era. In 1968 its economy became the world's second largest, behind that of the United States.
- Though in the late 1990s Japan suffered its most severe recession since World War II it is still the third largest market economy in the world after the United States and China. In 2007 Japan's GDP was estimated to be US$ 4.36 trillion.
- Japan has become politically more active and self-confident, globally as well as regionally and even sent its self-defense forces to Iraq.
- Japan is the second largest contributor to the regular United Nations (UN) budget and many special UN programmes are critically dependent on Japan's contribution. It is a member of G-8 grouping. Regionally, it has used its political and economic power to promote the cohesion of ASEAN and foster security dialogues at various levels.
- Japan is the second largest donor country among the Development Assistance Committee (DAC) members after the United States with net Overseas Development Assistance (ODA) of US$ 11.6 billion in 2006.
- Japan is among India's top five trading partners. Total trade between India and Japan was more than US$ 7 billion during 2006-2007. Japanese foreign direct investment (FDI) into India

during 2005-07 has been to the tune of US$ 1.8 billion. Equity investment from Japan into India is also on the rise, touching almost US$ 4.9 billion.

- India in 1958 was the first country to which Japan extended loan aid. Since fiscal 1986 Japan has been India's largest aid donor. In FY 2003 India became the largest recipient of the Japanese ODA.
- At the political level the two countries have initiated a "Global and Strategic Partnership" that involves closer political and diplomatic coordination on bilateral, regional, multilateral and global issues, comprehensive economic engagement, stronger defense relations, greater technological cooperation as well as working towards a quantum increase in cultural ties, educational linkages and people-to-people contacts.

The study of Japan is therefore not merely about Japan itself, but quite relevant to Indian resurgence in a globalised international order. In the words of Carol Gluck "not to know about Japan is no longer an option". The background for this study is rooted in the need to assess the trajectory of Japan's international relations since the end of the Cold War and the objective is to highlight the required focal points in India's interaction with Japan as a global and strategic partner. The idea being that 'India-Japan Global and Strategic Partnership' cannot be analysed in isolation from the dynamics of contemporary international relations. The fundamental question that needs to be answered is: what is driving Japan's recent attempts to raise bilateral relations to a higher level and impart stronger political, economic and strategic dimensions to its bilateral relations with India?

In the aftermath of World War II, when Japan was being "humiliated and trampled upon by the victorious powers" India had advocated the speedy economic recovery of Japan and insisted that the world concede to Japan a position of honour and equality among the community of free nations. India invited Japan to participate in the New Delhi Asian Games as an independent nation in 1951; India was a central player in lobbying for Japan's entry into the United Nations and for Japan's participation in the first Afro-Asian Conference in Bandung in 1955.[1] India also dissociated itself from the victorious powers and did not sign the San Francisco Treaty with

Japan in 1951 but signed a separate Peace Treaty in 1952, a few months after having established diplomatic relations, in which it waived any claim to war-reparations.

The relations between the two countries cooled considerably with the advent of the Cold War, as Japan and India set out on quite different paths. Japan's post-war position towards Asia was derived from the way Tokyo was firmly incorporated into the United States' global strategy, within which it took on the role of America's ally. Indian foreign policy, on the other hand, was focused on an entirely different perspective in international relations—non-alignment. This was the important difference that conditioned the responses of both India and Japan to international issues and influenced how they viewed each other. Bilateral relations therefore moved haltingly and warily and for a long time remained limited to economic and cultural matters.

From the Indian point of view, of particular concern were Japan's responses to the following issues[2]:

Liberation of Goa: The Japanese government fell in line with its allies and expressed regret that force was used to settle a dispute.

Border Clashes with China: In his foreign policy address to the Diet on December 10, 1962 the Japanese Prime Minister stated, "The reality of the armed Sino-Indian clashes in the border dispute has demonstrated how unrealistic are advocacy of neutralism and mere calls for peace".

Wars with Pakistan: In 1965 Japan declared that all aid promised for 1965-66 and all project aid was suspended till the conflict with Pakistan was settled. Japanese project aid was announced only during Prime Minister Indira Gandhi's visit in June 1969. Japanese aid was also suspended in 1971.

Idea of Indian Ocean as a Zone of Peace: Initially Japan gave its support to the Lusaka Declaration of 1970 that called for the Indian Ocean to be declared a "zone of peace". However in 1979 the Japanese position changed with regard to the question of the presence of outside powers in the ocean and Japan disassociated itself from the meeting in New York.

Nuclear Issues: In 1978, when India along with other concerned nations sought to move a resolution in the UN General Assembly declaring the threat of use of nuclear weapons as a crime against humanity, Japan abstained. In 1980 when the same resolution was moved again, Japan along with the members of NATO countries voted against it. In the case of non-proliferation, India and Japan initially agreed that there should be "mutuality of responsibilities and obligations of both nuclear and non-nuclear powers". In 1970, however, Japan affixed its signature to the Nuclear Non-Proliferation Treaty.

These developments created an Indian perception that Japan could not be looked upon as a nation sympathetic to the aspirations of the newly independent countries of Asia and Africa, and cast a dark their shadow on any meaningful bilateral political interaction.

The Cold War ended the strategic divide between the two nations and there appeared to be a convergence of interests between them in maintaining peace and stability in Asia. The beginning of the 1990s, therefore, saw India and Japan resume high-level contacts to establish close ties with each other. In May 1990, Japanese Prime Minister Toshiki Kaifu visited India as part of his sojourn to the South Asian region. Prime Minister Kaifu made a particular reference to the Kashmir issue and called upon both India and Pakistan to settle it bilaterally within the framework of the Shimla Agreement. His efforts led to the promotion of a South Asia Forum within the Japanese Foreign Ministry with a view to promoting relations with South Asian countries.

The Indian Prime Minister Narsimha Rao, who paid an official visit to Japan in June 1992 to commemorate the 40th anniversary of post-war bilateral relations, maintained the pace set by Prime Minister Kaifu. He and his Japanese counterpart Miyazawa Kiichi talked of "a unique opportunity to add several new dimensions to our relationship". The two leaders shared the view that India and Japan must "cooperate in restructuring international relations in a manner that permitted global and regional issues to be tackled both effectively and in a more democratic international environment".

The stagnancy which had been observed for many years in Indo-Japanese economic relationship was also broken in the early 1990s as India undertook major economic reforms and unveiled a "Look East" policy. Indeed, Japanese FDI commitment in 1997 reached a peak of US$ 531.5 million, with actual inflows being about one-third the committed level.[3] Big names of Japanese industry—Toyota, Honda, Sony, Mitsubishi, and Fujitsu—established their presence in

India. It appeared Japan's Ministry of International Trade and Industry (MITI) was taking direct interest in fostering ties with a MITI minister, for the first time, visiting India in 1995; the largest Japanese financial newspaper Nihon Keizai Shimbun actively promoted Indian economic reforms and Japanese airlines (JAL and ANA) established direct flights to India. According to a survey conducted by the Exim Bank of Japan in early 1998, India was regarded as the third most attractive investment destination in the long-term perspective (10 years) and the fifth most attractive destination in the medium-term perspective (5 years).

There was even talk of the need for a bilateral security dialogue between India and Japan during this period as both New Delhi and Tokyo started to view their ties in a regional context. In July 1997, K. Asano, Parliamentary Vice Minister of the Japanese Defense Agency visited India, till then the highest official ever to visit South Asia. In December of the same year, M. Hotsuki, Defense Counsellor of the Japan Defense Agency (JDA), visited India. The exchange of visits by the naval chiefs in 1997-98 broke new ground. In the words of the former Japanese Ambassador, Sakutaro Tanino, the two countries needed "to have more intense and wider political dialogue than (they) have had so far…Both India and Japan have a special responsibility and crucial role to play in contributing to peace and prosperity in Asia".[4]

India's nuclear explosions in May 1998, however, saw Japan taking an aggressive stand on the issue of proliferation, particularly nuclear proliferation. The day after India conducted the nuclear tests, Japanese Prime Minister Ryutaro Hashimoto indicated his readiness to review Japanese Official Development Assistance to India. The next day Japan's Chief Cabinet Secretary Muraoka Kenzo announced three "economic measures"—halt to new grant aid to India, with the exception of emergency, humanitarian and grassroots level aid; conditioning of new aid loans; and withdrawal of Tokyo as a venue for the World Bank India Development Forum. Following the second round of nuclear tests on May 13, Japan announced it would review its position on loans to India in international developmental institutions and also temporarily recalled its ambassador for "consultations" from New Delhi.

At the International level Japan, along with Sweden, Costa Rica and Slovenia, introduced what eventually became UN Security

Council Resolution 1172 that strongly deplored the nuclear tests by India and Pakistan, called on the two countries not to assemble or deploy nuclear devices, cease development of ballistic missiles, and unconditionally sign the Nuclear Non-Pro liferation Treaty (NPT) and Comprehensive Test Ban Treaty (CTBT).

Japan also sought to create a role for itself in promoting a dialogue between India and Pakistan and in facilitating international intervention in the Kashmir issue. There were reports during May 1998 that as an incentive not to conduct nuclear tests the Hashimoto government had promised Pakistan that Japan as a sitting member of the UN Security Council would immediately get Kashmir on the agenda. In June-July 1998 two offers were made by Japan's designated Prime Minister Keizo Obuchi to mediate to resolve the standoff between India and Pakistan. On June, 1, 1998, Obuchi, responding to a question about settling the Kashmir dispute at the Foreign Affairs Committee of the Lower House, spoke of inviting the concerned countries to help find a way out as a solution to this historical dispute.[5] During the Kargil crisis with Pakistan Japan projected Pakistan's incursions in terms of a larger dispute ignoring the fact that a unilateral violation of a mutually agreed Line of Control had taken place. Lack of evidence and absence of means of verification were cited as reasons not to pass judgment on who triggered off what in this dispute.

High-level political contacts since January 2000 have restored a degree of normalcy in bilateral relations. During Japanese Prime Minister Yoshiro Mori's visit to India in August 2000 the two countries agreed to establish a "Global Partnership in the 21st Century." Japan decided to lift all nuclear-related economic sanctions on India and Pakistan on October 26, 2001. In March 2004, at the Japanese Heads of Missions Meeting for Asia the highlight was the choice of "Emerging India" as the main subject of discussions. Some thirty Japanese Ambassadors of the region deliberated upon this topic from various angles, such as India's Look East policy viewed from the ASEAN perspective, a comparative analysis of the economic growth models of India and China, and the strength of the Indian IT industry in relation to the US outsourcing drive, among many others. The Asahi Shimbun, a highly influential newspapers in Japan, published in 2003-04 a series of feature articles about India and China, under the sub-title of "Dragon vs. Elephant".

In addition to this, many other articles and reports have appeared in the Japanese media, introducing India's economic dynamism and its social and political effects. Analysts have pointed out that the Indian and Japanese economies are complementary, not competitive, and that bodes well for enhanced engagement. There has been a perceptible increase in the number of Japanese business leaders expressing an interest in India. India's significant achievements in information technology, the steady pace at which its economy is growing and predictions that its population and hence market would outpace that of China by 2050 are among several reasons cited for the growing interest to do business in India. The Goldman Sachs BRICs report, which forecasts India's ascendance as the Number three economic power of the world by 2050, certainly appears to have had a certain impact on the Japanese attention towards India. In the words of Yasukoni Enoki, the Japanese Ambassador to India

> To begin with the changes on the Indian side, the first change is her high economic profile and, more importantly, the future prospect of a robust economic growth. While a little less than six per cent annual economic growth of India in the 1980s and 1990s is already an encouraging performance, India is now believed to be entering into a higher economic growth phase, possibly with a seven to eight per cent annual growth rate. Various attempts to legislate an outsourcing ban in the US Congress are paradoxically demonstrating India's high competitiveness and technological standard in the information technology (IT) industry. The Goldman Sachs' BRICs report impressed us with its forecast of the world economy in 2050, wherein India is expected to become the third largest economic power in the world, only after China and the USA, surpassing Japan as the fourth largest.[6]

The shift in Japanese ODA policy certainly is tangible evidence of a growing Japanese interest in India. India has been the largest recipient of Japan's Official Development Assistance (ODA) since 2003. This ODA is primarily geared towards Infrastructure Development, Poverty Reduction, Improvement of Healthcare Facilities, and Environmental Protection. Some of the key ODA projects funded in India are: Delhi Mass Rapid Transport, Irrigation Improvement Plan in Rajasthan, Ganga Action Plan in Varanasi,

Tamil Nadu Afforestation Plan, and the Super Thermal Power at North Karanpura. In March 2004 the Japanese government signed the Exchange of Notes for extension of ODA loan assistance worth more than 1 billion dollars to the Indian Government, thus upgrading India as the No. 1 recipient of Japanese ODA, surpassing China, which had been holding that position for many years. In 2006 India was once again the top recipient of Japanese loans for the third consecutive year, with 1.3 billion dollars marked for New Delhi till March 2007.

The "Outlook for Japanese Foreign Direct Investment," a study the Japan Bank for International Cooperation (JBIC) conducts annually, indicated that India has been gaining significance as "a promising destination of investments over the medium-term" as results of JBIC's 2005-06 survey rated India as the second most promising country after China. The India-Japan Joint Study Group (JSG), comprising government ministries, business leaders and academics, submitted a report on measures required for a comprehensive expansion of trade in goods and services, FDI and other areas of economic interaction. The JSG strongly recommended an India-Japan Economic Partnership Agreement (EPA).

According to the Joint Statement "India-Japan Partnership in a New Asian Era" issued during the visit of the Japanese Prime Minster Junichiro Koizumi to India in April 2005

> Shared democratic values and commitment to human rights, pluralism, open society, and the rule of law underpin the global partnership between the two countries. The global partnership between India and Japan reflects a broad convergence of their long-term political, economic and strategic interests, aspirations, objectives and concerns. Japan and India view each other as partners that have responsibility for, and are capable of, responding to global and regional challenges in keeping with their global partnership.

In order to realise the full potential of their global partnership, the two countries decided on an Eight-fold Initiative which comprises of measures for cooperation in eight key areas of interaction, namely: (i) enhanced and upgraded dialogue architecture, including strengthening of the momentum of high-level exchanges, launching of a High Level Strategic Dialogue and full utilisation of the existing dialogue mechanisms; (ii) comprehensive economic engagement, through expansion of trade in goods and services, investment flows and other areas of economic cooperation, and exploration of a Japan-India economic partnership agreement; (iii) enhanced security dialogue and cooperation; (iv) Science and Technology Initiative; (v) cultural and academic initiatives and strengthening of people-to-people contacts to raise the visibility and profile of one country in the other; (vi) cooperation in ushering a new Asian era; (vii) cooperation in the United Nations and other international organisations, including cooperation for the early realisation of UN reforms, particularly Security Council reform; and (viii) cooperation in responding to global challenges and opportunities.

And in December 2006 when Indian Prime Minister Dr. Manmohan Singh visited Tokyo it was decided to establish a "Strategic and Global Partnership" between India and Japan. The Strategic and Global Partnership will involve closer political and diplomatic coordination on bilateral, regional, multilateral and global issues, comprehensive economic engagement, stronger defense relations, greater technological cooperation as well as working towards a quantum increase in cultural ties, educational linkages and people-to-people contacts. "In India, Japan finds a partner that is both influential in the establishment of a regional order for East Asia and that shares common values such as freedom and democracy," opined the 'Yomiuri' newspaper in Japan calling for increasing Japanese economic support for India and described the new partnership as being "the heart of the Asian order".[7]

In fact, even before he became the prime minister of Japan in September 2006 Prime Minister Shinzo Abe in a strategic shift towards 'assertive diplomacy' signaled his strong commitment to building a new partnership with India. In his book, "Towards a Beautiful Country," published last July, Abe suggested that "it will not be surprising if in ten years time, Japan-India relations overtake Japan-US and Japan-China relations." Drawing India into the ambit of the new Japanese grand strategy Prime Minister. Abe emphasised the importance of a quadrilateral strategic dialogue involving Tokyo, Washington, Canberra and New Delhi to promote their shared values of freedom and democracy in Asia[8] and significantly injected the notion of 'shared political values' into the bilateral discourse.

Subsequently, Japan's Minister for Foreign Affairs Taro Aso unveiled the designing of an "arc of freedom and prosperity" along the outer rim of Eurasia as a new pillar in Japanese diplomacy.[9] This new emphasis on value-oriented diplomacy, which contrasts starkly with Japan's early postwar policy of seikei bunri (separation of politics and economics), means that Japan will aim to devote its economic and diplomatic resources toward what Foreign Minister Aso describes as "countries capable of partnering with Japan." The Indian response has been to state that India and Japan are "natural partners in this quest. India's External Affairs Minister Pranab Mukherjee has articulated the reasons[10] for this as:

- India and Japan share the common values of democracy, human rights and the rule of law.
- India and Japan are major engines of economic growth in Asia.
- India and Japan recognise that the key to ensuring long-term security and a stable equilibrium in Asia lies in the collective ability of Asian countries to build trust and confidence based on economic integration.
- The key to continued Asian economic prosperity lies not only in regional interaction but equally in the shared security of the sea-lanes of communication and India and Japan have individually demonstrated their capacities to contribute to maritime security.
- India and Japan have made a significant contribution to multilateral institutions, in particular to the United Nations.

No doubt, India-Japan relations are on an upward trajectory. However, a more nuanced understanding needs to be cultivated. Is it correct to say that the recent phase of "difficult relations" was an aberration brought on primarily because "our bilateral ties as yet do not constitute an adequate counterweight to restrain Japan"? Does a "mutuality of interests" bind the two countries and "demands that India and Japan engage substantially"? It has been variously suggested that India is no longer regarded by Japan as a local power, always hyphened with Pakistan. That "Japan wants to position India on a different paradigm and establish a new relationship, with a clear recognition that India is one of the three major powers of Asia, together with Japan and China. In this sense, there is a clear distinction between India-Japan relations in the past and those in the future". That 'India-Japan relations are poised to emerge as one of the most significant strategic partnerships in the world".

There are no straightforward answers. As one delves deeper a far more complex picture emerges. Linear correlations give way to a strategic web in which India-Japan political and strategic cooperation is a new entrant and the long-tem commitment of both sides remains to be tested. This book is an attempt to present a holistic understanding of Japan's security policy, its motivations and objectives through the prism of the proposed "India-Japan Global and Strategic Partnership". The focus is on five issues routinely identified as "common concerns"—Reform of United Nations, Disarmament, Rise of China, Protection of sealanes of communication, and Cooperation against International Terrorism. A critical appraisal of Japan vis-à-vis these issues is the necessary precondition for assessing the prospects for India-Japan bilateral relations evolving into a global partnership.

NOTES

1. Purnendra Jain and Mauree Todhunter, "India and Japan: Newly Tempering Relations" in Purnendra C. Jain (ed.) *Distant Aian Neighbours: Japan and South Asia*, (Sterling Publishers, New Delhi, 1996), p. 88.
2. For details see P.A.N. Murthy *India and Japan: Dimensions of their Relations. Historical and Political* (New Delhi: ABC Publishing House, 1986).
3. S. Jaishanker, "*India-Japan Relations after Pokharan II*", http://www.india-seminar.com/2000/487/487%20jaishanker.htm
4. S. Tanino, "Japan-India Relations and Cooperation: A Japanese Perspective" in Jasjit Singh (ed.) *Cooperative Peace in Asia* (IDSA, New Delhi, 1998), p. 143.
5. *Ibid.*
6. Yasukoni Enoki, "*The Japan-India New Partnership*", http://www.usiofindia.org/article_Jul_Sep04_1.htm
7. Cited in Suvendrini Kakuchi, "*Japan, India Set to Forge New Regional Order*", http://ipsnews.net/news.asp?idnews=35862

8. See C. Raja Mohan, "*Asia's New Democratic Quad*", http://www.isn.ethz.ch/news/sw/details.cfm?ID=17383
9. See Speech by Taro Aso, Japan's Minister for Foreign Affairs, on the occasion of the JIIA Seminar "Are of Freedom and Prosperity: Japan's Expanding Diplomatic Horizons" November 30, 2006. Available at http://www.mofa.go.jp/announce/fm/aso/speech0611.html
10. Address by India's External Affairs Minister, Pranab Mukherjee, at the Japan Institute of International Affairs, March 23, 2007. Available at http://meaindia.nic.in/speech/2007/03/23ss01.htm

1

The Japan-U.S. Alliance

The destruction of the Japanese military as an independent actor and the drawing up of the 1947 Peace Constitution were fundamental changes imposed on post-War Japan by the American occupation. Article 9 of this Constitution specifically stated

> "Aspiring sincerely to an international peace based on order, the Japanese people forever renounce war as a sovereign right of the nation and the threat or use of force as means of settling international disputes. In order to accomplish the aim of the preceding paragraph, land, sea and air forces, as well as other war potential, will never be maintained. The right of belligerency of the state will not be recognised."

However, the American vision of an unarmed Japan changed track with the advent of the Cold War in Asia. As the winds of containment gathered force, U.S. analysts, such as George Kennan, articulated the necessity of containing the Soviet Union and communism. Resuscitating Germany and Japan as the workshops of their respective regions was the initial thrust of U.S. containment policy, but the U.S. military and other conservative forces quickly transformed the theory of economic containment into a strategic military policy that became increasingly attractive to the Truman administration, particularly after 1949, when the Communist Party in China seized power and the Soviet Union successfully tested its own nuclear weapons.[1] The Korean War, which began on June 25, 1950, created new dynamics as the United States embarked on the quest for maximum access and flexibility for military operations from Japan. Thus, the peace offered to Japan in the form of the San Francisco Peace Treaty in 1951 was partially motivated by the U.S. desire to resuscitate Japan's economy but in exchange the U.S. also insisted on a new military arrangement with Japan that would allow it to keep its massive military installations already in Japan.

Under the terms of this treaty, Japan provided the U.S. with bases to allow for American power projection into East Asia. In return the Japanese received a U.S. security guarantee, including shelter under the U.S. nuclear umbrella. The treaty was more like a basing arrangement than a traditional alliance agreement stating that "Japan desires, as a provisional arrangement for its defense, that the United States of America should maintain armed forces of its own in and about Japan so as to deter armed attack upon Japan."[2] The Japanese motivations in signing the Security Treaty were articulated by Prime Minister Shigeru Yoshida

> The Japanese-American Security Pact…will assure the security of our country for the immediate future following our recovery of independence… to put Japan beyond the reach of aggression is one postulate to the peace of the Far East and to the peace…of the entire world. Herein lies the reason for our conclusion of a security pact with the *U.S.*...[3]

The "Yoshida Doctrine" as this approach came to be called was based on three pillars:

1. Economic rehabilitation and growth
2. Close cooperation with the United States
3. Avoidance of international political-strategic issues

Stressing *alignment* over *alliance*, the Yoshida Doctrine largely allowed Japan to walk a fine line between abandonment by the U.S. and entrapment in U.S. military actions.[4] Indeed, "Prime Minister Yoshida's decision to sign the security treaty with the U.S. in 1951, and to accept Japanese light rearmament through the formation of the Self-Defense Force (SDF) in 1954, reflected a pragmatic perception that alignment with and security guarantees from the U.S. were essential to Japan's survival in the midst of intensifying Cold War pressures in East Asia.

Subsequent Diet resolutions were, however, designed to limit Japan's military capacity. These included provisions to prevent the export of arms and to prevent the dispatch of troops outside the country as part of any collective security scheme. Japan also pledged to not become a nuclear power. This was delineated in Prime Minister Sato's three nuclear principles: "Japan would not produce, possess, or permit the introduction of nuclear weapons into its soil." The final addition became the practice of limiting defense spending to less than one per cent of the nation's GNP.

The Basic Policy for National Defense in May 1957 set out Japan's initial concept of "defensive defense". This included four points:

1. To support the activities of the United Nations and promote international cooperation, thereby contributing to the realisation of world peace;
2. To promote public welfare and enhance the people's love for the country, thereby establishing the sound basis essential to Japan's security;
3. To develop incrementally an efficient defense force pertinent to the nation's power and situation; and
4. To deal with external aggression on the basis of US-Japan security arrangements, pending the effective functioning of the United Nations in the future in deterring and repelling such aggression.

The Treaty of Mutual Cooperation and Security between the United States and Japan further reinforced the bilateral security alliance in 1960, which stated, *"Each Party recognises that an armed attack against either Party in the territories under the administration of Japan would be dangerous. to its own peace and safety and declares that it would act to meet the common danger in accordance with its constitutional provisions and processes."*[5] This division of roles has undergone "redefinition" over the years, with Japan assuming greater responsibility but there has been little support for a complete "reassessment" of the ties with the United States.

Burden-sharing during the Cold War

From the beginning the U.S.-Japan security relationship was asymmetrical. Not only was a joint response required only if an adversary attacked Japanese territory, asymmetry also existed in the context of the types of core alliance contributions each country was to provide. The Status of Forces Agreement (SOFA) in 1960 that governed the use of facilities and areas in Japan by the American forces stipulated the principle of cost sharing as Japan would provide "all facilities and areas and rights of way" "without cost to the United States and make compensation where appropriate to the owners and suppliers thereof." The United States would bear "without cost to Japan all expenditures incident to the maintenance of the United States armed forces in Japan except those to be borne by Japan as provided." Simply put, Japan provided the bases to the U.S. without cost and the U.S. paid the cost for operation of forces in the bases. With the result "U.S. government efforts to persuade Tokyo to increase its defense efforts and to improve upon its burden-sharing within the alliance are visible throughout the postwar period in some form or the other."[6]

A transformation of U.S.—Japanese security relations in the late 1960s and 1970s resulted from the Nixon—Kissinger strategy of détente with China. The "Nixon shocks," and the new American security objectives that attended them, set the alliance off in new directions and brought new prominence to the question of what role Japan should play in U.S. security policies for East Asia. Thinking within Japan's policy establishment shifted from the defence dilemma fearing entrapment to fearing abandonment and led the government to formulate the National Defense Programme Outline (NDPO) of 1976 and the Guidelines for U.S.-Japan Defense Cooperation of 1978.

A new division of labour was defined in the 1978 Guidelines of Japan-U.S. Defense Cooperation wherein Japan and the United States outlined the particulars of bilateral cooperation in both Japan's immediate defense and in regional contingencies in the Far East. The formulation of these guidelines was a significant development adding pith and substance to the treaty in that they drew out a mechanism for the implementation of the treaty, which did not have any operational rules till then.[7] According to Michael Green and Koji Murata's joint study, "The Guidelines for U.S.—Japan Defense Cooperation: Its Process and Impact," the origins of the Guidelines are rooted in the strategic changes of the Nixon era, as the United States, under the rubric of the Nixon or Manila Doctrine, and in conjunction with the draw down of U.S. forces in Vietnam, began pressing its allies in Asia to carry more of the burden for regional security and defense.

With the emergence of Japan as a prosperous economy another key component of the U.S.—Japan security relationship that emerged in the late 1970s and 1980s was defense technology sharing. Criticisms that the United States was selling the means of its own economic destruction to a putative ally in the name of the security alliance, sprinkled with concepts such as "techno-nationalism," "dual use," and "spin-ons versus spin-offs," focused public and political attention on the linkages that exist between security and economics.[8] Michael Chinworth[9] breaks down these arguments on the political economy of the bilateral security relationship into three distinct claims

- Japan has a "free ride" on defense, enabling the country to focus on economic development and expanded trade markets at the expense of the United States, its principal protector and benefactor.
- Japan has pursued defense research, development and production in order to further its domestic economic goals, including the development of "high tech" industries, often at the economic expense of the United States.
- Japan has utilised technology from U.S. defense systems to develop commercial spin-offs and import substitutes for the original imported military system.

Greater domestic attention in the United States also focused on the economics of deploying military forces in Japan with demands of evidence to show that Japan was contributing to the alliance in a manner commensurate with its economic power. Indeed underlying these claims was a deeper issue: "the degree to which the U.S. should subsidise the economic growth of a country that increasingly could rely on its own capabilities for prosperity."

Correspondingly by early 1978 there was considerable agreement within the Japanese policy establishment that some sort of accommodation of U.S. demands for greater cost-sharing would be necessary. Thus Japan's Host Nation Support (HNS) started in 1978 with the introduction of the concept of "*omoiyari yosan*" roughly translated as the "compassion budget" or the "generosity budget" for assisting with the maintenance of U.S. military forces in Japan. The Japanese government assumed responsibility for a host of maintenance costs and Japan's total military spending increased exponentially over the course of the 1980s.[10]

Yet, significant tensions continued between Japan and the United States in the 1980s concerning economic, political and security issues. The focus was on Japan's economic statistics:

> The trade imbalance stands at 50 billion dollars annually in Japan's favour; Japan's per capita income is higher than that of the United States; eight of the world's largest banks are Japanese; a single Japanese corporation, Nippon Telegraph and Telephone, is worth more than IBM, AT&T, General Motors, General Electric, and Exxon combined; nearly a third of the U.S. budget deficit is now shouldered by Japanese investors; Japan's share in the global financial and capital market stands at 40 percent.[11]

In the face of such 'Japan bashing' Tokyo's policy makers felt compelled to devise visible demonstrations of Japan's commitment to global security. It was with this mindset that in 1981 Prime Minister Zenko Suzuki for the first time publicly referred to the U.S.-Japan relationship as an "alliance" and stated that "within the framework of the Constitution" Japan would protect its sea-lanes of communication to 1000 nautical miles.

Prime Minister Yasuhiro Nakasone, too, highlighted Japan's closeness to the United States. Stating "unequivocal and active commitment to the U.S.-Japan alliance" Prime Minister Nakasone used noticeably bold language when he proclaimed in 1983 that Japan was an "unsinkable aircraft carrier against Soviet backfire bombers." He publicly pronounced that Japan would defend U.S. ships in the waters around Japan. Prime Minister Nakasone decided in January 1983 also to exempt the transfer of dual-use technologies to the United States. An exchange of notes was concluded followed by the "Detailed

Arrangement" in November 1983 concerning the transfer of such technologies. In September 1986, Japan announced it would cooperate with Washington in the Strategic Defense Initiative (SDI) and in July 1987 the "Agreement on Japan's Participation in SDI Research" was concluded. By 1988, Japan had also approved the transfer to the United States of SAM-technology related to the construction of naval vessels and technology for the modification of U.S. naval vessels. The most significant of the Nakasone initiatives were, however, in the area of defense budgets. In 1985 the Nakasone Cabinet approved the 1986-90 Mid-term Defense Estimate that prescribed defense spending in excess of the 1 per cent GNP limit, challenging one of Japan's important security norms. Though factional opposition within the ruling Liberal Democratic Party (LDP) prevented Prime Minister Nakasone from breaking this barrier in 1985 and 1986 he prevailed in 1987 when the 1 per cent GNP ceiling was exceeded and defense spending reached 1.004 per cent of GNP.

Yet the most active involvement of Japan in international security was economic in nature. No doubt during the Cold War period Japan upgraded its national military capabilities and range of missions in support of U.S. power projection functions in the Asia Pacific region. However, "Japan's military security role during the Cold War was geographically restricted to the area immediately surrounding Japan, and limited functionally to providing a defensive shield to support the U.S. offensive sword in Northeast Asia."[12] Simultaneously Japan implemented the concept of "comprehensive security" as the general direction of its security policy. The concept of comprehensive security was first articulated during the administration of Prime Minister Ohira Masayoshi (1978-80) with the commissioning of the National Institute for Research Advancement (NIRA) to produce a *Report on Comprehensive National Security.* The successor administration of Prime Minister Suzuki (1980-1982) later adopted elements of the report as national policy and established a new Comprehensive National Security Council in 1980.[13]

Comprehensive Security looked at Japan's security in a multi-level and multi-dimensional framework wherein potential threats were thought to include not only military developments (such as the Soviet military build-up) but also political events (such as the Arab-Israel conflict) and economic developments (such as the OPEC Crisis). Economic assistance in this context was portrayed as a contribution to international security, and called for the coordinated application of economic and political measures at three levels: global, within selected groupings of countries and in national self-help efforts. The key security objectives identified at each level were:

- At the global level: arms control, better North-South relations and free trade;
- At the intermediate level: maintenance of good relations with political allies and key economic partners;
- At the national self-help level: military defense, economic productivity and export competitiveness.

Articulated as a belief that economic growth held the key to state-building strategies, internal political and social stability and thus ultimately the prevention of conflict domestically and internationally, Japan's Official Development Aid (ODA) Policy also accepted the need to provide assitance to support key U.S. allies. And Japan during the Cold War extended sizeable "strategic aid" to frontline states such as South Korea, Thailand, Pakistan, Turkey and Egypt.

In this context many scholars suggested that Japan was a 'reactive state'. The main focus of the reactivist perspective was on the role of *gaiatsu* (foreign pressure) in Japanese policy-making. The argument being that *gaiatsu* provided a powerful stimulus to the Japanese domestic policymaking process—frequently characterised as immobile—and that *gaiatsu* was the foremost factor determining the direction of Japan's diplomacy. Dennis Yasutomo, for example, discussed four main tenets of the reactivist approach: (1) the external origin of reactivity, (2) the United States as the primary locus of reactivity, (3) the immobile domestic policymaking process as the fundamental causes of reactivity, and (4) the scope of reactiveness as both foreign economic policy and political-strategic diplomacy.[14] Some attributed Japan's sensitivity to US pressure to its heavy dependence on the US for trade and security.[15]

Others provided explanations based on Japan's fragmented bureaucracy where each ministry pursued its own interests.[16] The unanimous view, however, was that Tokyo's reactive policymaking involved minimalist, passive, and risk-avoiding diplomacy. In the words of Michael Blaker, Japan's foreign policy making involves "carefully assessing the international situation, methodically weighing each alternative, sorting out various options to see what is really serious, waiting for the dust to settle on some contentious issue, piecing together a consensus view about the situation faced, and then performing the existing situation with the fewest risk."[17]

Post–Cold War Developments

The collapse of the Soviet Union and the end of the Cold War in 1991 removed the main rationale for the U.S.-Japan security alliance. In the absence of the clear paradigm of Soviet containment, the U.S.-Japan alliance entered a period of uncertainty. The process was identified in the Armitage-Nye report as "post-cold war drift" and heightened tensions between the U.S. and Japan came to a head in the 1991 Gulf War. Japan's initial response to Iraq's invasion of Kuwait was in line with its traditionally passive stance in international affairs. It took Japan three weeks to formulate a positive commitment to help the United States and the Western Allies restore the status quo, and simply amounted to a monetary contribution of 13 billion dollars. A financial contribution had also been the Japanese response to the earlier threat to Gulf oil access during the 1987-88 Kuwaiti oil tanker flagging crisis. At that time Japan had provided economic assistance to construct shipping navigation aids in the Persian Gulf.

In August 1990, however, the situation was qualitatively different. Iraq's invasion of Kuwait raised the issue of how regional conflicts could be controlled after bi-polar super power competition had ended. The crisis was perceived as the first test to see how the United States and its allies could address regional conflicts jointly when their collective interests were at stake. The response of the Japanese government seemed to signal that it continued to expect the United States to protect Japan's interests without Japanese participation. The Japanese government scrambled to pass legislation establishing a UN Peace Cooperation Corps to provide logistic back up for the multinational forces in the Gulf, only to be defeated by concerted political opposition in the Diet. This Bill envisaged creating a UN Peace Cooperation Corps (UNPCC), which was to consist of non-

SDF government employees, private citizens directly subordinate to the Prime Minister, and members temporarily transferred from the SDF. It specified that activities of the corps could include overseeing cease-fire agreements, monitoring elections, medical activities, disaster relief measures, and transportation, telecommunications, and other logistical support. Thwarted in its efforts, the Kaifu government then initiated an attempt to dispatch air force transport planes to evacuate refugees. The Flight Squadron 401 of the First Air Transport Squadron at Komaki base in Aichi Prefecture was prepared for this mission, but this could not be realised as the Gulf War came to a quick end.

Eventually, in April 1991, the Japanese government sent six vessels including four minesweepers to the Persian Gulf to help clear the waterways of mines and for the first time SDF activity was described as a contribution to the international community and specifically a contribution in terms of personnel or human resources. According to the 1991 Japanese defense white paper, "ensuring safe ship traffic in that sea area at the earliest date possible was called upon by international society. Therefore, the dispatch of the minesweepers was of significance as a measure to contribute to the international community in terms of personnel for peace and humanity".[18]

But these measures earned Japan little credit, as they risked no Japanese lives. Rather "Japan was laughed off by the rest of the world as little more than a cash dispenser."[19] Nor were Japan's actions perceived to be spontaneous and voluntary. Infact Kuwait declined to include Japan in a list of allied countries it thanked for liberating the emirate.[20]

Importantly "Japan's failure to actively support its ally in the Gulf War, and to meet U.S. requests to participate more actively in security at the global level, was the first indication that the status quo in its security policy was no longer tenable."[21] The Gulf War debacle gave the Japanese serious reason to rethink their security policy and opened the door for new types of participation in the international security arena. This was illustrated by Japan's passage of the Peacekeeping Operations (PKO) Law in 1992, which allowed for Japan's Self Defense Forces' participation in United Nations peacekeeping operations and the subsequent participation in the U.N. Peacekeeping Operation (UNPKO) in Cambodia. According to Paul

Midford, it was participation in this U.N. mission that broke the Japanese domestic taboo on foreign military deployment.

A further series of events in the early 1990s served to remind Tokyo that the end of the Cold War did not eliminate all the possible sources of instability in East Asia These included Beijing's 1992 law reaffirming Chinese claim to the Senkaku Islands, the 1993-4 crisis over North Korea's nuclear weapons programme, Chinese nuclear tests in 1995 and 1996, Chinese military exercises in the Taiwan Strait in March 1996 and popular protests over the disputed Senkaku islands that broke out in Hong Kong and Taiwan in 1996. Particularly during the 1993-1994 North Korean nuclear crisis, in which North Korea threatened to withdraw from the Nuclear Non-Proliferation Treaty and conducted a ballistic missile test in the Sea of Japan, the Japanese policy establishment was unable to respond effectively to U.S. requests for active support in the event of an actual conflict on the Korean Peninsula. The alliance's lack of military operability induced a crisis of confidence in the bilateral relationship and raised fears that the United States might abandon Japan as an unreliable ally.[22] For example this is what, Chalmers Johnson, President of the Japan Policy Research Institute in the United States, had to say after the controversial Okinawan Rape Incident involving a U.S. soldier:

> "Today Japan has the most modern industrial structure in the world, it has not run a trade deficit with the United States for almost three decades, the dollar has lost nearly 80 percent of its original postwar value against the yen, and Japan faces no known military threat. The U.S. troops based in Japan cannot afford a bowl of noodles if they leave their bases, given the current yen-dollar exchange rate. It does not take a Thucydides to see that such a relationship is unstable.[23]

This created momentum for new Japanese initiatives to revise the country's military doctrine and to redefine the alliance with the United States. The report of the Advisory Group on Defense Issues in Japan or the Higuchi Report entitled '*The Modality of the Security and Defense Capability of Japan: The Outlook for the 21*st *Century'* released in August 1994 recommended that it would be necessary to take advantage of the alliance network, centreing around the US for security cooperation.[24] Besides, the report favoured a re-definition of the alliance oriented towards two objectives—ensuring smooth

Japan-US defense cooperation in the event of any military contingency in Japan and contributing to the stability of the region around Japan.[25]

In November 1995 Japan issued a revised National Defense Programme Outline that stressed the need for stronger Japan-U.S. alliance cooperation and inserted a new clause to state that if a situation impacting national peace and security should arise in areas surrounding Japan (*shuhen*), then Japan should seek to deal with the situation in cooperation with the UN and via Japan-U.S. security arrangements.[26] In April 1996 Japan and the United States issued a "Joint Declaration on Security"[27] that opened the way for a revision of the original 1978 Guidelines for Defense Cooperation. U.S. President Bill Clinton and Japanese Prime Minister Hashimoto reaffirmed the two countries, "strong determination, ... to build on the successful history of security cooperation." While agreeing upon the need for "continued US military presence in the region as being "essential for preserving peace and stability in the region," the declaration called for "studies on bilateral cooperation in dealing with situations that may emerge in the areas surrounding Japan."

The new Guidelines for Japan-U.S. Defense Cooperation[28], which were released in September 1997, were aimed at creating a solid basis for more effective and credible Japan-U.S. cooperation under normal circumstances and during contingencies and delineated cooperation in three circumstances:

- Cooperation under normal circumstances
- Actions in response to an armed attack on Japan
- Cooperation in situations in areas surrounding Japan that will have an important influence on Japan's peace and security

Fields of cooperation included:

- Cooperation in activities initiated by either Government, including relief activities, and measures to deal with refugees, search and rescue, non-combatant evacuation operations and activities for ensuring the effectiveness of economic sanctions for the maintenance of international peace and stability.
- In case of need, provision by Japan of additional facilities and areas in a timely and appropriate manner, and ensure the

temporary use by U.S. Forces of Self-Defense Forces facilities and civilian airports and ports.

- Rear area support by Japan to those U.S. Forces that are conducting operations for the purpose of achieving the objectives of the U.S.-Japan Security Treaty.
- Japan-U.S. operational cooperation in situations in areas surrounding Japan including surveillance, minesweeping and sea and airspace management.

Based on the September 1997 Cabinet Decision on ensuring the effectiveness of the Guidelines, the Japanese Government worked on the establishment of domestic mechanisms to this end, including legal aspects. This resulted in the April 1998 submission to the Diet of: (1) a draft law relating to measures for preserving the peace and security of Japan in the event of a situation in the areas surrounding Japan; (2) a bill to amend the Self-Defense Forces Law; and (3) an Agreement amending the Agreement between the Government of Japan and the Government of the United States of America concerning 'Reciprocal Provision of Logistic Support, Supplies and Services between the Self-Defense Forces of Japan and the Armed Forces of the United States of America (the so-called amended ACSA).'

Indeed the enactment and approval of these and other laws related to the 'Guidelines for Japan-U.S. Defense Cooperation' were highly significant steps in enhancing the credibility of the Japan-U.S. Security Arrangements and have broadened the mission of the SDF to provide logistical support to U.S. forces in order to deal with "situations in areas surrounding Japan that will have an important influence on Japan's peace and security."

The revised guidelines spell out the roles of the U.S. military and Japan's Self-Defense Forces (SDF) in the event of a crisis. The latter refers specifically to "situations in areas surrounding Japan that will have an important influence on Japan's peace and security" as the context in which the two governments could provide each other with supplies and services. In the context of modern warfare, the expanded regional scope of the new Japanese-U.S. defense cooperation arrangements has somewhat diluted Japan's traditional postwar policy against the use of force in the absence of a direct attack.[29] SDF operations, for example, will no longer focus solely on the defense of the Japanese home islands. Moreover, even though, the initial decision to revise the Guidelines and their function may have been prompted by and predicated upon a Korean Peninsula contingency, it is also clear that since the 1996 Taiwan Straits crisis the revised Guidelines have had a growing additional, if not equal, function designed to strengthen the U.S.-Japan alliance's deterrent potential versus China over the Taiwan issue.[30]

Post—9/11 Developments

Motivated by the desire to avoid a repeat of the 1991 Gulf War experience the centrepiece of Japan's response to the September 2001 terrorist attacks in the United States was the "Anti-Terrorism Special Measures Law". It was passed by the Diet on October 29 and authorised the Self-Defense Forces to implement "Cooperation and Support Activities", "Search and Rescue Activities" and "Assistance to Affected People" in support of the activities of foreign countries aiming to achieve the purposes of the UN Charter in response to the terrorist attacks of September 11 in the United States.[31] These included supply, transportation, repair and maintenance, medical services, communications, airport and seaport services and bases. The legislation was subjected to a debate that was almost perfunctory, amounting in total to 62 hours, as compared to 179 hours for the Peacekeeping Organization Cooperation Law of 1992 and 154 hours for the Guidelines legislation of 1999.[32] Effective for two years, the law mandated the prime minister, with Cabinet approval, to draft a Basic Plan regarding the types, areas, and duration of SDF activities and the scale and composition of the troops and equipment to be deployed.

Since then Japan's Self-Defense Forces (SDF) have provided logistical support for the war in Afghanistan, including intelligence collection, supply shipments, and medical and humanitarian relief, marking the first time Japan has lent military support to an international conflict since World War II. Japan began to provide transportation by the Air-Self Defense Force in late November 2001 and to supply fuel in the Indian Ocean in early December, following consultations with the U.S. government on the basic plan. The MSDF dispatched two Fast Combat Support Ships and three Destroyers, and was engaged in refueling U.S. and U.K. ships at sea without charge, with a total of 65 refuelings of approximately 114,000 kiloliters of fuel as of April 21, 2002.[33] As for support by the ASDF, C-130 transport airplanes and other aircraft transported goods such as spare parts between U.S. bases in Japan and the island of Guam with a total of 33 domestic missions and 14 overseas missions as of April 21, 2002.[34]

The Japanese Cabinet has twice amended the original Basic Plan. The first amendment extended the SDF deployment by one year, and the second amendment added to the activity list the dispatch of a landing (transportation) ship and an additional escort destroyer to transport heavy construction equipment and staff. On December 11, 2002, Japan's Vice Foreign Minister officially offered to transport heavy construction equipment for a 140-men strong Thai army engineering battalion to a port on the Indian Ocean setting a political precedent in transporting the troops of an Asian country, and on December 19 Japan moved its 7,250-ton Kirishima battleship, equipped with the high-tech Aegis missile detection system, from Yokosuka to the Indian Ocean. In 2003, the Diet approved a bill to extend the Special Measures Law by two years. In early March 2003 JMSDF ships began refueling Italian, Spanish, French, German, New Zealand and Dutch warships participating in Operation Enduring Freedom in addition to the U.S. and British vessels.

Japan has further indicated military support for the United States by passing on July 26, 2003 a Law Concerning Special Measures on Humanitarian and Reconstruction Assistance. This law is designed to enable the dispatch of the Self Defense Forces to provide logistical support for US and coalition forces engaged in Operation Iraqi Freedom (OIF). On December 18, 2003, Prime Minister Koizumi gave authorisation to send 1,000 non-combat SDF personnel to Iraq to assist reconstruction efforts, the nation's first troop deployment under its own flag rather than the UN's since World War II. The decision was especially bold since terrorists murdered two Japanese diplomats working in Iraq at the end of November 2003. Despite overwhelming opposition in Japan to the U.S.-led war on Iraq, the Koizumi government was one of the Bush administration's firmest backers from the outset and was listed as part of the so-called "coalition of the willing" that formally supported the invasion. Although ground troops were withdrawn in July 2006 Japan's lower house of parliament approved, in 2007, a two-year extension of the country's Air Force Transport Mission in Iraq.

The present cycle of policy change, once again, evolved in response to changing overall U.S. global strategy needs. The Bush administration has, especially since September 11, been seeking to activate its regional alliances to function for global security. The United States emphasised this shift in the *Quadrennial Defense Review Report* of September 2001, the *National Security Strategy* of September 2002, and the *National Defense Strategy* of March 2005. The White House now supports a move from "threat-based" regional alliances to "capabilities-based" global alliances that are capable of constructing flexible coalitions with interoperable military assets for missions in the "arc of instability" stretching from the Middle East to Southeast Asia. In addition, the Global Posture Review (GPR) of 2004 made clear that bases provided by regional alliances should be integrated into the U.S. strategy for the "surging" and global deployment of its forward forces. And Prime Minister Junichiro Koizumi made Japan's strategic calculations clear when he said, in a December 2003 press conference about his cabinet's decision to dispatch the SDF to Iraq that:

> ...In order to ensure the peace and security of Japan, and achieve greater prosperity, we must continue to enhance the Japan-U.S. alliance...Japan cannot alone secure its own peace and security...I believe that Japan must also be a trustworthy ally for the United States.[35]

Thus, Japanese policymakers appear to have come to the realisation that in order both to remain indispensable as an ally and to maintain political and strategic influence over the United States, Japan needs to move beyond the changes made in alliance cooperation in the mid-1990s and the immediate post-September 11 period, and further strengthen the alliance to respond to both regional and global security contingencies.[36] Consequently Japan has begun participating in U.S.—led multinational coalitions, including the dispatch of the JSDF to support the Afghan campaign and Iraqi reconstruction. Japan has predicated laws such as *The Anti-Terrorism Special Measures Law* (ATSML) passed to enable the dispatch of JSDF units to the Indian Ocean area and the *Law Concerning Special Measures on*

Humanitarian and Reconstruction Assistance (Iraq reconstruction law) that has enabled the dispatch of JSDF on non-combat reconstruction activities in Iraq and JSDF "out-of-area" dispatches upon linkages to relevant UN resolutions, wherein these security activities are strictly outside the geographical and functional scope of the U.S.-Japan security alliance. Nevertheless, the principal impetus behind the ATSML and Iraqi reconstruction law has centered on Japanese attempts to strengthen the range of U.S.-Japan alliance activities outside East Asia. As Christopher Hughes points out "Japanese policy-makers in responding to the U.S. expectation for military support in Iraq, in particular, have articulated a position which demonstrates that they view the dispatch of the JSDF as a means to shore up political confidence in the alliance so as to avoid the prospect of abandonment over the resurgent North Korean threat.[37]

Tokyo has become cognisant of Washington's expectations that U.S. regional alliances should function to support global security operations, as evidenced by specific base realignment proposals relating to Japan since 2004 that have emanated with the U.S. *Global Posture Review*. The clear ramification of these proposals was that Japan would serve essentially as a frontline U.S. command post for the Asia-Pacific and beyond, and that the increased concentration of command functions in Japan would also tighten military cooperation between U.S. forces and the JSDF.[38] This is also evident from the Joint Statement of the Japan-U.S. Security Consultative Committee[39] (SCC), or "2-Plus-2" meeting, on February 19, 2005 which clearly indicates the common strategic objectives in the region as:

- Ensure the security of Japan, strengthen peace and stability in the Asia-Pacific region, and maintain the capability to address contingencies affecting the United States and Japan.
- Support peaceful unification of the Korean Peninsula.
- Seek peaceful resolution of issues related to North Korea, including its nuclear programmes, ballistic missile activities, illicit activities, and humanitarian issues such as the abduction of Japanese nationals by North Korea.
- Develop a cooperative relationship with China, welcoming the country to play a responsible and constructive role regionally as well as globally.

- Encourage the peaceful resolution of issues concerning the Taiwan Strait through dialogue.
- Encourage China to improve transparency of its military affairs.
- Encourage Russia's constructive engagement in the Asia-Pacific region.
- Fully normalise Japan-Russia relations through the resolution of the Northern Territories issue.
- Promote a peaceful, stable, and vibrant Southeast Asia.
- Welcome the development of various forms of regional cooperation, while stressing the importance of open, inclusive, and transparent regional mechanisms.
- Discourage destabilising sales and transfers of arms and military technology.
- Maintain the security of maritime traffic.

Global common strategic objectives include:

- Promote fundamental values such as basic human rights, democracy, and the rule of law in the international community.
- Further consolidate U.S.-Japan partnership in international peace cooperation activities and development assistance to promote peace, stability, and prosperity worldwide.
- Promote the reduction and nonproliferation of weapons of mass destruction (WMD) and their means of delivery, including through improved reliability and effectiveness of the Non-Proliferation Treaty, the International Atomic Energy Agency, and other regimes, and initiatives such as the Proliferation Security Initiative.
- Prevent and eradicate terrorism.
- Coordinate efforts to improve the effectiveness of the United Nations Security Council by making the best use of the current momentum to realise Japan's aspiration to become a permanent member.
- Maintain and enhance the stability of the global energy supply.

The SCC statement is certainly significant in stressing the strengthened functions of the alliance for regional security and represents a more forthcoming statement than the revised guidelines concerning Taiwan's position as an object of alliance cooperation. Also the SCC statement's stress on countering threats, such as terrorism, that do not respect regional demarcations is a clear sign that Japan and the United States are creating greater leeway for the stretching of security treaty interpretations and for allowing the U.S.-Japan alliance to function in an increasingly global manner.

In order to implement the strengthened alliance cooperation allowed for by this new shift in policy described above, Japan is now seeking to acquire both new doctrine and more interoperable JSDF capabilities. These changes are being undertaken with an eye toward expanding military activities alongside the United States and in U.S.-led multinational coalitions on a global scale. Japan began this round of military modernisation with the issuance in October 2004 of the final report of the Prime Minister's Council on Security and Defense Capabilities, known as the "Araki Report" (after its chairman Araki Hiroshi). This panel—consisting of a range of business figures, academics, and former bureaucrats and JSDF officers—was notable in calling for an "Integrated Security Strategy" for Japan that would mandate a two-pronged approach for the JSDF: (1) the traditional function of preventing direct threats from having an impact on Japan and (2) a new emphasis on international cooperation outside Japan's own territory to prevent the rise of security threats.[40]

The Araki Report was followed in December 2004 with the release of the revised National Defense Programme Guideline (NDPG) and the simultaneous release of a new Mid-term Defense Plan (MTDP) for 2005-09. The latest defense guideline followed the 1995 defense outline (NDPO) in stressing Japan's regional security concerns and the importance of the U.S.-Japan alliance in responding to these issues. The new guidelines moved beyond its predecessor, however, by outlining a range of new threats to Japan, including ballistic missile attacks, guerrilla and special operations attacks, incursions into its territorial waters, and chemical and biological warfare. These concerns are a clear reflection of recent perceived regional threats from North Korea and China. In fact, the new defense guideline went further than the 1995 NDPO by not only identifying North Korea specifically as a destabilising factor in East Asia, but also by identifying for the first time concerns about China's impact on regional security, although the latter was couched in the oblique language of needing to "remain attentive" to China's future military modernisation. The NDPG also went beyond the 1995 NDPO in its new emphasis upon global—as opposed to regional—security interests. The report stated "the region spreading from the Middle East to East Asia is critical to Japan," thereby mapping Japan's own security interests onto those of the United States along the "are of instability." The report also focused upon the need for Japan to engage actively in "international peace cooperation" activities through the dispatch of the JSDF to support UN and U.S.-led multinational operations.

In order for Japan to fulfill these regional and global responsibilities, both the NDPG and MTDP advocated that the JSDF should seek to establish "multifunctional, flexible, and effective" forces. These forces should be characterised by mobility and rapid-reaction; enhanced joint command and control, including the capability to undertake joint operations amongst the three services of the GSDF, MSDF, and ASDF; increased interoperability with UN and U.S. forces; and the utilisation of state-of-the-art intelligence and military technologies. In terms of specific JSDF organisation and hardware, the MTDP has stressed a quantitative build-down from Japan's Cold War-style forces. Now, the MTDP is seeking to switch to a lighter and qualitatively strengthened JSDF, which would be capable of greater power projection and expeditionary capabilities.

There is also growing understanding that base realignment is crucial for cementing the foundations of bilateral military cooperation, and for enabling Japan and the United States to push ahead with their future plans for security cooperation. According to the current U.S. National Defense Strategy[41] , promulgated in March 2005 in line with the new threat-based approach American forces will now be based in three types of forward locations: *Main Operating Bases* which are the most important strategic sites; *Forward Operating Sites* are "warm sites" where a minimum number of personnel and pre-positioned stocks are deployed in time of peace and are used as staging areas in case of contingencies; and *Cooperative Security Locations* which are managed by an ally and where no US troops are stationed in time of peace. The perception in the Japanese defense establishment is that the United States may build what might be called "a triangle hub system" with Hawaii at the apex with Japan and Guam serving as mutually complementary strategic bases.[42]

By November 2004 Japan had formulated the basic position of being prepared to accept U.S. force dispositions with expanded "out-of-area" command functions as long as these could be demonstrated to in some way contribute to Japan's own security and the security of the Far East in line with Article 6 of the security treaty. After the "common strategic objectives" were identified in 2005 meeting of the Japan-US Security Consultative Committee the May 2006 meeting reached final agreement on the realignment of US forces in Japan. According to the "*Japan-U.S. Roadmap for Realignment Implementation*,"[43] which was issued after the meeting, the two countries will proceed with the integration of the Self-Defense Forces and U.S. forces, including the coordination of command centres, and, parallel with this, carry out by 2014 the construction of a replacement facility for Futenma Air Station, which is currently located in a built-up area in Ginowan and has been strongly criticised by the citizens of Okinawa Prefecture, and the transfer of 8,000 US marines from Okinawa to Guam, also by 2014.

The joint statement that was issued in relation to this agreement declared that this US military realignment "will lead to a new phase" in Japan-US alliance cooperation. Infact in May 2007 the Japanese Diet voted into law a bill to promote the realignment of U.S. forces in Japan, which will create a controversial system that offers financial rewards to municipalities that cooperate in the moves. The *Special Measures Law* will be effective for 10 years through 2017 and is designed to help the government carry out the realignment and also to finance the huge costs required. Under the law, the central government will introduce a system to provide subsidies to municipal governments that host U.S. military facilities. The size of the subsidies will depend on the progress of the realignment. The law will also enable the government to receive loans and investments from the Japan Bank for International Cooperation to secure Japan's share in the cost for relocating the U.S. Marines to Guam.[44]

Japan's engagement with Ballistic Missile Defense (BMD) is another significant step in forcing the pace of Tokyo's military modernisation plans and strengthening the U.S.-Japan alliance. Today BMD is Japan's prominent response to "new threats" in the revised National Defense Programme Guidelines (NDPG) of December 2004 and it is the major procurement item in the Mid-Term Defense

Programme for 2005-2009. Although Japan's interest in BMD dates back to the Strategic Defense Initiative (SDI) of the Reagan administration the August 1998 North Korean test firing of its Taepo Dong-1 ballistic missile that passed over Japanese territory ignited public concern about the country's vulnerability to ballistic missile. In December 1998 the Japanese government made an internal decision to engage with the United States in cooperative research and development of a ballistic missile defense system. Less than a year later, in August 1999, the U.S. and Japanese governments signed a memorandum of understanding covering a five-year programme of joint research and development on the then U.S. Navy Theater Wide (NTW) ballistic missile defense programme.

The decision of the Bush Administration in the Summer of 2001 to eliminate the distinction between national missile defense and other BMD programmes, and to re-designate the NTW project as the sea-based "mid-course" defense element of a seamless BMD capability created uncertainty in Japan about the benefits and constitutionality of participating in joint missile defense technology research. In particular, the Japanese government had serious qualms about the constitutionality of cooperating on the development of technology that effectively could become part of a system to defend U.S. territory from third countries. However after the September 11 terror attacks in the United States the Japanese government has revised its stance and in the background of the renewed North Korean nuclear crisis, Prime Minister Koizumi stated in May 2003 that Japan might 'accelerate consideration' of its participation in a joint BMD programme with the United States.

In December 2003 Japan decided to move beyond "joint research" with the United States regarding ballistic missile defense to actual plans for acquiring BMD systems. Referring to the proliferation of weapons of mass destruction, ballistic missiles, and to major technological advances, the Koizumi cabinet announced its plan to procure a two-layered ballistic missile system involving a sea-based Aegis system and the advanced land-to-air PAC-3 Patriot missile system. While noting the need to cooperate further with the United States both technologically and operationally, it stressed that these systems would be used only to defend Japan based on "an autonomous judgment" and not to protect a third country. In other words, acquisition of BMD capabilities would not violate the existing Japanese constitutional doctrine prohibiting the exercise of the right of collective self-defense.[45] In December 2004 Chief Cabinet Secretary Hiroyuki Hosoda stated that the missile shield would be excluded from the ban on export of weapons.

The Joint Statement of the Security Consultative Committee meeting in May 2007 *"Alliance Transformation: Advancing United States-Japan Security and Defense Cooperation"*[46] highlights key advances, in this context including:

- The operational deployment of a U.S. X-Band radar system to Air SDF Shariki Base, Japan, with associated U.S. delivery of radar data to Japanese forces.
- The operational deployment of a U.S. PAC-3 battalion to Kadena Air Base, Japan.
- The recent and continuing addition of Standard Missile (SM-3) defense capabilities to the forward-deployed naval forces of the U.S. Pacific Fleet.
- Japan's decision to accelerate modification of its Aegis ships with SM-3 capabilities. Japan will complete modification of DDG Kongo by the end of 2007, and will expedite modification of DDGs Chokai, Myoko, and Kirishima.
- Japan's decision to expedite the deployment of PAC-3, which resulted in deployment of the first PAC-3 fire unit in March 2007 and its goal to deploy 16 PAC-3 capable fire units by early 2010.
- Priority focus on U.S.-Japan cooperative development of the next generation SM-3 interceptor. The basic agreement on a framework for technology transfer reached by the two sides will facilitate progress on this project as well as in future U.S.-Japan technology cooperation projects.

Normal Japan

Changes in Japanese security policy have been accompanied by a reinvigorated domestic policy debate on security. At one extreme are the Japanese rightists who argue that Japan can only be "normal" by acting both more autonomously in relation to the United States and more assertive militarily against China and North Korea. At the other end of the continuum, the leftists and pacifists argue that real "normality" lies in renouncing military-centreed approaches to security and the bilateral alliance. Nonetheless there has been an increasing convergence of mainstream opinion in favour of a more proactive, or "normal," military role for Japan.[47]

The generation that experienced war, defeat, and occupation has largely exited the political scene, taking with it the reflexive pacifism and risk avoidance that had determined Japan's international posture for the last 50 years. The new generation is much less encumbered by history, more overtly nationalistic, and more willing to see Japan play an assertive international role.[48] The triad of economic diplomacy, engagement with international organisations, and a minimalist military posture predicated on a capable self-defense force with American guarantees of protection is no longer perceived by the post-war generation to be adequately achieving the national interests and influence that country seeks.[49]

There are two primary reasons for this.[50] The first reason is that Japan finds that in order to have a real voice among the major powers it must participate more actively and substantively in international security. The second reason from the realist perspective is that the security environment in which Japan now finds itself has changed dramatically, such that Japan cannot maintain the safety of its people and interests without substantive change in the way it conceives of self-defense.

Changes in the security environment and the rise of a new generation have ended the taboo on discussion on amending the 1947 'peace constitution. There has been a growing feeling in Japan that to meet the challenges of the post-Cold War world, Japan needs greater flexibility in its defense policy that may require not only further reinterpretation of the constitution but also its formal amendment. The issues in focus are:[51]

- Paragraph One of Article Nine of the Constitution that renounces war as a sovereign right and threat or use of force to settle international disputes.
- The need to legitimise military forces and clarify the right of self-defense.

- The right to collective self-defense, i.e., the right to respond to an attack against an ally or against a partner in a U.N. operation.

In August 2005, the Japanese Prime Minister, Junichiro Koizumi proposed an amendment to the constitution in order to increase Japan's Defence Forces' roles in international affairs. A draft of the proposed constitution was released by the Liberal Democratic Party (LDP) on 22 November 2005 as part of the fiftieth anniversary of the party's founding. Important changes include:

- New wording for the Preamble.
- First paragraph of Article Nine renouncing war is retained. The second paragraph forbidding the maintenance of "land, sea and air forces, as well as other war potential" is replaced by an Article Nine (2), which permits a "defense force" under control of the Prime Minister, which defends the nation and may participate in international activities.

In May 2007 the Japanese Parliament passed a bill outlining a referendum to amend the constitution's Article Nine. The law was the second piece of legislation passed during Prime Minister Shinzo Abe's administration that demonstrated his intention to cast off Japan's pacifist past, following the 2006's law upgrading the defense agency to a ministry. Earlier in a statement on May 3, 2007, the 60th anniversary of the Constitution's adoption, Prime Minister Abe called for "a bold review of the postwar regime all the way back to its origins and an in-depth discussion of the constitution" which has become "incapable of adapting to the great changes taking place."[52] In the meantime, a 13-member group led by Shunji Yanai, former Japanese ambassador to the United States, has begun looking at how the country might be able to embrace collective defense without modifying the constitution. The group will look at how Japan's Self-Defense Force could respond to four kinds of crises under current restrictions, and answer these questions:[53]

- Whether Japanese naval vessels are allowed to react when a U.S. warship is attacked.

- Whether Japan should be allowed to intercept ballistic missiles inbound to the United States.
- Whether Japanese forces are allowed to return fire after being attacked during peacekeeping missions in Iraq.
- Whether Japan can provide logistic support and transport of U.S. and other foreign troops.

Though the public will not vote on the amendment till 2010, support for constitutional amendment has been on the rise. For example in a April 2001 *Yomiuri* poll, 54 per cent of respondents supported constitutional revision while 28 per cent opposed; in the 2004 *Yomiuri* poll 65 per cent of respondents supported constitutional revision (highest percentage since the poll was first taken in 1981) while 23 per cent opposed. In 2006 the *Asahi Shimbun* national opinion poll found that 60 per cent favour constitutional revision.[54] In separate poll results published in May this year the *Mainichi Shimbun* and *Nikkei Shimbun* newspapers both said 51 percent of those surveyed were in favour of changing the constitution.[55] It is the first time those supporting a change topped fifty percent according to the Mainichi Shimbun.[56]

However "Normal Japan" will not be a Japan standing alone. Rather Japan's current path toward the "normalisation" of Japanese security policy is the incremental and cautious expanding of national military capabilities and responsibilities within the framework of a strengthened U.S.-Japan alliance. As Yoichiro Sato points out the proposed four scenarios being looked into by Group 13 suggest that the scope of collective defense the current government is willing to support is of limited nature — far from making Japan a "normal military power".[57] The current momentum for constitutional revision and collective self-defense is in no small measure designed to ease pressure from the United States that has been building on the issue. In 2000, the Armitage Report, had explicitly criticised Japan stating, "Japan's prohibition against collective self-defense is a constraint on alliance cooperation". In 2004 Richard Armitage, then U.S. Deputy Secretary of State, attempted to link Japan's quest for a U.N. Security Council seat with Tokyo's exercise of the right to collective self-defense.

Japan's policy-makers today consider security policy more

realistically. The solution, however, has not been to develop a strategy of self-reliance.[58] On the contrary, Japan has reaffirmed the importance of its alliance with the United States as the cornerstone of its security policy. Change in Japan's security posture is geared primarily towards becoming a "normal" and more reliable ally that shares "not only costs but also risks". As Michael Green points out Japan is a "reluctant realist".

As for what is driving this change there is hardly any doubt that it is China. To deal with a rising China "Japan has chosen to tie itself tighter to its time-honoured insurance-policy provider. Its force transformation, defense buildup, and participation in the U.S.-led war against terrorism can be viewed as costs of Japan's insurance policy upgrade. This tilt may turn out to be unnecessary in the long run if the risks are lowered once China's course settles on a more predictable direction."[59] In the interim, from a Japanese perspective, strengthening the Japan-U.S. alliance is the best option.

NOTES

1. John Price, "A Just Peace: The San Francisco Peace Treaty in Historical Perspective", JPRI Working Paper No. 78, June 2001. http://www.jpri.org/publications/workingpapers/wp78.html
2. Text of treaty available at http://www.yale.edu/lawweb/avalon/diplomacy/japan/japan001.htm
3. Extract from a Speech to the Japanese Diet by Prime Minister Yoshida on October 12, 1951. Available at http://www.niraikanai.wwma.net/pages/archive/yoshida51.html
4. Jacob Brown "Catalysts, Choices and Cooperation: Japanese Military Normalization and the U.S.-Japan Alliance" http://www.stanford.edu/group/sjeaa/journal52/japan2.pdf
5. Text of treaty available at Japan Ministry of Foreign Affairs website http://www.mofa.go.jp/region/n-america/U.S./q&a/ref/1.html
6. Sheila A. Smith "*Do Domestic Politics Matter? The Case of U.S. Military Bases in Japan*" http://www.gwu.edu/~nsarchiv/japan/smith_wp.htm
7. Hung-mao Tien and Tun-jen Chang, (eds.), *The Security Environment in the Asia-Pacific.* Armonk: M.E. Sharpe, 2000, p. 55.
8. Robert A. Wampler, "*Power and Prosperity: Linkages Between Security*

and Economics in U.S.-Japanese Relations Since 1960" http://www.ciaonet.org/pbei/igcc/igc03/

9. Michael W. Chinworth, "*Defense=Economics Linkages in U.S,-Japan Relations: An Overview of Policy Positions and Objectives*" http://www.gwu.edu/~nsarchiv/japan/chinworth_wp.htm
10. Sheila A. Smith, "*Do Domestic Politics Matter? The Case of U.S. Military Bases in Japan*" http://www.gwu.edu/~nsarchiv/japan/smith_wp.htm
11. Masao Miyoshi, *Off Centre: Power and Culture Relations between Japan and the United States* (Cambridge: Harvard University Press, 1991), p. 64.
12. Christopher W. Hughes, "*Japanese Military Modernization in Search of a Normal Security Role*", http://www.nbr.org/publications/strategic_asia/pdf/sa05xs_4japan.pdf
13. See M.W. John Chapman, Ian Gow and Reinhard Drifte, *Japan's Quest for Comprehensive Security; Defense, Diplomacy, Dependence* (London: Pinter Publishers, 1983).
14. See Dennis Yasutomo, *The New Multilateralism in Japan's Foreign Policy* (New York: St. Martin's Press, 1995), Chapter 2.
15. See R.M. Orr, *The Emergence of Japan's Foreign Aid Power* (New York: Columbia University Press, 1990) and A. Miyashita, *Limits to Power* (Lanham: Lexington Books), 2003.
16. See, K.E. Calder, "Japan's Foreign Economic Policy Formation: Explaining the Reactive State", *World Politics,* 40, (July 1998).
17. See, Michael Blaker, "Evaluating Japan's Diplomatic Performance," in Gerald L. Curtis (ed.), *Japan's Foreign Policy After the Cold War: Coping with Change* (Armonk, NY: M.E. Sharpe, 1993).
18. Defense Agency, *Defense of Japan*, 1991, pp. 138-39.
19. Comment by Senior Japanese Diplomat Okamoto Yukio Cited in Paul Midford "Japan's Response to Terror: Dispatching the SDF to the Arabian See" *Asian Survey***,** Vol. 43, No. 2, 2003, p. 338.
20. Paul Midford, "Japan's Response to Terror: Dispatching the SDF to the Arabian See", *Asian Survey***,** Vol. 43, No. 2, 2003, p. 338.
21. Christopher W. Hughes, *Japan's Re-emergence as a 'Normal' Military Power* (New York: Oxford University Press, 2004) p. 42.
22. See Yoichi Funabashi, *Alliance Adrift* (New York: Council on Foreign Relations Press, 1999, pp. 280-95 and Christopher W. Hughes, *Japan's Economic Power and Security: Japan and North Korea* (London: Routledge, 1999) pp. 93-97.
23. Chalmers Johnson "*The Okinawan Rape Incident and the End of the Cold War in East Asia*" JPRI Working Paper No. 16: February 1996 http://www.jpri.org/publications/workingpapers/wp16.html

24. Akio Watanabe, "Has Japan Crossed the Rubicon? Defense Policy Since the Higuchi Report", *Japan Review of International Affairs,* 17(4), Winter 2003, p. 241.
25. *Ibid.*
26. Christopher W. Hughes, "Japanese Military Modernization" In Search of a Normal Security Role", http://www.nbr.org/publications/strategic_asia/pdf/sa05xs_4japan.pdf
27. *Japan-U.S. Joint Declaration on Security: Alliance for the 21*st *Century,* April 17, 1996. Text available at http://www.mofa.go.jp/region/n-america/us/security/security.html
28. Text available at http://www.mofa.go.jp/region/n-america/us/security/guideline2.html
29. Peter J. Katzenstein and Nobuo Okawara, "*Japan. Asia-Pacific Security and the Case for Analytical Eclecticism*" http://www.arts.cornell.edu/tmpphp/publications/p153.pdf
30. Christopher W. Hughes, "*Sino-Japanese Relations and Ballistic Missile Defense*" http://www2.warwick.ac.uk/fac/soc/csgr/research/working papers/2001/wp6401.pdf
31. http://www.kantei.go.jp/foreign/policy/2001/anti-terrorism/1116 keikaku_e.html
32. Gavan McCormack "*Japan's Afghan Expedition*" http://www.iwanami.co.jp/jpworld/text/Afghanexpedition01.html
33. Fukushiro Nukaga, "Japan's Emergency Legislation and the War on Terrorism", *Heritage Lecture* 749, June 10, 2002 http://www.heritage.org/Research/AsiaandthePacific/HL749.cfm
34. *Ibid.*
35. "Press Conference by Prime Minister Junichiro Koizumi" December 9, 2003. Available at http://www.mofa.go.jp/region/middle_e/iraq/issue2003/pmpress0312.html
36. Christopher W. Hughes "Japanese Military Modernization" In *Search of a Normal Security Role*, http://www.nbr.org/publications/strategic_asia/pdf/sa05xs_4japan.pdf
37. Christopher W. Hughes "*Ballistic Missile Defense and US-Japan and US-UK Alliances Compared*" http://www.garnet-eu.org/fileadmin/documents/working_papers/1106.pdf
38. "Rikuji to no Kankei Kyoka" (Strengthening Relations with the GSDF), *Asahi Shimbun,* December 8, 2004. Cited in Christopher W. Hughes "Japanese Military Modernization" In Search of a Normal Security Role" http://www.nbr.org/publications/strategic_asia/pdf/sa05xs_4japan.pdf
39. Text available at http://www.mofa.go.jp/region/n-america/us/security/scc/joint0502.html

40. "*The Council on Security and Defense Capabilities Report: Japan's Vision For Future Security and Defense Capabilities*", October 2004. Available at: http://www.globalsecurity.org/wmd/library/news/japan/2004/041000-csdc-report.pdf
41. National Defense Strategy of the United States of America, March 2005. Available at: http://www.au.af.mil/au/awc/awcgate/nds/nds2005.pdf
42. See Chapter One "The Realignment of U.S, Forces and the East Asian Security" in *East Asian Strategic Review 2006* (Tokyo: National Institute for Defense Studies, 2006).
43. Text available at http://www.mofa.go.jp/region/n-america/us/security/scc/doc0605.html
44. These details are from "Diet passes 'incentive' bill to realign U.S. forces", *Asahi Shimbun*, May 24, 2007. Available at http://www.asahi.com/english/Herald-asahi/TKY200705240095.html
45. Statement by Japan's Chief Cabinet Secretary Regarding Acquisition of a Ballistic Missile Defense System and Related Matters], December 19, 2003. Cited in Mike M. Mochizuki "Japan" between Alliance and Autonomy" http://www.nbr.org/publications/strategic_asia/pdf/sa04_4japan.pdf
46. Text available at http://www.mofa.go.jp/region/n-america/us/security/scc/joint0705.html
47. Christopher W. Hughes "*Japanese Military Modernization" In Search of a Normal Security Role*" http://www.nbr.org/publications/strategic_asia/pdf/sa05xs_4japan.pdf
48. See Rust Deming "Japan's Constitution and Defense Policy: Entering a New Era", *Strategic Forum,* No. 213, 2004. Available at http://www.ciaonet.org/wps/der02/
49. See William E. Rapp, "*Paths Diverging? The Next Decade in the U.S.-Japan Alliance*", Available at http://www.strategicstudiesinstitute.army.mil/asia-pacific/japan/
50. *Ibid.*
51. Rust Deming, "Japan's Constitution and Defense Policy: Entering a New Era" *Strategic Forum*, No. 213, 2004. Available at http://www.ciaonet.org/wps/der02/
52. Sachiko Sakamaki, "*Japan Passes Constitution Revision Procedure Law*", http://www.bloomberg.com/apps/news?pid=20601101&sid=a14GLnjxq6SI&refer=japan
53. Wendell Minnick, "Japan Group 13 Seeks Article 9 Loopholes" *Defense News* May 28, 2007. http://www.defensenews.com/story.php?F=2780394&C=asiapac
54. Details from the "*Constitutional Revision Research Project 1997-2006*",

Reischauer Institute of Japanese Studies, http://www.fas.harvard.edu/~rijs/crrp/chronology/y1997-2006.html

55. "*Japanese Support Grows for Military Ammendment*" http://edition.cnn.com/2007/WORLD/asiapcf/05/02/japan.constitution.ap/index.html
56. *Ibid.*
57. Quoted in Wendell Minnick, "Japan Group 13 Seeks Article 9 Loopholes", *Defense News,* May 28, 2007. http://www.defensenews.com/story.php?F=2780394&C=asiapac
58. Soeya Yoshida "*Japan as a Regional Actor*" http://www.jcie.or.jp/thinknet/pdfs/asean_soeya.pdf
59. Tomohiko Taaniguchi, "*Whither Japan? New Constitution and Defense Buildup*" http://www.brookings.edu/fp/cnaps/papers/taniguchi20050530.pdf

2

Japan-China Relations

On April 3, 2005, angry Chinese crowds in Chengdu, Sichuan Province smashed the windows of a Japanese-owned supermarket as part of a protest against Japan's bid for a permanent seat on the United Nations Security Council. What began as a relatively small protest in central China soon developed into a series of full-scale anti-Japanese demonstrations. Tens of thousands people, across more than twenty major cities in China took part in the largest and most sustained mass protests since those at Tiananmen Square in 1989. Citing Japan's perceived lack of remorse for World War II atrocities, protesters vandalised Japanese restaurants and shops, damaged Japanese-made cars, and called for boycotts of Japanese goods.

This string of anti-Japanese protests in China represented mounting tensions between China and Japan, at once bitter political rivals and economic partners. Indeed the two countries have experienced a dramatic deterioration in political relations over recent years, with the Japanese displaying increasingly hostile attitudes toward China, even as the Chinese and Japanese economies have become increasingly intertwined and trade and investment has flourished.

Sino-Japanese Relations During the Cold War

During the post-Second World War period of United States-backed "containment" of China, there was a sharp divergence between official policy and popular attitudes in Japan. As an ally of the United States, the Japanese government was committed to non-recognition, whereas popular sentiments favoured diplomatic relations and expanded trade. Pro-Chinese sentiment found support not only in the desire of the business community[1] for a source of raw materials and a profitable market but also in the popular feeling of cultural affinity with the Chinese as well as a widespread feeling of guilt about Japanese aggression on the mainland.[2]

Even Prime Minister Yoshida believed that the promotion of economic relations with Mainland China was indispensable for Japan's economic development. He also felt that the Americans were wrong in regarding the Soviet Union and China as monolithic, and that the two communist countries would sooner or later become estranged given the differences in their civilisations, national character of their people, and political circumstances.[3] He wrote "Red or White: China remains our next door neighbour. Geography and economic laws will, I believe, prevail in the long run over any ideological differences and trade barriers."[4]

The Japanese government managed these tensions by proposing a separation of political and economic relations wherein "private trade" between Japan and China was regulated by the 1952, 1953 and 1955 agreements on Japan-China Non-governmental Trade and followed a general trend of expansion till early 1958. However when the fourth agreement in 1958 sought to propose that each side establish a private trade representative's office with some diplomatic privileges including the right to hoist its national flag in the capital of the other party, immense pressure from the United States forced Prime Minister Kishi's administration to backtrack. The Nagasaki Flag incident—when the Japanese government took the position that the action of a youth who pulled down the Chinese flag at a Chinese product fair in a department store in Nagasaki did not constitute damage to a foreign national flag-led Beijing to announce that it was breaking off all economic and cultural exchanges with Japan. Private trade between the two countries was resumed by the Liao-Takasaki agreement of 1962 and though the relationship continued to be strongly restrained by the Cold War Asia policy of the United States, the Japanese posture was far from being anti-

China. For example the famous "Taiwan clause" of the Nixon-Sato joint communiqué was inserted mainly in order to extract a US concession on Okinawa.

It was not until the United States' opening to China in 1971 that Japan was released from the bilateral and international structural constraint imposed by the US-Japan security alliance. US-China rapprochement took the administration of Prime Minister Sato with complete surprise, but the subsequent government of Prime Minister Tanaka quickly adjusted policy by normalising diplomatic relations in 1972. Prime Minister Tanaka visited China in September 1972 and in the subsequent joint statement Beijing was recognised as "the sole legal government of China" while Japan "fully understood and respected China's insistence that Taiwan was an inalienable part of the territory of the People's Republic of China."[5]

Prime Minister Tanaka later summarized his views toward Japan-China diplomatic normalisation in three points: First, the China issue was "a domestic issue rather than a diplomatic issue," and "the settlement of the China issue removes two-thirds of domestic problems." Second, the combined population of the two nations "comprises one-fourth of the world's population. Without the settlement of such relations, there would be no stability of Japan." Third, "Japan should establish friendly relations with China alongside with maintaining the Japan-US security treaty. With the formation of the triangular relationship among Japan, the United States and China, peace in the Far East is secured." Relations between the two nations deepened, as was seen with the presentation of giant pandas to Japan by the Chinese government and mutual visits by leaders and the Japan-China Treaty of Peace and Friendship was signed six years later in 1978.

China's economic importance to Japanese policy-makers rose in tandem with the market-oriented reforms and increased foreign interaction associated with the policies of Chinese leader Deng Xiaoping. Throughout the next decade, policy toward China continued to receive high priority as evident from (1) Japanese Prime Minister Ohira cabinet's comprehensive commitment to assist China after Deng Xiaoping launched the ambitious modernisation programme; and (2) expansion of the commitments by the Prime

Minister Nakasone and the succeeding Prime Minister Takeshita's cabinet in the mid-1980s. Ohira's commitment was composed of two central pillars—official development assistance (ODA) and the granting of most-favoured-nations (MFN) status which allowed Beijing a preferential tariff treatment. Specifically, assistance included Japan's first post-war governmental loan of up to 50 billion yen in fiscal year 1979 to assist six Chinese development projects including a grant to assist the construction of Japan-China friendship hospital at Beijing.

When Prime Minister Yasuhiro Nakasone visited Beijing in March 1984, his hands too were laden with presents. He promised a largely expanded volume of the second round ODA programme that was up to 470 billion yen during the next 5 years, and bank loans for oil and coal development amounted to 580 billion yen. The Japanese government also made an official announcement of "long-term economic cooperation" to Chinese modernisation efforts wherein Japanese funds were to be directly linked to the seventh five-year economic development plan of China.

Given Nakasone's subsequent visit to the Ysukuni shrine in 1985 and the textbook issue in 1986 Prime Minister Takeshita's largesse composed of the largest scale economic assistance in Japan's bilateral relations and the settlement of an investment guarantee agreement. The total amount of the third round ODA programme (1990-1995) rose up to 810 billion yen regarding 41 projects (almost double of the second round programme). Takeshita cabinet's decision was a political choice based on the logic of 'balance by expansion' which means that symbolic conflicts could be resolved through an aggressive expansion of bilateral partnership in the areas of economic cooperation.[6] From 1972 to 1989 under the shared umbrella of partners in the Cold War the Japanese confidently expected that the two countries would become increasingly accustomed to cooperation, even if indirect, on security and Japanese developmental assistance and expanded trade would forge close economic networks.

The strategic rationale, bringing together China, Japan, and the United States against their mutual enemy, the Soviet Union, ended abruptly in 1989 with the collapse of the Berlin Wall and the subsequent breakup of the Soviet Union. According to Gilbert Rozman the "Japanese counted on China's international isolation and continued need for economic growth as a basis for legitimacy at a time of collapsing world communism to give their country unprecedented leverage."[7] The idea was that just as Eastern Europe was drawing closer to the West to share in its prosperity, China would elect to draw closer to Japan, whose abundant capital and advanced technology would be indispensable to China's future. When the Tiananmen Square incident occurred in 1989, Japan was reluctant to apply sanctions and joined the other G-7 countries at the Paris summit in a declaration criticising China after successfully arguing for the inclusion of a passage on the importance of not isolating China. At the 1990 G-7 summit in Houston the Japanese Prime Minister Kaifu stated:

> "While we strongly criticized the suppression of human rights during the Tiananmen incident and continue to do so, we consider it important to keep China from falling into isolation and to encourage it to continue its reform process and open-door policy. Our aim is for China to become an integral part of the regional framework of peace and prosperity…I feel that we should take appropriate note of the positive steps that the Chinese have taken and let them know that we expect further progress. It is on this basis that Japan has decided to go ahead with the gradual implementation of a package of yen loans to China that was agreed upon before the Tiananmen incident, through which we hope to contribute to China's economic development and the improvement of living standards in that country. Economic progress, in turn, is expected to encourage China's process of democratisation."[8]

However, with China's rapid implementation of a market-based economy and ongoing high level of growth, Japanese worries about the long-term rise of Chinese power, including the negative impact on regional strategic relations have increased. Difficulties in managing the relationship between the two countries have gradually become salient since the late 1990s and voices have been growing among Japanese in recent years that Japan should assert its national interests more frankly vis-à-vis China. The resulting state of affairs is frequently characterised as "economically hot and politically cold" wherein increasing economic co-operation and integration has occurred in tandem with growing levels of political discord and animosity between the two governments over a broad range of problems including, most significantly, increasing nationalism on both sides and mutual suspicion over each country's long-term ambitions and goals.[9]

Rising China

The relative balance of power between China and Japan underwent a dramatic shift in the 1990s. The Chinese economy began its rapid takeoff, while the Japanese economy descended into a decade of stagnation.[10] Often referred to as the "lost decade," this era saw the economic bubble burst and Japan's archaic financial system break down. Companies went out of business, banks failed, and unemployment soared. In 1997 with the advent of the Asian economic crisis, Japan officially entered into a period of severe recession. Even though Japan remained well ahead of China in absolute economic and technological capabilities, China started to narrow the gap at an impressive pace. China's real GDP grew by 9.7 per cent a year on average from 1990 to 2003.[11] In 1990, its share of world exports was 1.9 per cent; that grew to 4 per cent in 2000 and 6 per cent by 2003. It's share of world imports grew from 1.5 per cent in 1990, to 3.6 per cent in 2000 and 5.7 per cent by 2003.

The implications for Japan were not just numerical. In the early 1990s, China was perceived as a threat to its Southeast Asian neighbours in part due to its conflicting territorial claims over the South China Sea and past support of communist insurgency. This perception began to change in the wake of the Asian financial crisis of 1997/98 when China resisted pressure to devalue its currency, which would have exacerbated devaluations in Thailand and Indonesia, and portrayed its decision as standing up for other Asian nations.[12] Since then, in statements and speeches, Chinese leaders have enunciated a doctrine of "win-win" relations, highlighting that Southeast Asians can benefit from their relationship with China even as China benefits from its relationship with them. Moreover rhetoric has been backed with real initiatives.

Over the past five years, China has ended nearly all of its old border disputes and has signed Southeast Asia's Treaty of Amity and Cooperation that commits the signatories to mutual respect for sovereignty and equality. Beijing has committed to creating a code of conduct on the South China Sea. It has enthusiastically signed bilateral cooperative agreements with several Asian states and also reversed its previous reluctance towards multilateral organisations. As a dialogue partner with ASEAN, China works closely with the organisation, trying to strengthen it and, according to Asian diplomats, initiating far more joint projects than other partners, such as Japan or the United States.[13] As a result perceptions of China in Southeast Asia have shifted significantly, so much so that elites and publics in a majority of the 10 members of the Association of Southeast Asian Nations (ASEAN) now see China as a constructive actor—and potentially the preeminent regional power.[14] Though Japan remains the predominant source of investment, retains the larger trade relationship, and drives the currency negotiations within the region its initiatives have been largely a reaction to Chinese moves. In the words of a senior Southeast Asian diplomat "Japan doesn't know what it wants. They have no consensus on what their role is."[15]

Consequently today "China is a source of existential angst for Japan's political class."[16] For, hierarchical constructs of international relations are critical to Japanese perspectives on national identity and, as Masaru Tamamoto points out, "China's rise has robbed Japan of its identity as the world's economic miracle." The foundation of Japan's postwar role has been its economic success and pre-eminent standing within the region. China's rise is not only a challenge to the structure of regional politics, but to Japan's national identity, too. And driven by the desire to preserve its status as a powerful nation in the global system the Japanese policy establishment is increasingly focused on the "China threat".

Economic Interdependence

Japan has long used its economic capabilities as one of the principal instruments in the conduct of foreign policy wherein economic interaction with China has been dictated by three interconnected reasons—commercial importance, a feeling of guilt for past aggression and strategic calculations of interdependence. According to Suh, Seung Won Japanese economic diplomacy towards China from early 1979 to the mid-1997 can be divided into four typical stages in terms of the successive cabinets' major decisions:

1. Ohira cabinet's comprehensive commitment to assist China right after Deng Xiao-Ping launched its ambitious modernisation programme;
2. expansion of the commitments by the Nakasone and the succeeding Takeshita cabinet in the mid-1980s;
3. participation into the Western economic sanctions against China after the Tiananmen incident in June 4, 1989; and
4. independent economic sanctions after the Chinese nuclear tests in 1995.

These decisions have included various economic measures such as governmental loans, grants in aid, technical assistance, MFN status, governmental bonds, COCOM measures, foreign direct investments and others.[17]

During the year immediately prior to Sino-Japanese diplomatic normalisation, the two countries, bilateral trade stood at about 900 million dollars, approximately 4 per cent of China's total external trade at the time.[18] Normalisation was quickly followed by a sharp rise in China's imports of Japanese goods, first mainly of textile goods and various machinery tools, and later of household electronics, cars and light trucks, etc. In December of 1979, Japan announced that it would begin providing China with governmental support for development (ODA). The purpose of Japan's policy toward China was to support the modernisation of its physical infrastructure, to encourage the reform and liberalisation of its policies, and to establish political and economic relations between China and Japan. More generally, it was also meant to give special attention, within in its overall ODA initiative, to a country that turned down war reparations.

Politically, the Japanese leadership, particularly the Prime Minister and the Ministry of Foreign Affairs held the view that proactive economic assistance employing governmental loans and other economic instruments would be an effective policy alternative to contribute to peace and stability in Asia and encourage the Chinese leadership's pragmatic and moderate behaviour in contrast to the ideology-centered approach.[19] Japan was, therefore, a prime source of economic assistance to China through its overseas development assistance (ODA), exports of capital equipment, flows of investment funds, technology transfers, and technical assistance. Since as early as 1981 Japanese firms contributed to the Chinese economy a total of US$ 36.34 billion in foreign direct investment (FDI) through 2002, making Japan China's largest foreign investor. Japan's FDI and financial aid to China consistently exceeded 10 per cent of China's annual FDI inflow.

The idea of economic engagement gained further momentum in the immediate post-Cold War period. Trade frictions between the United States and Japan combined with a perceived 'fluidity' in American military commitment to East Asia helped to consolidate the view within the Japanese policy establishment that China was best steered towards a peaceful and sustainable path with economic policy tools. In April 1991 the Japanese Prime Minister announced four principles for disbursement of ODA including consideration of democratisation and human rights situation in the recipient countries but the government was careful to indicate that these were not "conditions".

In 1992 two-way trade between the two countries reached US$ 29 billion making Japan the second most important trading partner of China after Hong Kong while China was Japan's second largest source of imports.[20] In 1993 the two-way total trade stood at US$ 37.8 billion and Japan became China's number one trading partner while China was Japan's number-two trading partner after the United States.[21] Also in 1992 Japanese investment made up 11 per cent of the total investment in China and Japan's contribution constituted 46 percent of China's total bilateral ODA.[22] Even with China's nuclear test in 1995 Japanese retaliation was minimal as Japan cut off only the grant portion of its ODA to China, a small portion of its total ODA package.

Correspondingly, the growth in bilateral trade between China and Japan in the 1990s was rapid and more or less steady. This is not to suggest that economic relations between Japan and China were trouble-free. However a combination of skillful high-level diplomacy together with an underlying commitment to the economic relationship on both sides mitigated conflict. Since the opening of the Chinese economy in the early 1990s, trade between China and Japan increased at an average of 16 per cent per annum[23] exceeding the growth of China's external trade over the same period (15 per cent).[24] Japan became China's largest trading partner in 1993 and sustained this status through 2003, only exceeded by the U.S. and the European Union in 2004. Meanwhile, China leapfrogged the U.S. to become Japan's largest trading partner in 2004.[25]

Indeed, since Japan's slump in the late 1990s, China has taken on ever-greater importance to Japan as the primary driver of its economic recovery. Even as Japan's exports to the U.S. have remained flat in recent years, exports to China have grown at a striking rate of 30 percent per year.[26] According to the *Economist*, the two economies are indeed strikingly complementary, with cheap Chinese goods delighting Japanese shoppers and sophisticated Japanese equipment humming away in Chinese factories.[27] However the fact that China skipped over the U.S. to become Japan's largest trading partner the same year that Japan slipped from first to third place in China's trading partner rankings has been greeted in Japan with some alarm over a potential "China threat" arising from Japan's increased dependence on the Chinese economy and gave momentum to calls for safeguards and other import restrictions.

In general, when China is said to pose a threat, a sense of danger is often expressed in the following three phrases[28]:

(a) China makes great progress and will soon become a world's major economic power.
(b) Chinese products have strong international competitiveness. China is going to become the "factory of the world" in the near future.
(c) The increased imports from China cause the hollowing-out of the Japanese industry.

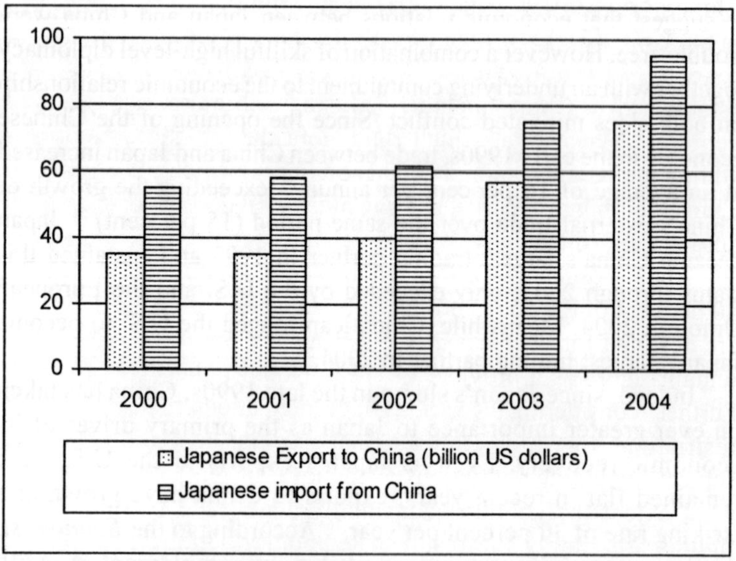

Source: Embassy of Japan in China, http://www.cn.emb-japan.go.jp/english/e-jcdata.htm

The optimistic view, on the other hand, is that at present, the Sino-Japanese trade relations are more complementary than competing. For this reason, the growth of China within the international multilateral framework, will bring a new business opportunity to Japan. In the words of Prime Minister Koizumi: "China should not be perceived as a threat to Japan but rather an opportunity. We must not overwhelm our minds with thoughts of preventing imports from China, but instead, look more at the positive aspects such that Japan too can export to China. Japan also should not be taken in by the 'China threat' theory, but on the contrary, consider the development of China as an opportunity and chance for Japan. This exact phenomenon can be seen today. Trade between Japan and China is drastically increasing, in both exports and imports. I believe that both Japanese and Chinese economic circles as well as the people of both countries fully understand our mutually interdependent and mutually beneficial relations for each economy."[29]

Clearly the fortunes of Japan Inc are already seriously tied to

China. Between 1999 and 2003, Japan's foreign direct investment in the United States dropped by 52 per cent, while its FDI in China rose by 314 per cent. [30] Countless Japanese firms are now established in China, including Mitsui, with more than 110 joint ventures; Matsushita, which runs more than 49 factories and is adding more; and Canon, Hitachi and Sharp, which intend to make China their biggest market and site of their biggest factory. Japanese auto giants Honda and Toyota are already top players.

Analysis such as Kazuo Ogoura[31] do point out that some 30 to 40 per cent of the goods produced by Japanese companies in China are destined for overseas markets. Thus the country's significance remains more as a provider of cheap labour rather than a market. Further "considering the various rules, regulations, and market-entry restrictions to which China's financial and capital markets are subject (including restrictions on money transfers), one must ask to what extent the country's apparently huge trade and investment figures are simply the result of temporary action by companies anxious to ensure that they do not miss the boat."[32]

At the same time China's economic growth and military modernisation has led many Japanese to question why their government continues to provide ODA to China. Japan was China's largest bilateral aid donor during the two decades between 1979 and 1998. But criticism has led the government to scale back some of its assistance to China for the first time in the postwar period. The amount of yen loans to China have been cut annually by 24.7 per cent (for 2001), by 24.8 per cent (for 2002), by 20.2 per cent (for 2003), and by another 10 per cent (for 2004), In March 2005, the Japanese government announced its intention to terminate Japan's yen loans to China by the year 2008.

In addition two main reform measures implemented by the Ministry of Foreign Affairs have changed the procedure and priority of Japan's ODA to China. First, starting in 2001, aid to China has been negotiated and disbursed on a single-year basis, rather than in multiyear lump-sum packages, a practice that was unique among Japan's ODA recipients. Second, Japanese ODA's priority has been shifted from infrastructure building in coastal areas towards areas such as conservation of environment and eco-systems, the improvement of living standards and social development in the inland regions, human resources development, institution building, and technology transfers.

Japan and China are also becoming increasing rivals for trade with other Asian countries. China was the first country to have a free trade agreement (FTA) with the 10-member Association of Southeast Asian (ASEAN) bloc with both sides agreeing in 2002 to establish a free-trade area creating a market of 1.8 billion consumers and a projected economic activity totaling more than US$ 2 trillion. At present, trade between China and ASEAN is growing at nearly 40 per cent a year and is predicted to reach US$ 200 billion a year by 2010.[33] Japan proposed the same to ASEAN in November 2004. Officially dubbed a Comprehensive Economic Partnership it will cover trade in goods, services, investments, rules of origin, dispute settlement, technical barriers to trade, economic cooperation and, intellectual property rights. In the meanwhile Japan has concluded bilateral agreements with Singapore, in 2002, Malaysia, in December 2005 and the Philippines, in September 2006. Japan has also been negotiating FTAs with South Korea and Indonesia. In mid-February 2005, Japan and Vietnam held preparatory talks in Hanoi for formal FTA negotiations. The governments of Japan and India started negotiating a comprehensive Economic Partnership Agreement in January 2007.

It is also felt that China's economic development has disturbed the balance of global supply and demand in natural resources and is making it more difficult for Japan to secure these resources. In a striking example just days after Japanese Prime Minister Koizumi's visit to Uzbekistan and Kazakhstan in August 2006, the first visit by a Japanese Prime Minister to these countries, China National Petroleum Corp., China's largest oil producer, said that together with Korea National Oil Corp., Malaysia's Petronas, Lukoil of Russia, and iocal group Uzbekneftegaz, it had obtained a 20 percent stake in a joint oil and gas exploration project in Uzbekistan's Aral Sea.[34] Both countries have lobbied hard for alternative routes for a pipeline from eastern Siberia's oilfields to Pacific Rim nations. It has been reported that Japan plans to seek the inclusion of a pledge to preferentially supply crude oil to Japan, even in emergencies, like war in the proposed FTA with GCC, the customs union comprised of Saudi Arabia, Bahrain, Kuwait, Oman, Qatar and the United Arab

Emirates that accounts for more than 70 per cent of Japanese oil imports.[35]

Worsening Political Ties

Growing economic interdependence between China and Japan in the post Cold War period has not been matched by a corresponding improvement in relations in other spheres. In the words of Michael Yahuda "To be sure the economic interdependence between China and Japan is crucially important to the relationship as a whole. The leaders are particularly conscious of its beneficial significance. It also ensures that both sides can point to underlying positive value in the relationship. Arguably, the economic interdependence acts as a constraint against allowing relations to deteriorate unduly. But so far there is little evidence of these considerations spilling over into other aspects of their relations."[36]

Sino-Japan relations are still coloured by historical animosity and territorial disputes and have led to considerable political friction and historic tension as well as occasional naval clashes. The tensions date to 19th-century disputes and Japan's 1931-45 occupation of China. They play out in recurring cycles of Chinese anger over Japan's perceived lack of contrition for war-time crimes and ongoing disputes over islands in the East China Sea the Chinese call Diaoyutai and the Japanese refer to as the Senkaku.[37]

The greatest obstacle to effective Sino-Japanese cooperation stems from Chinese memories of Japanese atrocities during World War II. Estimates are that China suffered over 1.3 million military deaths and perhaps as many as 13 million civilian deaths as a result of Japan's invasion of China in 1937 and the subsequent eight-year war that only ended with Japan's surrender to the U.S. in 1945. The extent and number of atrocities on civilians committed during this war also remains a point of contention between the two countries. In "The Rape of Nanjing," in December 1937, perhaps as many as 300,000 civilians lost their lives in several days of rampage, brutality, rape, and murder by uncontrolled Japanese troops. About 10,000 Chinese as well as Russian, Korean, and Mongolian civilians were used as guinea pigs, infected with plague, cholera and anthrax bacteria in biological weapons experiments by the infamous Unit 731 near

Harbin. These memories linger and are still used as a yardstick by many among the Chinese to judge postwar Japan—In a 2000 public opinion survey of adults concerning images of the other country, although about a majority of Chinese saw Japan "prosperous" as a country and its people "diligent" and "courteous," only 9 per cent saw the country as "peaceful" and 16 per cent "democratic," and only 6 per cent saw its people as "peaceful," 5 per cent as reliable, even while 44 per cent saw them as "headstrong," and 27 per cent saw them as "aggressive.[38]

Trouble over the historical record first broke out in the summer of 1982 in a dispute over Japanese textbooks. According to Japanese and Chinese press reports of the time, Japan's Ministry of Education instructed history textbook authors to delete, reword, or tone down passages referring to Japan's wartime record. Chinese anger also focused on the August 1985 visit by Japanese Prime Minister Nakasone to the Yasukuni shrine in Tokyo, where war criminals are commemorated alongside Japan's war dead. Since then the debate on Japanese militarism and the question of Japan's responsibility has remained central to the relationship between the two countries.

A series of apologies by Japanese leaders has made only marginal progress towards healing the historical wounds including the Japanese Emperor's statement of regret in Beijing in 1992, Prime Minister Hosokawa's unequivocal admission in July 1993 that Japan's conduct during the war was "aggressive and wrong", and apology to the victims of war by Prime Minister Murayama on the occasion of the fiftieth anniversary of the end of the Second World War. The issue arose again in 1998, after Korean President Kim Dae-jung visited Japan in October and obtained written expression of Japan's "remorse and apology." At a China-Japan summit meeting in Tokyo later that year, Chinese President Jiang Zemin demanded a similar written statement. Although Prime Minister Obuchi verbally expressed "remorse and apology," the eventual document only stated that Japan accepts "responsibility for the serious distress and damages caused to the Chinese people through its aggression."

The Japanese government has taken some formal steps to address the issue of historical grievances. Chief among these has been the recognition of the problem of chemical weapons left behind in northeast China. In 1995, Prime Minister Murayama personally recognised this issue and expressed Japan's determination to assist in defusing this threat. In addition, in late 1994, the Japanese government established a foundation using both government and private funding to compensate former "comfort women." In 2004, after the Chinese Foreign Ministry complained that artillery shells from the Japanese Imperial Army were still injuring Chinese citizens, Japan acknowledged that the shells belonged to its erstwhile army and dispatched a weapons excavation team to central China. In the same year the Hiroshima High Court awarded full damages to Chinese wartime forced labourers based on the violation of the plaintiffs' human rights.

Increasingly, however, generational changes in both countries are spinning new social threads and political dynamics and Japanese public, politicians, and officials have become far less patient with China over its playing of the "history card". The Japanese Prime Minister Koizumi emerged as the most visible face of this new political generation, repeatedly visiting the Yaskuni Shrine despite vehement Chinese protests. Koizumi was only the third Japanese leader to visit the shrine in the post-war era, and the only leader to do so more than once. Prime Minister Koizumi's decision to pay his respects at the Yasukuni Shrine for four consecutive years after taking office in 2001 brought unprecedented intensity to the debate.

While Japanese nationalists' denial that events like the "Rape of Nanking" is a minority opinion, there is a growing apology fatigue within the mainstream, which believes that Japan has already expressed enough remorse. Others worry that the type of statement China desires would expose Japan to further financial liability. Some see the issue as part of the Chinese Communist Party's efforts to use history as domestic propaganda to maintain its hold on power. According to Kobayashi Yotaro, Chairman of Fuji Xerox Company and co-chair of the New Japan-China Friendship Committee for the 21st Century "In the eyes of the Japanese, the Chinese government has been trying to divert attention of the Chinese people away from domestic problems and channel their dissatisfaction into complaints about Japan."[39]

Japanese analysts are increasingly questioning China's own history education as being exceedingly focused on the Sino-Japanese

War (1937-1945), while China sharply criticises certain history textbooks in Japan. Thus arguments linking the Chinese Communist Party's domestic legitimacy challenges and biased Chinese education with the "history problem" are no longer regarded as extreme in Japan. For example Kitaoka Shin'ichi, Japan's Deputy Permanent Representative to the United Nations bluntly asked, "How much do Chinese schools teach about the Great Leap Forward and the Cultural Revolution…When it comes to highlighting the glorious episodes in one's history and glossing over the negative chapters, Japan cannot hold a candle to China."[40]

Finally, a good deal of public sentiment in Japan holds that while the actions of the 1930s were wrong, they were not particularly different from those of the imperial powers in other regions of the world. The Japanese view that the history issue is primarily of utilitarian value for China in terms of exploiting it for economic and political ends has once again received impetus with China's recent campaign against Japan's bid for a permanent Security Council seat at the United Nations.

The deadlock over Prime Minister Koizumi's visits to the Yasukuni shrine issue, combined with the large-scale, anti-Japanese demonstrations in major Chinese cities in the spring of 2005, cut off much of the senior-level contacts between Tokyo and Beijing. Chinese President Hu Jintao reiterated China's bottom line on its policy toward Japan in March 2006: There would be no summit between the two countries as long as Japan's prime minister visited Yasukuni Shrine.[41] In an attempt to break the diplomatic impasse Prime Minister Abe did travel to Beijing within weeks of forming his new cabinet in 2006 but he remained vague about the Yasukuni visit, and the controversy at the fundamental level is by no means resolved. New reports suggested that Prime Minister Abe simply told the Chinese side during the summit that he would handle the issue "appropriately." As Haruko Satoh points out "That the manner of honouring the war dead from 60 years ago should become a condition for a meeting of the leaders of two global powers today only goes to show how the 30 years of supposed goodwill had been merely cosmetic."[42]

Increasing Security Concerns

Closely tied to the nationalism conundrum in Sino-Japan affairs is China's ongoing military modernisation. In the early 1990s, some Japanese scholars envisioned that China's enhanced military capability, highlighted by its renewed claims over disputed territories, was evidence of emerging Chinese hegemony and its ambition to fill the power vacuum generated with the end of the Cold War. Masashi Nishihara, for example, warned that, "China appears ready to protect by force its own territorial interests, a move that could create new tensions with Japan and other Asian countries in the future."[43] Official views were however inclined to "build relations of trust" on the assumption that "Beijing's top priority was economic growth and Chinese military modernisation could proceed only gradually."[44]

The tuning point was China's nuclear testing in May 1995 that Japan called "extremely regrettable". In March 1996 when China fired ballistic missiles near Taiwan and conducted military exercises in the Taiwan Straits prior to Taiwan's first democratic presidential election Japan joined the United States in condemning China's missile diplomacy.

The Japanese *Defense White* Paper of 2000 stated "China's recent modernisation of its nuclear, naval, and air forces, and the expansion of the scope of its maritime operations...demand continued scrutiny."[45] Regarding Japan's concerns about the lack of transparency in China's military buildup, the *Defense White Paper* of 2004 expressed clearly: "...the problem is that China does not disclose specific information on the weapons that it possesses, its procurement programmes, unit-level organizations, major operational plans, exercises, or the details of its defense budget." The *Defense White* Paper of 2005 noted that China's military modernization, including apparent plans for a deep-water navy needs to be monitored closely to determine whether it exceeds requirements for self-defense.

The paper also reflected a fundamental change announced by the Japanese Defense Agency in December 2004 as part of a policy review conducted once every decade.[46] The agency decided to shift its strategic focus from the Cold War threat of invasion by the Soviet Union to the potential threat of missiles from North Korea and Chinese incursions around Japan's southernmost islands. The *National Defense*

Programme Guideline for FY 2005 and After—which outlines Japanese defense policy in medium to long-term—affirmed that "...China, which has a strong influence on the security in this region, has been modernizing its nuclear and missile capabilities as well as naval and air forces, and expanding its area of operation at sea. We have to remain attentive to its future course."

Indeed today while North Korea represents the most immediate threat to security, from a Japanese perspective China poses the greatest challenge for Japan's security over the medium to long terms. These concerns focus not on China's military modernisation *per se*, but upon signs that China is now willing to project military power beyond its borders. Over the years Japan has noted the increasing frequency of incursions by Chinese 'observation' and 'scientific' vessels into its Exclusive Economic Zone (EEZ), the gradual encroachment on its EEZ through oil and gas extraction a few miles from the median line between the two countries and China's claims in the South China Sea through which many of Japan's sea-lanes of communication run. The fear is that Beijing could use its small blue-water surface, submarine, and amphibious naval capacities to assert China's territorial claims to the South China Sea and thereby disrupt Japan's sea lines of communication (SLOC).[47] Therefore China's frequent dispatch of "research ships" and warships into Japan's exclusive economic zone (EEZ) around the disputed Senkaku Islands are viewed by many in Japan as evidence of aggressive intent.

Such concerns about China were heightened when a Chinese nuclear-powered submarine passed through Japanese territorial waters on November 10, 2004. Presently the dispute revolves around China's drilling in the Chunxiao field, which is three miles west of the median line, with Japan contending that China is tapping natural gas reserves that extend past the median line. After the November 2004 incursion of the Chinese nuclear submarine into Japanese territorial waters Japan has responded in February 2005 with a declaration of formal possession of the Senkaku Islands and the announcement that it has placed under state control and protection a lighthouse erected by Japanese right-wing activists in 1988. Japan has also decided to accept applications from companies planning to drill for natural gas in the East China Sea near the disputed territories. In September 2005 the dispute turned dangerous when five Chinese naval vessels including a guided missile destroyer were observed near the Chunxiao gas field.[48] Japan intercepted Chinese reconnaissance planes 107 times in the first three months of 2006 as opposed to 13 times in all of 2005.

Then there is Taiwan. There are two principal ways in which Taiwan represents a strategic determinant in Sino-Japanese relations.[49] First, Taiwan is seen as a critical gateway to Japan for Chinese blue-water naval advances from the south. Hence, the island represents a defensive imperative for Japan. Taiwan stands guard as a natural gateway to Japanese waters and losing Taiwan could allow Chinese submarines into Japanese waters from the south, thus facilitating a naval encirclement of Japan from the South China Sea. Second, Taiwan represents an important part of the American strategic security umbrella of Japan, South Korea, Taiwan, the Philippines and Australia which Japan seeks to maintain against its big neighbour.

In this context many Japanese analysts have noted, that Taiwan's democratisation and the indigenisation of Taiwanese politics have pushed Taiwan away from China toward independence, made China's aspiration for Taiwan's peaceful reunification with the mainland more difficult, and thus increased the prospect of China's use of force to achieve Taiwan's reunification. They view the 1995-96 Taiwan Strait crises including China's intimidation of Taiwan through the test-firing of ballistic missiles as indicators of Chinese aggression. Specifically, Japan is worried about China's willingness to project military power in pursuit of its national interests, to possibly challenge the United States militarily in the region over the longer term, and to even use ballistic missiles to strike against U.S. bases in Japan and against rear area support facilities provided by Japan in the event of a full-blown conflict resulting from any Taiwanese move to declare independence. Japanese security planners also fear that in a Taiwan Strait crisis China might attempt to seize offshore islands, such as parts of Okinawa Prefecture, in order to disrupt U.S.-Japan military cooperation.

In 1996, when the US-Japan mutual security treaty was upgraded, Japan vaguely defined its expanded military operational sphere as "Japan's surrounding areas"—and refused to clarify the geographic boundaries. But now Japan is displaying a new overt posture the U.S.-Japanese inclusion of Taiwan as a "common strategic objective". The declaration in conjunction with the Japanese government's identification of the People's Republic of China (PRC), together with North Korea, as a potential national security threat in its December 2004 release of Japan's *National Defense Programme Outline* (NDPO) underlines a new assertiveness on part of Tokyo's *vis a vis* Beijing's rising might in the region. The NDPO posited three scenarios in which China could attack Japan: a confrontation over marine resources, territorial conflict in the Senkaku Islands, and an extension of a China-Taiwan conflict.[50] This uncharacteristically clear statement by the Japanese government of how, in security terms at least, it currently perceives the PRC is a strong indicator of how much Japanese strategic perceptions of China have changed over the last decade.

Implications for India

As pointed out in the previous chapter the United States is a pivotal player in the China-Japan relationship. It is in the context of China that Japanese efforts to redefine the relationship with the United States encounter in the clearest terms the alliance dilemma of abandonment and entrapment. A U.S.-Japanese alliance that is too aggressive alarms China, whereas one that is too weak raises abandonment anxieties in Japan.[51] The sudden reversal of U.S. policy under President Nixon in 1972 was a minor form of abandonment by the key ally and is still very much on the minds of Japanese policymakers and analysts.[52] In order to counteract the uncertainties about China's future path Japan has opted to deepen the military alliance with the United States. To this end, from the perspective of many Japanese policy makers, Japan has no choice, but to maintain and strengthen its alliance with the United States. In the words of Defense Agency Chief Shigeru Ishiba, "Japan can not (afford) to be without allies and who can it really trust except the U.S.? Why? The U.S. bases here in Japan have proven America's commitment to Japan."[53] As Prime Minister Koizumi himself explained, "Japan cannot ensure its own peace and stability by itself. That's why the Japan-U.S. alliance is so important."[54]

Meanwhile, the United States and India have made significant progress in their relationship. U.S. interaction with India has grown rapidly since President Clinton's much-publicised visit to India in March 2000, the subsequent security and counter-terrorism dialogues and extending economic and commercial relations. Under the then new Bush administration Indo-U.S. relations developed at a still faster pace with Secretary of State, Colin Powell, stating in January 2001 "India has the potential to help keep the peace in the vast Indian Ocean area and its periphery. We need to work harder and more consistently to help India in this endeavor".[55] The appointment of Dr. Robert Blackwill as American Ambassador to India indicated the importance that the Bush administration then placed on its relations with India, and his words in September 2001 "President Bush has a global approach to US-India relations consistent with the rise of India as a world power ..."further emphasised India's geo-strategic importance to America.

The September 11, terrorist attacks in the United States 2001 shifted the overall dynamics of U.S. foreign policy discourse and provided a springboard for solidarity and understanding between the two countries. The *National Security Strategy*[56], released in September 2002, stated:

> The United States has undertaken a transformation in its bilateral relationship with India based on a conviction that U.S. interests require a strong relationship with India. We are the two largest democracies, committed to political freedom protected by representative government. India is moving toward greater economic freedom as well. We have a common interest in the free flow of commerce, including through the vital sea-lanes of the Indian Ocean. Finally, we share an interest in fighting terrorism and in creating a strategically stable Asia.

The extent to which India will associate itself with U.S. power and global policies is still a subject of debate within the Indian strategic community. Nonetheless, in June 2005 the United States and India signed a 10-year military cooperation agreement that calls for expanded joint military exercises, increased defense-related trade, and establishing a defense and procurement production group. Expectations are high in Washington that the Indo-U.S. civil nuclear agreement of March 2006 will deepen American military cooperation, trade links, and geopolitical engagement with New Delhi.

Correspondingly, the graph of India-Japan relations has been on an upward trajectory. In the words of Masanori Kondo, "In order to find a political and economic counterbalance to China, the Japanese government has also put effort in vitalizing the Japan-India relationship."[57]

Japan and India agreed to establish "Japan-India Global Partnership in the 21st Century" when Prime Minister Mori visited India in August, 2000. Prime Minister Vajpayee visited Japan in December 2001, and both Prime Ministers issued "Japan-India Joint Declaration", which consists of high-level dialogue, exchange in IT, joint counter-action against proliferation of WMD and terrorism. The Security Dialogue between the two countries was set up in 2001 and four rounds of dialogue have been conducted since then. High level exchange is continuing between the defense authorities. Between the coast guards, combined exercises on anti-piracy, search & rescue, etc. have been conducted every year since the year 2000.

When Japanese Prime Minister Koizumi visited India in April 2005 the two countries decided on an Eight-fold Initiative which comprises of measures for cooperation in eight key areas of interaction, including enhanced and upgraded dialogue architecture, launching of a high level Strategic Dialogue, cooperation in ushering a new Asian era and cooperation in responding to global challenges and opportunities. In December 2006 when Prime Minister Dr. Manmohan Singh visited Tokyo it was decided to establish a "Strategic and Global Partnership" between India and Japan. India and Japan have also set-up a bilateral energy dialogue with five working groups on 1) Electricity and Power Generation, 2) Energy Efficiency, 3) Coal, 4) Renewable Energy and 5) Petroleum and Natural Gas to identify specific projects for cooperation.

Though not explicitly mentioned in any of these initiatives the "China factor" unmistakably provides the context. Even the highly publicised China-Japan diplomatic wrangling over India's inclusion in the first East Asia Summit (EAS) in December 2005 was essentially due to the Japanese interest in balancing China's influence in the grouping. Especially since the United States was excluded from this "Asians only" grouping regional diplomacy leading up to the EAS in

Kuala Lumpur saw China and Japan locked in a bitter struggle for supremacy, with Beijing attempting to gain the leadership position in the planned EAC, and Tokyo trying to rein in its rival with the help of other "China-wary" nations in the Asia-Pacific.[58] Articulating Japan's position that the EAS reflect the principles of "openness, transparency, inclusiveness and conformity with global norms and systems" Japan's Foreign Minister Nobutaka Machimura stated in March 2005 "India should be welcome…the organization should be an open community."[59]

There is no talk now of the idea of Japan, China, India axis to promote peace and prosperity in Asia that was put forward by the Japanese ambassador Enoki in May 2004. Rather the Ambassador now says that "Indo-Japanese strategic partnership" could become "the driving force behind an emerging Asia".[60] The Japanese embassy in New Delhi had scrambled to suggest that Ambassador Enoki did not use the word "axis" in the traditional negative sense. Formalised cooperation and consultation between the three nations makes eminent political sense was all he meant, it was said.[61] Nonetheless, while making the suggestion, Japanese ambassador Yasukoni Enoki said it "had been discussed informally with the Indian side" and news reports suggest that External Affairs Minister Natwar Singh exchanged views on the subject with his Japanese counterpart when they met on the sidelines of the Asian Cooperation Dialogue in China in June 2004.[62]

Recent formulations of democracy as a new pillar of Japanese foreign policy are another attempt at involving India to challenge Chinese attempts at leadership of Asia. In line with this thinking has been Japanese Prime Minister Shinzo Abe's declaration that Japan, as a democracy, "will engage with strategic dialogues, at the leaders level, with countries that share fundamental values" with the objective of "widening the circle of free societies."[63] Benjamin Self refers to this "enhanced affinity for democracy" as the "the core of the contemporary strain" between Japan and China.[64] Drawing India into the ambit of this new Japanese grand strategy Prime Minister Abe has emphasised the importance of a quadrilateral strategic dialogue involving Tokyo, Washington, Canberra and New Delhi to promote their shared values of freedom and democracy in Asia.[65] As Yasukoni Enoki, Japan's ambassador to India, points out "India is very clearly positioned in our Asian diplomacy."[66]

On the Indian side the expectation is that this strategic importance of India for Japan will translate into economic and political benefits—"While China will remain the key partner for Japan, the new line says Tokyo must invest in another important economic relationship."[67] During his visit to Tokyo in December 2006 Prime Minister Manmohan Singh also stressed his desire to see more investment by Japanese companies coming into India, referring to "disproportionately low levels" of Japanese trade and investment toward India. Japan's economic relationship with India remains weak relative to the two countries' economic sizes. Though rising yearly, bilateral trade is US$ 6.5 billion, a tiny fraction of Japan's worldwide trade and one-thirtieth of its trade with China.[68] About 350 Japanese companies are operating in India, but their numbers are less than one fiftieth of those doing business in China. Japan is also lagging behind other countries, such as the U.S., China and South Korea, in capitalizing on India's fast expanding domestic market. Both the U.S. and China have doubled their trade with India in the past five years, but Japan's trade with India was one quarter of the U.S.'s in 2005.

The joint study group, which was set up during the Japanese Prime Minister Koizumi's visit to India in 2005, has given the green signal for a Comprehensive Economic Partnership Agreement (CEPA) between India and Japan. In December 2006 the two countries released a joint statement calling for the immediate start of negotiations aimed at reaching a free-trade agreement within two years. The accord would address trade issues and also promote increased Japanese investment in India as well as cooperation in the South Asian country's banking, insurance and capital markets sector. News reports quoted Prime Minister Manmohan Singh saying "The India-Japan comprehensive economic partnership marks a new phase in our economic relations, which will enable us to develop full potential and promise,"[69]

Indeed, Japanese and Indian policymakers have great designs for the relationship between the two countries, but "it is only when Japanese firms step up and make the needed large-scale commitment in India that Indo-Japanese trade will start to grow."[70] It is hoped that Japanese political and strategic interests can prompt a cautious business community into strengthening its position in India.

NOTES

1. According to the average statistics of the 1930s China was the largest destination for Japan's exports with a total share of 26 per cent and the third largest as a source of imports with a total share of 12 per cent. Cited in Seiichiro Takagi "In Search f a Sustainable Equal Partnership: Japan-China Relations in the Post-Cold War Era", *Japan Review of International Affairs* Vol. 13, No. 1, Spring 1999, p. 18
2. In a public opinion poll in 1952, the year Japan concluded the peace treaty with Taipei, 57 per cent of the respondents favoured restoring diplomatic relations with mainland China.
3. Yoshida Shigeru, *Kaiso junen (Ten Years in Retrospect)* Vol. 3 (Tokyo: Shinchosha, 1957; reprint, Tokyo: Chuo Koron Sha, 1998), p. 83 of reprint edition. Cited in Kamiye Matake "Japanese Foreign Policy Toward Northeast Asia", in Inoguchi Takashi and Purnendra Jain (ed.), *Japanese Foreign Policy Today* (New York: Palgrave, 2000) p. 227.
4. Shigeru Yoshida, "Japan and the Crisis in Asia", *Foreign Affairs*, January 1951, p. 179.
5. Wolf Mendl *Japan's Asia Policy: Regional Security and Global Interests* p. 81
6. Suh, Seung Won "More Carrots than Sticks: Economic Assistance and Economic Sanction in Japan-China Relation, 1979-1997" http://www.isanet.org/archive/Suh%20Seungwon.doc
7. Gilbert Rozman "Sino-Japanese Relations: Mutual Images and the Balance between Globalization and Regionalism", in The Asia Programme Special Report: *The US-Japan-China Triangle: Who's the Odd Man Out?* July 2003 http://wwics.si.edu/topics/pubs/asia_rpt113.pdf
8. *Ibid.*
9. Michael Heazle "Sino-Japanese Relations and Japan's Emerging Foreign Policy Crisis", http://www.gu.edu.au/centre/asiainstitute/pdf/SinoJapaneseRelations.pdf
10. Minxin Pei and Michael Swaine "Simmering Fire in Asia: Sino-Japanese Strategic Conflict" *Carnegie Endowment Policy Brief* No. 44, November 2005. Available at http://www.ciaonet.org/pbei-2/ceip/cei015/cei015.pdf
11. Data in this para from "*China and the Global Economic Recovery*", Keynote address by Anne O. Krueger, from the International Monetary Fund, at American Enterprise Institute Seminar, Washington, January 10, 2005. Available at http://www.imf.org/external/np/speeches/2005/011005.htm
12. Joshua Kaurlantzick "China's Charm Offensive in Southeast Asia"

Current History September 2006. Available at http://www.carnegieendowment.org/files/Kurlantzick_SoutheastAsia_China.pdf
13. *Ibid.*
14. *Ibid.*
15. Quote from Bronson Percival "Japan-Southeast Asia Relations: Playing Catch-up With China", *Comparative Connections,* Vol. 8, No. October 3, 2006, http://www.csis.org/media/csis/pubs/0603qjapan_seasia.pdf
16. Masaru Tamamoto, "Japanese Discovery of Democracy", *Policy Forum Online,* 06-38A, May 16, 2006. http://www.nautilus.org/fora/security/0638Tamamoto.html
17. Suh, Seung-Won, "*More Carrots than Sticks: Economic Assistance and Economic Sanction in Japan China Relation 1979-1997*" http://www.isanet.org/archive/Suh%20Seungwon.doc
18. He Liping, "Sino-Japanese Economic Relations: A Chinese Perspective" *China and World Economy,* No. 5, 2003 http://www.iwep.org.cn/wec/2003_9-10/heliping.pdf
19. Suh, Seung-Won, "*More Carrots than Sticks: Economic Assistance and Economic Sanction in Japan China Relation 1979-1997*", http://www.isanet.org/archive/Suh%20Seungwon.doc
20. These figure are cited in Seiichiro Takagi "In Search of a Sustainable Equal Partnership: Japan-China Relations in the Post-Cold War Era", *Japan Review of International Affairs,* Spring 1999. p. 24-25.
21. *Ibid.*
22. *Ibid.*
23. He Liping "Sino-Japanese Economic Relations: A Chinese Perspective", *China and World Economy,* No. 5, 2003 http://www.iwep.org.cn/wec/2003_9-10/heliping.pdf
24. *Ibid.*
25. "Sino-Japanese Trade Investment Grow", *China Daily,* March 7, 2005, http://www.chinadaily.com.cn/english/doc/2005-03/07/content_422432.htm
26. Martin Fackler "China Takes on Greater Import for Japan", *The Wall Street Journal,* December 27, 2004.
27. "So Hard To Be Friends", *Economist,* March 23, 2005 http://www.economist.com/displaystory.cfm?story_id=3786409
28. Economic and Social Research Institute Report of the Study Group on China, *Issues in the 21*st *Century and Influences on the International Economy*, January 2003. http://www.esri.go.jp/en/archive/hou/abstract/hou007-e.html
29. Text of speech available at http://www.kantei.go.jp/foreign/koizumispeech/2005/01/04press_e.html
30. Dick K. Nanto and Emma Chanlett Avery, "The Rise of China and Its

Effect on Taiwan, Japan and South Korea: U.S. Policy Choices", *CRS Report for Congress*, January 13, 2006, http://www.fas.org/sgp/crs/row/RL32882.pdf

31. Kazuo Ogoura "*Japan-China Relations: Four Fallacies Masquerading as Common Sense*", http://www.ciaonet.org/pbei/mitcis/mitcis015/mitcis015.pdf
32. *Ibid.*
33. *International Herald Tribune*, November 2, 2006.
34. "*Oil Raises China, Japan Rivalry*", September 6, 2006. http://www.peakoil.com/article18677.html
35. "*China vs Japan: FTAs, Oil and Taiwan*", January 27, 2007. http://www.bilaterals.org/article.php3?id_article=7022
36. Michael Yahuda, "*The Limits of Sino-Japanese Economic Interdependence*", http://www.isanet.org/archive/yahuda.doc
37. Lionel Beehner "*China-Japan Rift*", http://www.cfr.org/publication/8025/asia.html
38. Yumiko Hara and Takehiro Shioda, "Images of the Other Country and Media Coverage," NHK Broadcast Culture Research Institute, *Features No. 12* (Summer 2000), http://www.nhk.or.jp/bunken/bcri-news/bnl-s-feature.html
39. Kobayashi Yotaro, "A Time to Rebuild: A New Era for Japan-China Relations", *Gaiko Forum* (Winter 2006).
40. Kitaoka Shin'ichi, "Answering China's Japan Bashers", *Japan Echo* (Special Issue, 2005), p. 17.
41. *People's Daily*, April 1, 2006. http://politics.people.com.cn/BIG5/1024/4260505.html
42. Haruko Satoh "*Japan and China: Reaching Reconciliation or Stuck in the Past*", http://www.chathamhouse.org.uk/pdf/research/asia/BP1006japanchina.pdf
43. Masashi Nishihara "Northeast Asia and Japanese Security", in Danny Unger and Paul Blackburn (ed.) *Japan's Emerging Global Role* (Boulder: Lynne Rienner Publishers, 1993), p. 92.
44. *Defense of Japan*, Japan Defense Agency, Tokyo, 1994.
45. *Defense of Japan*, Japan Defense Agency, Tokyo, 2000.
46. "Japan Wary of China's Growing Military", *International Herald Tribune*, August 3, 2005. http://www.iht.com/articles/2005/08/02/news/japan.php
47. See Lyle Goldstein and William Murray, "*Undersea Dragons: China's MatThe fear is that uring Submarine Force.*" *International Security, Vol.* 8, No. 4, Spring 2004. pp. 161-96.
48. *Japan Times*, September 10, 2005.
49. This analysis draws upon Eric Teo Chu Cheow "Taiwan's Role in the Sino-Japanese Rivalry", *China Brief*, March 29, 2005. Available at http://www.ciaonet.org/pbei-2/jfcb/jfcb_v5_7/jfcb_v5_7b.html.old

50. "Agency Anticipates China Attack on Japan" *Tokyo Shimbun,* November 8, 2004.
51. Michael Mastanduno, "*Back to Normal: The Promise and Pitfalls of Japan's Economic Integration*", http://www.nbr.org/publications/strategic_asia/pdf/sa06xs_Mastanduno.pdf
52. Reinhard Drifte "U.S. Impact on Japanese-Chinese Security Relations", *Security Dialogue,* Vol. 31(4) 2000. p. 455.
53. Cited in Kevin Cooney, *Japan's Foreign Policy Maturation*, (New York: Routledge, 2002), p. 104.
54. Cited in 'SDF Dispatch decision like a double-edged sword', *The Japan Times*, January 1, 2004.
55. Colin Powell "U.S. Looks to Its Allies for Stability in Asia and the Pacific", *International Herald Tribune,* January 27, 2001.
56. Text available at http://www.globalsecurity.org/military/library/policy/national/nss-020920.pdf
57. Masanori Kondo "*Japan and an Asian Economic Community*", RIS Discussion Paper No. 106, January 2006. http://www.ris.org.in/dp106_pap.pdf
58. See Mohan Malik "*China and the East Asia Summit: More Discord than Accord*", http://www.apcss.org/Publications/APSSS/ChinaandEastAsiaSummit.pdf
59. "*Japan and China at Odds on Summit*", http://www.asahi.com/english/Herald-asahi/TKY200504010205.html
60. Quoted in "*The New Great Game: Why the Bush Administration has Embraced India*", http://www.encyclopedia.com/doc/1G1-156090916.html
61. C. Raja Mohan, "A New Asian Axis", http://www.hindu.com/2004/05/24/stories/2004052407111100.htm
62. See Sultan Shahin, "*India, Japan Eye New Axis*", http://www.atimes.com/atimes/South_Asia/FH24Df03.html
63. See P.S. Suryanarayana, "*Abe and Japan's Quest for a New Identity*", http://www.thehindu.com/2006/12/25/stories/2006122502410900.htm
64. See Benjamin Self, "China and Japan: A Façade of Friendship", *The Washington Quarterly,* Winter 2002-03, pp. 77-88.
65. See C. Raja Mohan, "*Asia's New Democratic Quad*", http://www.isn.ethz.ch/news/sw/details.cfm?ID=17383
66. Quoted in "*Japan Hoping to Improve Ties with Manmohan Singh's Visit*", http://www.hindu.com/2006/08/08/stories/2006080811880600.htm
67. C. Raja Mohan, "*Visit of the Rising Ties*", http://www.indianexpress.com/story/18476.html

68. Economic Data in this para from *Japan Brief,* Foreign Press Centre Japan, December 18, 2006. http://www.fpcj.jp/e/mres/japanbrief/jb_693.html?PHPSESSID=2cdd5d7e509d7c24ff5becbc2f9c2afa
69. http://www.bilaterals.org/article.php3?id_article=6719
70. Masanori Kondo "*Japan and an Asian Economic Community*", RIS Discussion Paper No. 106, January 2006, http://www.ris.org.in/dp106_pap.pdf

3

Japan's Maritime Security Perspectives

The geographical fact of being an island nation has meant that the sea has been both a source of danger as well as a lifeline to prosperity and stability for Japan. Japanese maritime strategy, therefore, has two components—one of defense against the outside world and secondly of management to ensure long-term access to the sea. In fact the Japanese often describe their key national characteristic in maritime terms, with the familiar notion that "Japan is a small island nation lacking resource endowments and is thus highly dependent upon sea borne commerce for its well being." Clearly, Tokyo must always be mindful of the surrounding oceans.[1] And, since its defeat in World War II, Japan has relied primarily on its alliance with the United States to achieve these objectives.

The destruction of the Japanese military and the 1947 'Peace Constitution' were fundamental changes imposed on post-War Japan by the American occupation. Article 9 of the Japanese Constitution specifically stated that the Japanese people forever renounce war as a sovereign right of the nation and the threat or use of force as a means of settling international disputes" and then that "land, sea, and air forces, as well as other war potential will never be maintained." As Cold War tensions escalated the United States changed course and on January 1, 1950, General Douglas MacArthur recognised the right of Japan to establish self-defense. In 1951 the two countries signed the United States-Japan Security Treaty which stated that

"Japan desires, as a provisional arrangement for its defense, that the United States of America should maintain armed forces of its own in and about Japan so as to deter armed attack upon Japan" and that *"Japan will itself increasingly assume responsibility for its own defense against direct and indirect aggression, always avoiding any armament which could be an offensive threat"*.[2]

The Treaty of Mutual Cooperation and Security between the United States and Japan further reinforced the bilateral security alliance in 1960, which stated, *"Each Party recognises that an armed attack against either Party in the territories under the administration of Japan would be dangerous. to its own peace and safety and declares that it would act to meet the common danger in accordance with its constitutional provisions and processes."*[3] This division of roles has undergone "redefinition" over the years, with Japan assuming greater responsibility but there has been little support for a complete "reassessment" of the ties with the United States. It is therefore imperative that we assess Japan's role in maritime security in Asia within this framework, specifically the issue of "burden sharing".

Sea as the Lifeline of the Japanese Economy

The sea occupies an important position in the Asia Pacific, and maritime issues play a major role in shaping its international relations. Southeast Asia has a vast span of water with the South China Sea, extending over 1800 miles from Sumatra to Taiwan, linking the Indian and the Pacific Oceans.[4] The shores of Northeast Asian countries are washed by the East China Sea, the Yellow Sea, the Sea of Japan, the Sea of Okhotsk, the Bering Sea, and in a broad sense by the Pacific Ocean.[5]

Sea lanes of communication connect world countries with one another. In peacetime, these ocean routes serve as commercial trade routes; in times of conflict, they become strategic pathways. The Asia Pacific roughly has two significant sea lanes of communication, one passing through the South China Sea to the Indian Ocean and the Middle East, the other passing through the East China Sea and the Sea of Japan to the Pacific Ocean and the Pacific coast of the U.S. and Canada.[6] In terms of ship movement, the seas in the Asia Pacific are among the busiest in the world. Keeping the sea lines of communication secure and stable is therefore an important economic and security interest for Asian countries. The other challenge is to prevent maritime conflicts between states due to resource and trade competition as the region and their navies grow.

As for Japan after the end of the Second World War the economy lay in total ruin. Recovery, however was rapid and analysts used the term 'miracle economy' to highlight Japan's combination of high growth and equitable income distribution. The principal source of growth was the outward-looking and open-development strategies followed by the Japanese government. The primary emphasis being on state direction, active industrial policy and an export oriented growth pattern. Japan's economic prosperity is therefore crucially linked with overseas markets. Japan's major export markets are Asia (41 per cent), the United States (30 per cent) and the EU (16 per cent). Japan's major import partners are Asia (42 per cent), the United States (19 per cent) and the EU (12 per cent). Almost 85 per cent of trading goods pass through the sea lanes of Southeast Asia and 15 per cent of the goods go through Pacific routes.[7]

The fact that Japan is a country with extremely limited natural resources further compounds dependency on sea borne trade. In the words of Joseph M. Dodge, "The fundamental problem of the Japanese nation can be expressed in the simple terms of too many people, too little land, and too few natural resources."[8] Crucially, Japan imports most of the natural resources necessary for its economic activities. Japan's dependency rate for foreign energy resources was 80 per cent in FY2000, and Japan imports 86 per cent of its oil from the Middle East.[9] Japan has made efforts to diversify its energy supply, but these dependency rates are not likely to change significantly in the foreseeable future. Japan is therefore a crucial player in the maritime security arena.

However a coordinated regional response is continually challenged by the principle of state sovereignty. The freedom of the seas principle today was set out in UNCLOS (UN Convention on the Law of the Sea) in 1982, which came into force in November 1994. In reality, differences in understanding and interpretation have resulted in a host of unresolved navigational issues—the right of innocent passage of warships and submarines in territorial waters; archipelagic sea-lanes passage; the freedom of action of foreign navies within

Exclusive Economic Zones; the legal issues relating to the shipment of nuclear wastes, etc. For instance, regional countries like Bangladesh, Myanmar, China, India, Indonesia, South Korea, North Korea, and Pakistan require authorisation or notification for the innocent passage of foreign warships. Indonesia wants that submarines must sail on the surface, weapons and surveillance radars must be switched off and aircraft-carriers must keep their planes deck-bound while using the Java Sea.[10] Also in declaring her new archipelagic sea-lanes it has proposed to limit passage to only three north-south sea-lanes while a spokesman for the Gerakin Aceh Merdeka (GAM), or Free Aceh movement is reported to have said "Ships using the Malacca Strait should seek permission from the separatist rebels in Indonesia's Aceh Province."[11] The issue of restricting the passage of "vessels carrying nuclear or other hazardous cargoes through the Malacca Strait has often been raised by states littoral to the Strait." "There have been various proposals by regional straits states to go beyond the International Maritime Organization safety regulations and traffic lane demarcations and to impose additional restrictions on passing ships including even tolls for the use of these recognised straits".[12] Both China and North Korea have attempted to control freedom of passage by proclaiming military zones for national security.

Then, there are several potential flash points along the SLOCs, in the form of unresolved territorial and boundary disputes with overlapping claims topping the list. The most troublesome disputes are those in the South China Sea, where Indonesia, Malaysia, Brunei, the Philippines, Vietnam, China, and Taiwan assert conflicting claims to sea and island territories. These claims are deemed to be of vital importance, because the archipelagic seas may have vast petroleum resources and the islands are strategically positioned for support of sea-lane control or amphibious warfare. With incidents of claimants clashing violently the current situation is "volatile and could, through an unexpected political or military event, deteriorate into open conflict."[13] Any escalation could disrupt the South China Sea's huge volume of shipping, with grave consequences. An Indonesian initiative bringing all claimants together in a conflict management dialogue has been unable even after ten years to resolve the issue. In conjunction with "creeping jurisdiction" or "ocean enclosure" concerns there exist a wide range of non-military threats, which include terrorism, piracy, narcotics trade, and environmental pollution. Of these, piracy, linked closely with terrorism after September 11, is the region's chief concern.

Several Southeast Asian guerrilla and terrorist groups possess substantial maritime capabilities. Since 2000, al-Qaida, the Moro Islamic Liberation Front, the Abu Sayyaff Group, Jemaah Islamiyah, the Kumpulan Militan Malaysia, the Gerakan Aceh Merdeka, and Laskar Jihad have all been suspected of planning or executing maritime attacks.[14] Other groups have used the sea to transport weapons, move forces, and raise funds. The most successful has been Abu Sayyaff, which has conducted dozens of successful maritime operations in the southern Philippines, metropolitan Manila, and East Malaysia. Abu Sayyaff gained global notoriety in 2000 and 2001 when it kidnapped dozens of people, among them Filipinos, Malaysians, Chinese, Europeans, and Americans, in a series of raids on villages, resorts, and ships in and near the Sulu and Celebes Seas. Despite a large-scale government offensive backed by American forces, Philippine officials have confirmed Abu Sayyaff claims of responsibility for the February 26, 2004 sinking of *Superferry 14* near Manila, in which 116 people were killed.[15]

Al-Qaida and its close regional allies Jemaah Islamiyah and the Kumpulan Militan Malaysia have stated intent to conduct large-scale operations against the U.S. Navy and global trade. Since 2000, regional security forces have disrupted half a dozen plots to attack American warships transiting narrow waterways or visiting ports in Southeast Asia.[16] There has also been increasing concern that al-Qa'ida or its affiliates might use a merchant vessel to administer an attack—perhaps a nuclear bomb, radiological "dirty nuke," or other weapon of mass destruction—in a shipping container. Alternatively, a large petroleum, liquefied gas, or chemical carrier could be hijacked and either sunk in a key waterway or crashed into a port facility or population centre, turning the vessel's cargo into a gigantic bomb. Many of these scenarios could cause unprecedented loss of life and economic disruption.[17]

From a Japanese perspective there are seven factors that contribute to current instability in the maritime sphere in the Asia Pacific.[18]

- The first is the proliferation of WMD and ballistic missiles, and the failure of mechanisms to prevent proliferation has forced nations like the U.S. and Japan to resort to developing ballistic missile system as a defensive measure.

- The second factor is the growth of 'indiscriminate terrorism' by regional terrorist organisations that continue to thrive.
- The third factor is China's rapid military build up, as evidenced by the increases in national defense budgets and the quick pace of military modernisation efforts.
- The fourth factor is the continued impasse on the Korean peninsula and the Taiwan Straits, both of which appear to defy resolution in the near term.
- The fifth factor is the continued existence of territorial disputes and ethnic conflicts in the region with long historical roots.
- The sixth factor is the confrontational posture adopted by regional states to resolve conflicting ocean interests and how naval power is used to assert rights over disputed areas.
- The seventh factor is the increasing incidences of organised piracy that continues to plague and endanger maritime traffic.

Coastal Defense to Sea Lane Defense

It was in the late 1960s that the idea of extending the range of Japan's maritime defense began to emerge in both the United States and Japan. On the Japanese side, Hideo Sekino, a former imperial navy officer, put forward the idea of sea-lane defense in the early 1970s. Sekino suggested that Japan's defense policy be reordered so that "the protection of the sea communications of Japan should be given first priority in the national defense of Japan, and the prevention of direct invasion of Japan should be made the secondary function of the maritime defense force of Japan."[19] The idea made strategic sense. With the Soviet Union engaging the U.S. in the diplomacy of détente it was unlikely that the Japanese territory would face a direct assault. Expanding the maritime forces within the framework of the U.S.-Japan alliance, and with a definite strategic purpose that was complementary to regional stability was also politically viable. The 1973 Arab oil embargo lent credence to Sekino's basic premise and to his recommendation that Tokyo procure the wherewithal to defend sea-lanes as far away as northern Indonesia.[20] Sekino insisted that such a posture would be fully compatible with American regional strategy in Asia.

Also the Japanese economy was growing while the American economy was straining under fiscal and monetary pressures. There was worry among U.S. defense planners that the United States was perhaps dangerously overextended in military obligations. As pointed out by Peter Woolley there was a tendency to superficially compare Japanese and U.S. defense spending amounts and by implication link these to unemployment rates, poverty rates, funding for education, inflation, trade deficits, etc. in the United States.[21] U.S.-Soviet détente and Nixon's dramatic opening to China in the early 1970s fed Japanese fears that Washington was preparing to abandon the alliance. In response, the Japanese government issued its first comprehensive report on how the MSDF would meet Tokyo's national security objectives.

The 1976 National Defense Programme Outline (NDPO) provided guidelines for the MSDF to defend against a direct invasion of the home islands; provide warning and defense against threats to Japan's coastal areas; protect major ports and straits; and conduct active air reconnaissance and surveillance of the seas adjacent to Japan's Pacific coast and in the Sea of Japan. Two years later, Tokyo and Washington signed Guidelines for Defense Cooperation that formally committed Japan to maintaining "peace and stability" across the Asia Pacific region. The expansiveness of the outline and the guidelines sealed the ascendance of Sekino's vision, emphasising the complementary role Japan could play in American security strategy.[22]

In this way sea-lane defense appeared tailor-made as a strategic role to rationalise increased defense spending by Japan that would also complement U.S. strategy in the Asia Pacific. The stage was, therefore, set "for an agreement on what role Japan's defense forces should play to ameliorate the argument over how much money Japan spent on defense."[23] During his visit to the United States in 1981 Prime Minister Suzuki formally declared that a "division of roles" between Japan and the United States in the northwest Pacific was desirable and that Japan would "seek to make even greater efforts for improving its defense capabilities in Japanese territories and in its surrounding seas and air space." Though, later, Prime Minister Suzuki denied having made any concrete commitment, there were reports that Japan had agreed to defend sea-lanes within a 1,000 nautical mile radius. In 1983, after the former director general of the JDA, Nakasone became Prime Minister, a formal decision-making group undertook a study and in 1984 the responsibility to defend sea-lanes to 1,000 nautical miles was incorporated into the five-year defense plan. This redefinition of the JMSDF mission facilitated a corresponding improvement in equipment and training. By 1990 Japanese naval forces were first rate in quality and no longer overshadowed in quantity by other Pacific fleets.

The collapse of the Soviet Union and the end of the Cold War once again brought the issue of Japan's "burden sharing" into sharp focus. The United States once again appeared to be turning inward. In 1990, the U.S. announced that it would make a ten per cent reduction of its forces in the region. The U.S. troop presence in Asia steadily declined from 141,000 in 1988 to 98,000 in 1992. Japan's traditional "cheque-book diplomacy" during the Gulf War in 1990 came in for sharp public criticism from the United States. Moreover, a series of events served to remind Tokyo that the end of the Cold War did not eliminate all the possible sources of instability in East Asia and brought renewed attention to the importance of the U.S.-Japan alliance. These included Beijing's 1992 law reaffirming Chinese claim to the Senkaku Islands, the 1994 crisis over North Korea's nuclear weapons programme, Chinese nuclear tests in 1995 and 1996, Chinese military exercises in the Taiwan Strait in March 1996 and popular protests over the disputed Senkaku islands that broke out in Hong Kong and Taiwan in 1996.

This created momentum for the revision of the Guidelines for Japan-U.S. Cooperation from 1997 onwards, and then the passage in May 1999 of legislation to enable the SDF to provide logistical support to U.S. forces in order to deal with "situations in areas surrounding Japan that will have an important influence on Japan's peace and security." Japan's response to the September 11 and subsequent participation in the U.S. actions in Afghanistan and Iraq have further enhanced the scope of Japan's security measures. The US-Japan statement of "Common Strategic Goals" adopted on February 19, 2005 is an important step reaffirming a decade of deepening security ties between the two countries. A new cycle of change is therefore underway in Japanese security strategy primarily in response to changing overall U.S. global strategy needs following the September 11 terrorist attacks. The Bush administration has been seeking to activate its regional alliances to function for global security. The United States emphasised this shift in the *Quadrennial Defense Review Report* of September 2001, the *National Security Strategy* of September 2002, and the *National Defense Strategy* of March 2005. The White House now supports a move from "threat-based" regional alliances to "capabilities-based" global alliances that are capable of constructing flexible coalitions with interoperable military assets for missions in the "arc of instability" stretching from the Middle East to Southeast Asia. In addition, the Global Posture Review (GPR) of 2004 made clear that bases provided by regional alliances should be integrated into the U.S. strategy for the "surging" and global deployment of its forward forces.

Japanese policy-makers have faced pressure to respond to these changes in U.S. strategy and the international security environment. This need, moreover, has been intertwined with the ongoing and wider debate in Japan regarding the next steps in Japanese security policy. No doubt this debate on security in is still subject to a variety of divisions, but there has been an increasing convergence of mainstream opinion in favour of a more proactive, or "normal," military role for Japan.[24] There is a realisation that the new framework of international security is the "coalition of the willing". As Daisuke Kajimoto points out "Within the arrangement, each nation participates in coalition freely and provides through the means that are agreeable and feasible to it. On the other hand, the level of contribution to coalition by each nation is consistently compared with other nations, usually by the United States that leads the coalition."[25] A situation similar to the stock market, in which the value of participating nations constantly goes up or down depending on the level of contribution.

Japan and the New Maritime Order in Asia

At the same time Japan has been careful to avoid entrapment in American military strategy. The key, as Ralph Cossa points out, has been "defining adequate support to the satisfaction of both nations, and in a manner not threatening to Japan's neighbours."[26] Because the "Japan Problem," i.e. Japan's history of aggression and colonialism in the region makes neighbouring states extremely wary of any increases in Japan's military activities in the region and continues to constrain Japanese security policy. These constraints operate across both Northeast and Southeast Asia. And a key response to this dilemma of "adequate support" vis-à-vis regional concerns has been Japan's initiative for the protection of sea-lanes.

From Tokyo's perspective, both economic and strategic considerations make it imperative that the regional maritime dynamics evolve in a positive direction. Moreover, freedom of navigation appears to be taking on a new meaning in U.S. defense plans. A report by the U.S. Defense Department concluded that a sea-based component will be critical to the success of both the national and the theater defense systems that the United States is considering building to defend itself and its allies, including those in the Asia-Pacific region, from ballistic missile attack.[27] Missiles launched from sea-based systems could avoid being misled by decoys by destroying an enemy missile in its boost phase, shortly after liftoff. But to do so the surface ships and submarines carrying the anti-ballistic missiles would have to be rather close to the launch site. The U.S. Navy is, therefore, increasingly concerned with freedom of navigation issues in the Asia Pacific wherein Washington's policy has evolved from active neutrality to active concern.

Given the unwillingness to radically alter the military component of its security policy it therefore appears that Japan has creatively interpreted burden sharing in terms of a growing role in Asian maritime security. There are clear advantages to doing so:

1. It resonates with the spirit of the October 2000 Armitage/Nye report that called on burden sharing by Japan to evolve into power sharing.
2. There is greater domestic acceptance for such a role than sending troops abroad.
3. It allows Japan to delicately distinguish itself from the larger American military strategy in Asia.
4. It mitigates regional antagonism that tends to regard any change in Japan's security profile as a revival of militarism.

In 1995 Rear Admiral (Ret.) Sumihiko Kawamura of Japan made a proposal for establishing an international cooperative SLOC security scheme, placing the U.S. at its core (key strategic player) and having the Asia-Pacific countries share the responsibilities of areas and function in accordance with their capabilities and geographic conditions.[28] In accordance with capabilities and geographic locations of the regional states, Kawamura presented the following model: (1) maintenance of sea control throughout the Pacific Ocean by the U.S.; (2) protection of shipping, surveillance and search and rescue (SAR) in regional areas such as the Northeast Pacific, South Pacific or the ASEAN area, etc. by the concerned regional states; and (3) surveillance of coastal seas and local shipping protection by littoral states.[29]

Such a strategy envisages a Japan-led International Ocean Peacekeeping Force, which would be primarily concerned with activities that are necessary to fulfill obligations under the 1982 UN Convention on the Law of the Sea so as to maintain maritime order and prevent armed conflict at sea. The force would conduct joint monitoring activities to protect the environment and resources in waters beyond state control, as well as to combat illegal activities that span international maritime boundaries, including illegal fishing, illegal entry and piracy. It would have both "benign" military duties, such as search and rescue, and constabulary functions. The long-term vision has the peacekeeping force providing a framework for a regional maritime security regime.[30] In 1996, at an international conference sponsored by the National Institute for Defense Studies, Japan proposed the idea of a Japan-led international Ocean Peacekeeping Force to combat piracy in the South China Sea and surrounding straits. The proposal included the participation of China, South Korea, Indonesia, Malaysia and Singapore. The purpose of OPK was to maintain maritime order and prevent armed conflict at sea. The Japan Coast Guard would practice and conduct joint maneuvers with the militaries and coast guards of Southeast Asian nations in order to better secure freedom of navigation and combating piracy and terrorism.

Initial steps towards realising this vision have been taken with Japan taking the lead in regional anti-piracy measures. Japan has recently pushed for the multilateral anti-piracy pact "Regional Cooperation Agreement on Combating Piracy and Armed Robbery against Ships in Asia." It was signed by 14 Asian countries and an information-sharing centre has been established in Singapore that is headed by a Japanese. Simultaneously concrete cooperative approaches are being worked out to deal with non-conventional issues like humanitarian assistance, search and rescue (SAR) cooperative maritime surveillance, and mine-countermeasures. These include the following[31] :

- **August 1999:** Japan and South Korea staged a joint search and rescue operation in the East China Sea.
- **November 1999:** Japanese Prime Minister Obuchi proposed a meeting of related parties at the ASEAN + 1 (Japan) Summit in Manila. Japan also proposed a regional coast guard to combat piracy in the Strait of Malacca and Singapore, as well as in the South China Sea. Tokyo suggested that other participants in the force include China, South Korea, Indonesia, Malaysia and Singapore.
- **April 2000:** The Regional Conference on Combating Piracy and Armed Robbery against Ships was held in Tokyo. The conference adopted a Model Action Plan that indicates specific action guidelines that should be followed by maritime policy authorities and private sector maritime parties like shipping companies, as well as Asia Anti Piracy Challenges 2000, which are guidelines for strengthening international coordination and cooperation.
- **May 2000:** Tokyo and Singapore concluded a bilateral military agreement that permits Japanese patrol ships and aircraft to be stationed in Singapore to evacuate Japanese nationals in disturbed areas as also to assist UN peacekeeping operations in Southeast Asia. Earlier, during the Indonesian crisis leading to the fall of President Suharto, Tokyo dispatched transport planes and patrol ships to Singapore on standby for the possible evacuation of Japanese citizens in Indonesia.
- **June 2000:** JMSDF exercised submarine rescue operations with the Singaporean Navy together with the navies of United States and South Korea.
- **September 2000:** Following a proposal by then Minister of Foreign Affairs Yohei Kono, the Japanese government dispatched the Mission for Combating Piracy and Armed

Robbery against Ships to the Philippines, Malaysia, Singapore and Indonesia.

- **November 2000:** Prime Minister Mori proposed the holding of the Asian Cooperation Conference on Combating Piracy and Armed Robbery against Ships at the ASEAN + 3 (Japan, China, Republic of Korea) summit in Singapore.
- **June 2001:** Japan's MSDF sent three vessels to the first Western Pacific minesweeping exercise hosted by the Singapore Navy.
- **September 2001:** Japan-Russia search and rescue exercise in Japan.
- **October 2001:** Japan and China agreed on much closer cooperation to combat crimes like piracy, smuggling of people, drugs and weapons. Katsuhiko Nawano (head of the Japan Coast Guard) and Zhao Yongji (China's vice public security minister) signed an agreement on full-scale joint-operations to that effect.
- **October 2001:** Japan and the Philippines conducted an anti-piracy exercise.
- **October 2001:** The Asian Cooperation Conference on Combating Piracy and Armed Robbery against Ships took place in Tokyo and came to the conclusion that multilateral regional cooperation was indispensable to combat piracy. It suggested that a working group of experts should be convened to develop a regional cooperation agreement.
- **November 2001:** Prime Minister Koizumi proposed the convening of a working group of government experts to study the formulation of a regional cooperation agreement related to anti-piracy measures at the ASEAN + 3 summit in Brunei.
- **December 2001:** Anti-piracy training exercise held between the Thai Marine Police and the Japanese coast guard.
- **April to May 2002:** Japan hosted Pacific Reach 2002, the second Western Pacific submarine rescue exercise, for the first time with five countries taking part in the exercise.
- **January 2003:** Speaking at a lecture in Singapore Prime Minister Junichiro Koizumi highlighted piracy as one of the main initiatives for future cooperation between Japan and the ASEAN nations. Koizumi said that more cooperation between the respective coast guards could be part of a formal agreement on Asia-wide cooperation to combat piracy.

- **March 2003:** The Philippines, Japan and Indonesia carried out a joint Sea borne Anti-oil-pollution Exercise.
- **August 2003:** A group of Japanese naval vessels visited Manila Harbour in the Philippines.
- **April 2004:** Two Japanese warships visited the Vietnamese Ho Chi Minh City.
- **May 2004:** China's largest patrol vessel, the Haixun 21 attended a two-day joint maritime exercise hosted by the Japan Coast Guard.
- **November 2004:** Sixteen countries including ASEAN members plus China, Japan, South Korea, Bangladesh, Sri Lanka and India concluded the Regional Cooperation Agreement on Combating Piracy and Armed Robbery Against Ships in Asia (ReCAAP), first proposed by Japanese Prime Minister Koizumi in 2001.
- **March 2005:** Japan held the second "ASEAN-Japan Seminar on Maritime Security and Combating Piracy" in Tokyo to exchange information with ASEAN countries on efforts to implement the International Ship and Port Facility Security (ISPS) Code.
- **October 2005:** Japan conducted a training course for maritime law enforcement officials from ASEAN countries, China and the Republic of Korea.
- **June 2006:** Japan decided to extend to Indonesia a grant aid up to a total of 1,921 million yen for the project for construction of vessels for the prevention of piracy, maritime terrorism and proliferation of weapons.
- **February 2007:** Japan, Malaysia and Thailand held anti-piracy exercises in the Andaman Sea.

Mindful of resistance from Southeast Asian nations to the Ocean Peacekeeping Force the Japanese idea is that specific SLOC management efforts would be crucial confidence building measures for multilateral regime building on the lines outlined above. That progress on "hard" maritime security issues depends on successful development of a "soft", essentially civil, maritime safety regime.[32] For example a softening of national sovereignty issues via cooperative measures to combat piracy could lead to greater flexibility in addressing concerns about the impact of the Southeast Asian Nuclear Weapons Free Zone (SEANWFZ) agreement on high seas freedom of navigation. As a paper commissioned by the Ship and Ocean Foundation, Tokyo, points out "it would be a mistake to conceive of naval co-operation in the region in tactical terms as if the problem were simply one of assembling the right blend of co-operative measures, and as if the larger strategic context of the security dilemma did not exist. Confidence and security building measures (CSBMs) are stepping stones or building blocks, not ends in themselves. As such, they should have realistic, pragmatic, clearly defined objectives...Gradual, methodical, incremental approaches work best. The best approach is to start small; use a gradual, incremental, building block process; avoid over formalizing the process; and use unilateral and bilateral measures as steps towards multilateral confidence building."[33]

Rear Admiral Kawamura himself propounds that "Maritime counter terrorism cooperation should be promoted on a burden-sharing basis between the flag (user) states and the coastal states aiming at building of the capacity of the latter and the establishment of regional mechanisms for operations' coordination and intelligence sharing, instead of requesting the coastal states to comply with regulations. Capacity building in the coastal states should include financial and equipment support, technological and training assistance by the flag states. In order to foster effective security cooperation in the region, it is essential to ensure greater burden sharing between and among the coastal states and the flag states in the form of capacity building."[34]

Thus in sharp contrast to the three major unilateral initiatives of the United States—the Container Security Initiative (CSI), the Proliferation Security Initiative (PSI), and the Regional Maritime Security Initiative (RMSI), Akio Suda, Ambassador in charge of International Counter-Terrorism cooperation, at the September 2006 Kuala Lumpur meeting on the Straits of Malacca and Singapore clearly stated

> It is a firm position of the Government of Japan that, as a matter of principle for this cooperation, we should fully respect the sovereignty of the littoral states of the Straits of Malacca and Singapore, endorsing them to play a central and primary role in

> various programmes and activities to be carried out in the straits. Upon this principle, it is also of essential importance that the user states cooperate in these programmes and activities in the spirit of burden sharing by beneficiaries. The initiatives of and close cooperation between the littoral states, as well as the strong support of the user states for the initiatives of the littoral states, are both necessary to solve problems and improve conditions in the Straits of Malacca and Singapore.[35]

Underscoring this approach is the use of the Japanese Coast Guard as the agent of change. To avoid a dominant and objectionable presence, for example, Japan's proposal for a regional anti-piracy force suggested that its participating ships be drawn from the civilian-controlled coast guard, the Japan Maritime Safety Agency, rather than from the navy. For, Coast guards offer advantages over navies for cooperative activities in terms of overcoming sensitivities that inhibit naval cooperation.[36] The Japanese Maritime Safety Agency (JMSA) was renamed the Japan Coast Guard (JCG) on April 1, 2000, although the name JMSA has been retained in the Japanese language. It is a very considerable organisation with a fleet of over 400 patrol vessels, patrol craft, surveying ships, navigational aid tenders, and special service craft.

Indeed the JCG is an excellent example of a paramilitary marine constabulary force established by a major power with extensive maritime interests"[37] as a "foot in the water"[38] given the reluctance to involve conventional military forces. Japanese Coast Guard vessels and aircraft now regularly visit other countries in the region for exercises and for anti-piracy patrols. The JCG has provided training, equipment, and funding to all the coastal states of the South China Sea, and has conducted joint training exercises with six Southeast Asian states. The JCG has funded the installation and maintenance of navigational aides and buoy-tenders; it has also provided technical assistance to upgrade marine safety data management systems and hydrographic surveys. Students from Asian countries have been enrolled in the JCG Academy as a contribution to fighting piracy. In a further diplomatic initiative, the JCG sponsored the Indian Ocean (Bangladesh, India, Pakistan, and Sri Lanka) Maritime Safety Practitioners' Conference in Tokyo in November 2001. Japan hosted the "Heads of Asian Coast Guard Agencies Meeting" in Tokyo in

June 2004 to build cooperative relations among agencies and share information on maritime security in the Asian region.

Humanitarian initiatives have further raised the Japanese navy's profile in the region. Prime Minister Koizumi seized the opportunity provided by the tsunami disaster in December 2004 to push Japan to the forefront of aid efforts. The JSDF used its dispatch on this non-combat humanitarian mission under the International Disaster Relief Law, which, involving 1,500 personnel, was its largest overseas mission ever. Maritime Self-Defense Force (MSDF) ships en route to return to Japan after service as part of the U.S.-led coalition in the Indian Ocean were first diverted to the vicinity of Thailand for relief assistance immediately following the tsunami. Then in January 2005 an MSDF flotilla, including an *Osumi*-class transport, was dispatched to Sumatra. This flotilla carried five GSDF helicopters and twenty GSDF trucks, and acted as a "floating camp" for joint MSDF and GSDF operations. Tokyo has also pledged to back development of a regional tsunami early warning system and put its substantial knowledge in development and disaster prevention and relief to work on behalf of the region.

Implications for India

The journey from "Global Partnership" in 2000 to "Strategic and Global Partnership" in 2006 between India and Japan has been a quick one and is reflective of a new willingness on part of Japan to engage with India. And maritime cooperation has been an integral part of this process. In the words of Yasukoni Enoki, the Japanese Ambassador to India, "Once the Japanese vessels cross the Malacca Strait and navigate westbound, they find that India is literally the only country that has a reliable navy."[39] Cooperation in ensuring the safety and security of sea-lanes of communication, combating piracy and terrorism, search and rescue, and disaster relief is bringing India and Japan closer. Some of the shared "objectives" of the "partners in peace" to meet the many challenges across the new security landscape in Asia and beyond have been spelt out.[40] These include:

(i) Maintenance and promotion of peace and stability in Asia and at the global level, creating an international climate conducive to the continued economic growth and development;

(ii) Promoting confidence building measures in Asia, including promotion of transparency and frank exchange of views among defense authorities;
(iii) Countering terrorism and violent extremism;
(iv) Preventing the spread of weapons of mass destruction and related materials, equipment, technologies and means of delivery;
(v) Contributing to the safety and stability of regional maritime traffic;
(vi) Promoting international cooperation in the areas of disaster management and provision of relief operations;
(vii) Developing cooperative relationships with nations of Asia and in the world; and
(viii) Promoting the development of various regional cooperation mechanisms, in an open and inclusive manner.

The key "mechanisms" of cooperation include:

(i) Holding of meetings between the Defense Minister of India and the Minister of State for Defense of Japan at regular intervals, alternately in the two capitals or elsewhere; also making use of opportunities at regional and multilateral meetings;
(ii) Holding of a Defense Policy Dialogue at the Defense Secretary/ Administrative Vice Minister level from time to time, alternately in India and Japan;
(iii) Holding of regular Comprehensive Security Dialogue and Military-to-Military Talks, alternately in India and Japan;
(iv) Regular exchange of visits at the Chiefs of Staff and Joint Staff level and Staff level of each service.
(v) Exchange of ship visits between the Indian Navy and the Japan Maritime Self Defense Force;
(vi) Holding of goodwill exercises between the Indian Navy and the Japan Maritime Self-Defense Force of progressively advanced nature that takes account of future possible exercises in areas of mutual interest;
(vii) Inviting officials of the other side to witness designated military activities;
(viii) Mutual exchange of student officers (including civilian officials)

and researchers from defense establishments for various courses (such courses may be identified based on areas of interest of each country); and

(ix) Participating in security conferences and seminars hosted by their defense establishments, and cooperating in the relevant existing regional and multilateral fora.

No doubt there is considerable enthusiasm within the Indian security establishment regarding recent defense exchanges with Japan. These include the following:

- **January 2000**: Indian Defense Minister George Fernandes visited Japan at the invitation of the Director General of the Japanese Self-Defense Agency. It was the first visit to Japan by an Indian defense minister.
- **April 2000**: India participated in the Japan-hosted "Asia Anti-Piracy Challenges 2000" conference in Tokyo.
- **May 2000**: The JMSDF Training Squadron visited Mumbai.
- **June 2000**: Indian Defense Minister George Fernandes visited Japan.
- **September 2000**: Two Indian naval ships, INS Delhi and INS Kora visited Japan.
- **November 2000**: Japanese Coast Guard vessel PLH Shikishima visited India to take part in the first India-Japan Coast Guard joint exercise held at Chennai.
- **February 2001**: Japan participated in the International Fleet Review held at Mumbai. The ship JDS Amagiri and Vice Admiral N. Makimoto were present.
- **May 2001**: A training squadron of two ships "Kashima" and "Yamagiri" of the Japan Maritime Self-Defense Forces visited Chennai Port.
- **May 2001**: Indian Coast Guard vessel "Sangram" visited Japan to participate in the second joint Coast Guard exercises held at Kagoshima.
- **July 2001**: India and Japan held security and defense discussions in Tokyo as part of their efforts to establish a regular dialogue.
- **July 2002**: Indian Defense Minister George Fernandes visited Japan.

- **October 2002**: Indian Naval Ship INS Mysore visited Japan to participate in the Japanese Maritime Self-Defense Force Fleet Review. Indian Vice Chief of Naval Staff was present.
- **November 2002**: Japanese Coast Guard ship Yashima visited India for the third India-Japan Coast Guards Joint Exercises held at Chennai.
- **May 2003**: Visit of Mr. Ishiba, Defense Minister of Japan, to India.
- **July 2003**: Visit of Mr. Horimura, Ambassador in charge of International Counter-terrorism, to India.
- **September 2003**: India and Japan hold the fourth joint Coast Guard series of maritime search and rescue and anti-piracy exercises off the Kobe Coast in Japan.
- **November 2003**: Friendly Joint Training between Japanese Maritime Self-Defense Force and the Indian Navy.
- **January 2004**: The Second Japan-India Security Dialogue held in New Delhi.
- **January 2004**: The Indian Coast Guard entered into a pact with the U.S. and Japan to ensure scrutiny of shipping lanes stretching from the Indian Ocean to the western seaboard of America.
- **May 2004**: Takemasa Moriya, vice minister of the Defense Agency visited India for five days for talks with Defense Secretary Ajay Prasad.
- **November 2004**: Japanese Coast Guard Ship Mizuho visited Mumbai to participate in the 5th Indo—Japan Coast Guard Combined Exercise.
- **December 2005:** Japan proposed a military exchange programme to India in which it can use Japanese naval and coast guard bases for joint exercises in the Asia-Pacific region. In return, Japan wanted similar facilitation for the Japanese navy and coast guard in Indian bases, where they can conduct rescue operations, joint exercises against terrorism, and provide security to transport ships.
- **February 2006:** Japan's Naval Chief Admiral Takashi Saito's visit to India.
- **May 2006:** Visit of Indian Defense Minister Pranab Mukherjee to Japan. It was indicated that the two countries have decided to hold goodwill exercises between the Indian Navy and the

Japanese Maritime Self-Defence Force (JMSDF) with "progressively advanced content of future possible exercises in areas of mutual interest".

- **June 2006:** India and Japan agreed to conduct joint search and rescue operations, annual coast guard talks, joint anti-piracy exercises
- **November 2006**: Japan coast guard Ship Shikishima visited Mumbai to participate in Indo-Japan Coast Guard Combined Exercise SAHYOG—KAIJIN 2006.
- **March 2007:** First strategic dialogue between Indian External Affairs Minister Pranab Mukherjee and his Japanese counterpart Taro Aso.

It has also been suggested that in terms of a promising future in bilateral relations important ground was broken by the Japanese government in two recently-issued policy documents. The 2003 revision of the ODA Charter calls for the disbursal of aid from, among other angles, a strategic perspective too. The JDA's Defense Guidelines issued in December 2004, meantime, for the first time refers to sea lanes of communication in the context of "international peace cooperation activities. Together, the two afford a unique opportunity to route ODA towards India's ports, maritime infrastructure and shipyards, much of which is geared towards dual commercial and military servicing. With India committed to an ambitious ocean security programme, and with Indo-U.S. naval cooperation making rapid strides forward, strategically-oriented ODA channeled towards functional areas such as marine transport, oceanographic surveys, sea bed exploration, ship-lift capabilities, etc. would lend additional focus to what is already the single, largest ODA country disbursal.[41]

However as the popular saying goes there are wheels within wheels. One cannot overlook the fact that during the same period military cooperation between India and the United States has made rapid advances. As pointed out earlier Japan is actively engaged in the creation of an Asian maritime order. It is doing so to shoulder greater responsibility within the U.S.-Japan alliance without provoking a hostile regional response. The potential for cooperation with India was always there given India's strategic location at the head of the Indian Ocean.[42] With the entry of the United States what has changed is Japan's willingness to harness this potential.

A New Democratic Alliance?

India's growing economic and strategic profile have brought into sharp focus complementary interests with the United States. These interests can be summed up in three words: terrorism, energy, and China. In the past, U.S.-Indian relations have been marked by divergent world views but since the advent of the second Bush administration, there has been a warming in relations between the two countries. It is increasingly being argued that this appraisal of India's position has came from the U.S. administration stance that China was no longer just a major trading partner but had become a strategic competitor that needed to be contained in Asia and India is being seen as a useful partner in this endeavor. The United States has to "strengthen political, economic and military-to-military relations with those Asian states that share our democratic values and national interests. That spells India," stated the former U.S. ambassador to India, Robert Blackwell, a strong advocate of a U.S.-Indian alliance.

Major proponents, like Ashley Tellis argue that a partnership between India and the US is vital for the success of US geopolitical objectives, and that the Bush Administration's decision to accommodate India on the issue of nuclear cooperation, provide access to space-related and dual use high technology is desirable because it would speed up India's pace of economic transformation and growth, strengthen India's geopolitical importance, enlist its enthusiasm for counter-proliferation efforts in the Indian Ocean, and buttress its potential utility as a hedge against a rising China (and) encourage it to pursue economic and strategic policies aligned with U.S. interests.[43]

It therefore appears the United States is considering relations with India in the wider strategic context of Asia. For example a restricted October 2002 report sponsored by the Director, Net Assessment, Office of the (U.S.) Secretary of Defense, on India-U.S. military relations, some details of which have appeared in the press, said: "The U.S. military seeks a competent military partner that can take on more responsibility for low-end operations in Asia, such as peacekeeping operations (PKO), search and rescue (SR), humanitarian assistance (HA), disaster relief (DR), and high-value cargo escort, which will allow the U.S. military to concentrate its resources on high-end fighting missions." Two American Lt. Generals were quoted as saying: "Access to India would enable the U.S. military to be able to touch the rest of the world and to respond rapidly to regional crises." "The (U.S.) Air Force would benefit from having access closer to areas of instability (such as Central Asia, South-East Asia, and the Persian Gulf). India's well-developed infrastructure could be useful for the U.S. power projection into these areas." A South Asia Foreign Affairs Officer (FAO) said: "India's strategic importance increases in the event the U.S. relationships with other traditional allies (Japan, South Korea, and Saudi Arabia) become more acrimonious or politically uncomfortable for both parties...or if our traditional relationships collapse resulting in a U.S. military withdrawal. The United States needs to develop alternatives in Asia — India is the optimal choice if we can overcome the obstacles in building the relationship."[44]

Accordingly the United States has come to acknowledge that it has a common interest with India in "securing the vital sea lanes of the Indian Ocean, in fighting terrorism and creating a strategically stable Asia". According to the report "Indo-U.S. Military Relationship: Expectations and Perceptions", prepared for the Net Assessment Office of the U.S. Defense Secretary, "naval cooperation is perhaps one of the more promising and "non-threatening areas of service-to-service cooperation for the U.S. and India".[45] The U.S., thus, now refers to the Indian Navy as a "stabilizing force" in the Indian Ocean region and wants a closer working relationship with it as it straddles the strongest area of strategic convergence—sea-lane protection. Such cooperation has begun with the Indian Navy conducting joint patrols with the U.S. Navy in the Strait of Malacca in 2002.

The high points of defense cooperation between the two countries have been joint exercises and U.S. high-tech arms sales to India, while a dialogue for a framework of strategic cooperation, including on missile defense, transfer of high-technology weapon systems, and counter-terrorism, as well as a strategic partnership between the two navies is underway. It is a highly institutionalised and structured affair: with an Indo-U.S. Defense Policy Group overseeing it and three steering groups guiding it for the three services. Indian naval ships mounted escort patrols for U.S. ships through the Malacca Straits in support of Operation Enduring Freedom.

From the Japanese side a statement clearly linking U.S.-India military cooperation with Japan has come from someone no less than the foreign minister. In a special talk organised by the Federation of Indian Chambers of Commerce (FICCI) on January 8, 2003, in New Delhi, Ms. Yuriko Kawaguchi, Japanese Minister for Foreign Affairs said "Within the new strategic environment, India has been working to strengthen its ties with the United States and other major countries with which it had limited engagement during the Cold War era. And its recent advances in defense cooperation with the United States are of particular note. This Indian initiative will contribute towards peace and prosperity in the Asian and Pacific region through the Japan-U.S. Alliance."[46]

In line with this thinking has been Japanese Prime Minister Shinzo Abe's declaration that Japan, as a democracy, "will engage with strategic dialogues, at the leaders level, with countries that share fundamental values" with the objective of "widening the circle of free societies."[47] In order to create a "beautiful country" Prime Minister Abe proposes to engage in "Proactive Diplomacy" founded on three pillars: (a) strengthening partnerships with countries that share the fundamental values of freedom, democracy, basic human rights and rule of law, (b) creating an Asia that is open and rich in innovation, and (c) contributing to global peace and stability.[48] A theme that was present in the Joint Statement issued at the end of Prime Minister Manmohan Singh's visit to Tokyo in December 2006:

> The two leaders affirm that Japan and India are natural partners as the largest and most developed democracies of Asia, with a mutual stake in each other's progress and prosperity. Indeed, a strong, prosperous and dynamic India is in the interest of Japan, and likewise, a strong, prosperous and dynamic Japan is in the interest of India. They have responsibility for, and are capable of, responding to global and regional challenges, and they must play an active role in the promotion of peace and stability in Asia and world at large.[49]

Indeed, while the Japanese policy establishment has stated in no uncertain terms that it considers building an enhanced relationship with India as one of the cornerstones of a new policy for Japan the shadow of the United States is not difficult to detect. After the navies of the U.S., India, Japan, and Australia formed a "core group" to help Southeast Asia face the tsunami crisis of December 2004, several analysts have regarded the four as potential allies or new friends with compatible strategic goals. Infact, the March 2007 Japan-Australia security declaration is widely seen as part of U.S. efforts to implement a four-way "strategic dialogue" among Japan, the U.S. and Australia plus India because of relations between the U.S. and South Korea deteriorating in recent years.[50] According to news reports this is an initiative of US Vice-President Dick Cheney, and the idea reflects the neo-conservative belief that China will inevitably become a serious threat to US strategic primacy in Asia. Vice President Cheney apparently considers the best way of hedging against China's rising power is to bring together a coalition of like-minded, democratic nations united by a common desire to limit China's influence.[51] The official confirmation has come with the May 2007 Joint Statement of the Security Consultative Committee of Japan and the United States—"Alliance Transformation: Advancing United States-Japan Security and Defense Cooperation"[52] that lists as common objectives:

> "Further strengthening trilateral cooperation among the United States, Japan, and Australia in the region and around the world, including in the areas of security and defense, based on shared democratic values and interests."

And,

> "Continuing to build upon partnerships with India to advance areas of common interests and increase cooperation, recognizing that India's continued growth is inextricably tied to the prosperity, freedom, and security of the region."

As a start the first trilateral naval exercise between India, Japan and the United States was held on April 16, 2007 off the western coast of Japan. And for evidence of India's willingness to be part of the "alliance of democracies" consider this—"During the upcoming trilateral exercise … the most powerful democracy, the most populous democracy and the most prosperous democracy will come together to promote inter-operability," said India's Flag Officer Commanding,

Eastern Fleet Rear. Adm. R.K. Dhowan before the exercise took place.[53] As C. Raja Mohan points out "From being a "lone ranger" of sorts during the Cold War, Indian military forces are now ready to join others in contributing towards regional security. India's changing security policy has now begun to feed into the search for a new balance of power in Asia."[54] It is however a strategic accommodation on part of Japan not a wholehearted embrace.

NOTES

1. Toshi Yoshihara and James R. Holmes, "*Japanese Maritime Thought: If not Mahan, Who*?", http://www.nwc.navy.mil/press/review/2006/summer/pdfs/art1-su06.pdf
2. Text of treaty available at http://www.yale.edu/lawweb/avalon/diplomacy/japan/japan001.htm
3. Text of treaty available at Japan Ministry of Foreign Affairs website http://www.mofa.go.jp/region/n-america/U.S./q&a/ref/1.html
4. Ji Guoxing, "*SLOC Security in the Asia Pacific*", Occasional Paper, Asia-Pacific Centre for Security Studies, February 2000. http://community.middlebury.edu/~scs/docs/Ji%20Guoxing-LOC%20Security%20in%20the%20Asia%20Pacific.htm
5. *Ibid.*
6. *Ibid.*
7. Hideki Yamaji, "Future Japanese Security Policies: Contending Approaches", *Brookings Northeast Asia Survey 2003-04,* http://www.brookings.edu/dybdocroot/fp/cnaps/papers/survey2004/3japan.pdf
8. J.B. Cohen, Japan's *Postwar Economy,* (Minneapolis: University of Minnesota Press), 1958, p. 11. Cited by Warren S. Hunsberger, "Japan's Economy: From Resource Constraints to External Surpluses" in Warren S. Hunsberger (ed.) *Japan's Quest: The Search for International Role, Recognition, and Respect*, (New York: M.E. Sharpe, Inc., 1997), p. 37.
9. *Ibid.*
10. *Far Eastern Economic Review*, February 29, 1996.
11. Dato'Noor Azuman Othman, "Malaysia's Perspective", presented to the 4th Meeting of the ICC International Maritime Bureau Meeting on Piracy and Phantom Ships, June 2001, p. 7. Cited in Takaki Susumu "Suppression of Modern Piracy and the Role of the Navy" *NIDS Security Reports,* No. 4 (March 2003),
12. Stanley B. Weeks, "Sea Lines of Communication (SLOC) Security and

Access", *Institute on Global Conflict and Cooperation Paper*, February 1998. Available at http://www.ciaonet.org/wps/stm02/pp33-5.html

13. Mark Valencia, "Building Confidence and Security in the South China Sea: The Way Forward," in *Non-Traditional Security Issues in Southeast Asia*, ed. Tan and Boutin, (Singapore: Select, for IDSS, 2001), p. 536.
14. John F. Bradford, "*The Growing Prospects for Maritime Security Cooperation in Southeast Asia*", http://community.middlebury.edu/~scs/docs/Maritime%20security%20cooperation%20in%20Southeast%20Asia.pdf
15. James Hookway, "A Dangerous Alliance," *Far Eastern Economic Review,* May 6, 2004, and "Abu Sayyaf Planted Bomb in 'Superferry,' says GMA," *Manila Times,* October 12, 2004.
16. Tanner Campbell and Rohan Gunaratna, "Maritime Terrorism, Piracy and Crime," in *Terrorism in the Asia-Pacific: Threat and Response,* ed. Rohan Gunaratna (Singapore: Eastern Universities Press, 2003), pp. 78-79.
17. Michael Richardson, *A Time Bomb for Global Trade: Maritime-Related Terrorism in an Age of Weapons of Mass Destruction* (Singapore: ISEAS, 2004), pp. 49-72.
18. Presentation by Hideaki Kaneda at the conference "Maritime Security in the Asia Pacific" organised by the IDSS at Singapore from May 20-21, 2004. Report Published by IDSS.
19. Cmdr. Hideo Sekino, "Japan and Her Maritime Defense", *U.S. Naval Institute Proceedings*, May 1971, p. 119, Cited by Peter J. Woolley, pp. 68-69.
20. See Toshi Yoshihara and James R. Holmes, "*Japanese Maritime Thought: If not Mahan, Who?*", http://www.nwc.navy.mil/press/review/2006/summer/pdfs/art1-su06.pdf
21. Peter J. Woolley, *Japan's Navy: Politics and Paradox, 1971-2000*, (London: Lynne Rienner Publishers, Inc., 2000), p. 67.
22. Toshi Yoshihara and James R. Holmes, "*Japanese Maritime Thought: If not Mahan, Who*?", http://www.nwc.navy.mil/press/review/2006/summer/pdfs/art1-su06.pdf
23. Peter J. Woolley, p. 70.
24. Christopher W. Hughes, "*Japanese Military Modernization: In Search of a Normal Security Role*", http://www.nbr.org/publications/strategic_asia/pdf/SA05Hughes.pdf
25. Daisuke Kajimoto, "*Proliferation Security Initiative—A Case Study of US-Japan Alliance Cooperation within the Coalition of Willing*", http://www.stimson.org/japan/pdf/Kajimotopresentation.pdf
26. Ralph A. Cossa, "U.S.-Japan Security Relations: Separating Fact from Fiction" in Ralph A.Cossa (ed.) *Restructuring the U.S.-Japan Alliance:*

Toward a More Equal Partnership", (Washington DC: CSIS, 1998), p. 46.

27. Reference in Mark J. Valencia "Beijing is Setting the Stage for Trouble in the South China Sea", *International Herald Tribune,* July 3, 2000.
28. Seo-Hang Lee "Security of SLOCs in East Asia" *Institute on Global Conflict and Cooperation Paper*, February 1998. Available at http://www.ciaonet.org/wps/stm02/pp33-6.html
29. Sumihiko Kawamura, "*Maritime Transport and Communications including Marine Safety and SLOC Security,*" paper presented at the CSCAP Working Group Meeting on Maritime Cooperation, June 2–3, 1995, Kuala Lumpur.
30. Mark J. Valencia, "*International Co-operation in Anti-piracy Efforts in Asia: Some Considerations*" www.glocomnet.or.jp/okazaki-inst/doc/0313ValenciaPaper.doc
31. This chronology was constructed primarily from reports available at a website maintained by Mark Bruyneel, http://www.geocities.com/Tokyo/Garden/5213/index.html
32. See Mark J. Valencia, "*The U.S. position on Co-operative Maritime Security Frameworks*", http://www.iips.org/Valencia_paper.pdf
33. *Asian Sea Lane Security and International Relations,* Paper commissioned by the Ship and Ocean Foundation, Tokyo, Japan, 2001. Section "Forward and Japan's role", Available at http://nippon.zaidan.info/seikabutsu/2001/00800/contents/00008.htm
34. Sumihiko Kawamura, "*International Cooperation in Marine Counter-Terrorism: A Japanese Perspective*", http://www.observerindia.com/reports/maritime/japanese.pdf
35. Text of statement available at http://www.mofa.go.jp/policy/terrorism/state0609.html
36. See Sam Bateman, "*Coast Guards: New Forces For Regional Order and Security*", Analysis from the East-West Centre, No. 65, January 2003. Available at *http://www.ciaonet.org/pbei/ewc/bas01/bas01.pdf*
37. *Ibid.*
38. Nayan Chanda, "Foot in the Water", *Far Eastern Economic Review*, March 9, 2000, pp. 28-29.
39. Yasukoni Enoki, "*The Japan-India New Partnership*", http://www.usiofindia.org/article_Jul_Sep04_1.htm
40. Joint Statement, *Visit of Shri Pranab Mukherjee, Minister of Defense to Japan*, May 25, 2006. Available at http://meaindia.nic.in/speech/2006/05/25js01.htm
41. See "Manmohan Singh's Visit to Japan: Recent Trends, Historical Perspectives", *Hitachi Research Institute Report*, http://www.hitachi-hri.com/english/research/areareport/us01.html

42. A fact highlighted particularly when in 1999, the Indian Coast Guard rescued the Japanese cargo ship "Alendra Rainbow" which had been seized by pirates in the Malacca Strait along with 7000 tons of aluminum ingots on board.
43. Ashley J. Tellis, "*India as a New Global Power, An Action Agenda for the United States*", Washington, D.C.: Carnegie Endowment for International Peace, 2005, p. 27.
44. "U.S. military wants India to undertake low-end operations in Asia", *The Hindu,* online edition July 4, 2003. http://www.hinduonnet.com/thehindu/2003/07/04/stories/2003070403241200.htm
45. Cited in Rahul Bedi "Weighed Down by History", *Frontline,* Vol. 20, issue 10, May 10-23, 2003.
46. Text of speech available at the FICCI website http://www.ficci.com/ficci/media-room/speeches-presentations/2003/Jan/jan8-japan.html
47. See P.S. Suryanarayana, "*Abe and Japan's Quest for a New Identity*", http://www.thehindu.com/2006/12/25/stories/2006122502410900.htm
48. See Policy Speech by Prime Minister Shinzo Abe to the 166th Session of the Diet on January 26, 2007. English translation available at http://www.kantei.go.jp/foreign/abespeech/2007/01/26speech_e.html
49. Full text available at http://www.in.emb-japan.go.jp/PDF/joint0612.pdf
50. For example see Hisane Masaki, "*The Emerging Axis of Democracy*", http://www.atimes.com/atimes/Japan/IC15Dh01.html
51. Alan Dupont, "*Quadrilateral Alliance Runs Counter to Post-Cold War Multilateralism*", http://www.usyd.edu.au/news/84.html?newsstoryid=1645
52. Full text available at http://www.mofa.go.jp/region/n-america/us/security/scc/joint0705.html
53. Quote in "*Interoperability Focus of Trilateral Exercise*" http://www.c7f.navy.mil/news/2007/april/27.htm
54. C. Raja Mohan, "*Asia's New Democratic Quad*", http://www.isn.ethz.ch/news/sw/details.cfm?ID=17383

4

Japan and the United Nations

For Japan, admission to the United Nations in 1956 was a major step towards rejoining the international community after the defeat in World war II. The UN membership was extremely popular with most Japanese and when Japan joined the UN, it did so with great enthusiasm and broad public support, for the international organisation was seen to embody the newly pacifist country's hopes for a peaceful world order. On February 4, 1957, the Japanese Prime Minister Nobusuke Kishi in a speech to the Japanese Diet outlined the three pillars of the country's postwar foreign policy: (1) to centre foreign policy around the United Nations, (2) to cooperate with the free, democratic nations of the Western Alliance and (3) to identify closely with Asian nations.[1] The first White Paper on foreign policy, issued in 1957, also mentioned 'UN-centered diplomacy' as one of the three pillars of Japan's foreign policy. The Japanese government inserted into the 1951 and 1960 security treaties with the United States, references to Article 51 of the UN Charter that stipulates the right of individual and collective self-defense and also created articles which explicitly hoped that the UN may in future take over Japan's security (article 4 in the 1951 treaty and article 10 in the 1960 treaty).

Yet, as Hisashi Owada, Permanent Representative of Japan to the United Nations has pointed out "Japan's UN-centreed diplomacy was never clearly defined…it was used rather as a slogan to mean that Japanese diplomacy would follow any decision made by the

United Nations. Defeated in the Second World War, the main aim of Japanese foreign policy was to integrate well into the international community."[2] Japan strove, above all, to replace the global view of it as a defeated enemy state with the image of a respected member of the international community, giving priority to peaceful economic development.[3]

It was in the background of the Japanese application for membership of the United Nations having been rejected thrice by the Soviet Union that Japan's Foreign Minister Shigemitsu stated, "Japan, after its defeat in World War II, sincerely wishes for peace and believes that the United Nations would be a central force in promoting world peace".[4] Similarly, Yasushi Akashi, former UN Under-Secretary General for Humanitarian Affairs, has argued "UN-centrism was a cover or an excuse for the lack of a well defined and specific foreign policy in the postwar era."

Indeed, given the UN's paralysis with the advent of the Cold War as well as Japan's firm commitment to the security alliance with the United States, there was not much scope for a UN-centered policy, and in the 1959 Diplomatic Blue Book the idea disappeared from the beginning section. Prime Minister Yoshida referred to Article 51 as the "silk hat" which dressed up the unattractive reality of leasing military bases to the United States after the end of the occupation. In conformity with this ethos, in the early years of its UN membership Japan kept a low profile, paying its dues and generally following U.S. voting patterns.[5]

Rather, it was permanent membership of the UN Security Council that soon claimed the attention of Japanese policymakers. Leading them, according to Reinhard Drifte, was the Ministry of Foreign Affairs, which had been spared the ravages of the purge during the American occupation, where personnel continuity from pre-war days to post-war days was largely maintained and therefore where institutional memory was strongest. With its growing economic stature, the Japanese government not only came to feel even more entitled to a permanent Security Council seat, but also started to become more politically active. In his speeches to the General Assembly Foreign Minister Kiichi in 1969 and 1970 strongly argued that the mechanism of the Security Council was outdated and should be reformed and for the fist time asked for the removal of the "enemy clauses". "Although Japan's bid was not mentioned it was made clear by him and Japanese UN diplomats in background briefings to the press that Japan was a suitable candidate."[6]

In 1973 a joint communiqué announced by U.S. President Nixon and the Japanese Prime Minister Tanaka stated that the United States supports a permanent seat on the UN Security Council for Japan. Again in 1977, U.S. President Carter and Japanese Prime Minister Fukuda announced a joint communiqué stating that the United States believed that Japan was qualified to be a member of the UN Security Council. By the 1980s the goal of pursuing a permanent Security Council seat had become established policy in the Japanese foreign ministry, and was supported by Prime Minister Nakasone. In 1985, Nakasone referred carefully to the revision of the UN Charter in the context of mentioning the proposal about the establishment of a "Group of Wise Men" and said "We must not shrink from the task of continually reviewing and improving the functions of our United Nations in order to maximize its effectiveness." In 1987, Nakasone once again spoke of UN centrism as being one of the pillars of Japan's diplomacy and urged UN reform in the context of the increased number of member states.

The core points of the initial bid remain valid even today and can be summarised as:[7]

- Japan's high contribution to the United Nations budget and its voluntary contributions to many UN organizations. By 1973, Japan was assessed the third largest financial contributor.
- Japan's status as the second largest economy in the world and its major contribution to development assistance.
- Japan's non-nuclear status, which predestines the country to permanent membership in order to balance the fact that all other permanent members are declared nuclear powers.
- Japan as a permanent member would afford better regional representation of Asia in the Security Council.

The quest for permanent membership of UN Security Council, therefore, has always had more to do with the Japanese policy establishment's perceptions of the country's economic strength and the high financial contribution made to the international body rather than any clear intent to enhance Japan's multilateral diplomacy. The desire for a permanent seat on the UN Security Council has been consistently linked to notions of international prestige and recognition rather than any perceptions that a multilateral framework was more suited to address Japan's foreign policy and security issues. Just as UN membership was a symbol of an accepted independent country in the international community after defeat in the Second World War, permanent membership of the Security Council is seen as "a ticket to being recognised as a major power in the international arena.[8] And Japan has remained unrelenting in the pursuit of this goal.

The was a brief interlude of independence from the United States policy in the Middle East following the first oil crisis as, the nation most dependent on Middle Eastern oil, Japan found itself singled out for special pressure to take a more pro-Arab position in order to achieve classification as a "friendly" nation entitled to an uninterrupted flow of oil. The Japanese cabinet issued in 1973 a statement stating opposition to the acquisition of territory by force, a consequent demand for withdrawal of Israeli forces from all territories occupied in 1967, and support for the "legitimate rights" of the Palestinians.[9] When this failed to satisfy the boycotting nations, a second statement was issued adding a promise to contribute to a peace based on these principles, and which deplored "Israel's continuing occupation of Arab territories," and threatened to "reconsider its policy toward Israel" in light of future developments.[10]

However, "the Japanese declaration was little more than a stylistic verbal change in existing Japanese policy, and made little or no difference on the ground."[11] It has been noted that during the 1980s, when Japan was in theory following a declaratory policy somewhat more sympathetic to the Arab side of conflict than that of the United States, its voting record on Arab-Israeli issues in the United Nations actually moved closer to the U.S. position.[12]

In the changed international environment after the end of the Cold War Japan has once again declared its desire for a permanent seat on the UN Security Council. In 1993 the Japanese government clearly suggested that, as part of a restructuring of the UN Security Council the body should be enlarged from 15 (including the P5 and the non-permanent members) to 20 members. Foreign Minister Kono justified Japan's quest saying "In the maintenance of international order, it is not the overwhelming military might of some countries that is playing a major role, but concerted international action towards such destabilizing factors as nuclear proliferation and various conflicts that threaten peace. It is therefore inappropriate that a country like Japan which is playing a prominent role in such international cooperation is not engaged in the UNSC which makes decisions regarding concerted international action." Similarly in the words of Ambassador Hatano, former Japanese Permanent representative to the UN, "some critics argue that Japan can play an important role without a permanent seat. However, the reality is that unless one is a member of the core organ, the Security Council in the case of the United Nations, one looses opportunities to speak."

However, for Japan to become a permanent member of the Security Council revision of the UN charter is necessary, a process that requires two thirds approval by the UN General Assembly and concurring votes of the Permanent Members of the Security Council. And here a "legitimacy deficit' has consistently dogged Japan's bid. During the Cold War Japan was seen as a subordinate of the United States, given the comprehensive security alliance between the two countries wherein a permanent seat on the Security Council for Japan was widely perceived as akin to strengthening American control over the United Nations. In the 1990s therefore both Japanese financial contributions and the country's involvement in UN peacekeeping operation have aimed to highlight the trend of increasing engagement with international security.

"International Contribution", "Proactive pacifism", "An Integrated Approach to Peace-building", etc., are the new buzzwords in Japanese initiatives and pronouncements as Japan has been in the forefront of organising international gatherings on global and regional issues such as development assistance, the environment, nuclear disarmament and arms control. In 1989, Japan invited the U.N. Disarmament Conference to Kyoto and in 1991 hosted a meeting in Tokyo to discuss the Missile Technology Control Regime (MTCR) guidelines. A joint initiative of Japan and the European Union established in 1993 the "UN Register of Conventional Arms" to increase transparency in the transfer of arms and weapon systems. The Tokyo Meeting on Cambodia was held in 1990 and in September 1991, Japan took the initiative to host a conference aimed at promoting democratisation in Mongolia.

Additionally, Japan hosted the Tokyo Meeting for Assistance to the Former Soviet Union in October 1992, as well as the Tokyo Special Session on Partnership for Democracy and Development in March 1993. As a part of its efforts in regional economic development, Japan hosted the second meeting of the International Conference on the Reconstruction of Cambodia in 1994 after chairing the first meeting in Paris in 1993. Japan also hosted the Tokyo International Conference on African Development (TICAD) twice, in both 1993 and in 1998. Japan, hosted the Tokyo Conference on Anti-personnel Landmines in 1997, and the Kyoto Conference on Climate Change.

Financial Contribution

The meteoric rise of the Japanese economy from the ruins of the Second World War and the pacifist Constitution meant that economic assistance has been the cornerstone of post-war Japanese foreign policy. With respect to the United Nations this translated into high Japanese contribution to the regular UN budget and voluntary contributions to many UN organisations. In 1986, Japan became the largest contributor after the United States, contributing almost 11 per cent of the regular UN budget. In 2004 Japan's assessed share was 19.46 per cent. Japanese officials constantly question why their country remains outside the UN's most important policy body and speak of "no taxation without representation".[13] In 1994 a senior Japanese diplomat was quoted as having said, "The UN question is basically one of money. We shall be raising our contribution soon and that should give us a right of entry".[14]

Simultaneously, Japan's aid policy constitutes an integral part of its efforts to effect the 'internationalisation' of the country. In addition to bilateral overseas development aid (ODA) Japan provides multilateral aid through multilateral development institutions such as the World Bank, the International Development Association, and Development Banks worldwide as well as a range of United Nations Agencies, particularly the United Nations Development Programme (UNDP, The United Nations High Commissioner for Refugees (UNHCR), the World Food Programme (WFP), the Fund for Population Activities (UNFPA), and more recently to the United Nations Environment Programme (UNEP).

Sueo Sudo points out that within the Japanese policy establishment there are two implementers of the official aid policy—one represented by the Ministry of International Trade and Industry (MITI) and the other by the Ministry of Foreign Affairs (MOFA).[15] MITI emphasises economically oriented aid based on Japan's short-term economic interests, such as "expansion of export market" or "security of natural resources" as well as long-term interests, such as the "strengthening of economic relations between Japan and developing countries" or "maintaining and developing a stable world economy." On the other hand, MFA emphasises politically oriented aid based on such ideas as "responsibility as a member of the West" and "enhancing the political stability of developing countries," or "promoting democracy."[16] Interest and responsibility are however not two separate trends and Japanese overseas development assistance is an important element of Japan's bid to become a permanent member of the UN Security Council. It is worth noting that MOFA receives the largest ODA budget in the aid administration.

Since being elevated to the status of the world's leading aid donor in 1989 Japan has worked vigorously, both in terms of ideas and geographical diversity, to shed the image of a 'mercantilist nation' whose overseas development assistance was designed solely to promote its domestic interests in Asia. This was necessary as this notion had persisted notwithstanding the fact that in the 1970s Japan diversified its ODA from traditional industrial infrastructure projects to those related to basic human needs (BHN), including education, health, housing, public services, and human resource development or that the *International Cooperation Initiative* announced by Prime Minister Takeshita, in May 1988, identified aid as one of the major elements of Japan's contribution to the world. The international aid community, represented mainly by the Development Assistance Committee (DAC) of the Organization for Economic Cooperation and Development (OECD), pressed the Japanese government to improve its existing ODA programme so that it would be more beneficial to the recipient countries as well as to the entire world. This pressure particularly targeted Japan's infrastructure oriented aid policy.

In 1992, Japan adopted the so-called Overseas Development

Assistance (ODA) Charter[17], which stresses four basic principles in the disbursement of aid:

1. Environmental conservation and development should be pursued in tandem.
2. Any use of ODA for military purposes or for aggravation of international conflicts should be avoided.
3. Full attention should be paid to trends in recipient countries' military expenditures, their development and production of mass destruction weapons and missiles, their export and import of arms, etc.
4. Full attention should be paid to efforts for promoting democratisation and introduction of a market-oriented economy, and the situation regarding the securing of basic human rights and freedoms in the recipient country.

There followed in the next few years a comprehensive review of the aid policy. The Ministry of Foreign Affairs embarked on efforts to deal with the challenges to Japan's ODA in the post-cold war era by providing four reforms to overcome these challenges:

1. Coping with the fiscal crisis by prioritising certain regions,
2. Integrating "soft" aid (emphasising basic human needs and poverty alleviation) into Japan's ODA,
3. Pursuing an untied aid policy, and
4. Collaborating with NGOs.

It was announced that Japan would no longer have the goal of increasing its total ODA, but would instead improve the quality of ODA it provides. One such government measure had been the decision to step up as the world's "environmental donor"18, a commitment that resulted in Japan's US$ 7 billion pledge at the 1992 Rio Earth Summit. Apart from singling out support for aid packages for environmental issues in developing countries, Tokyo has been leaning toward a regional strategy to settle problems such as acid rain. The Ministry of Foreign Affairs *Consultative Committee on ODA Reform Toward the 21st Century* issued a report in January 1998, which in turn led to the proactive 1999 "*New Medium-term Aid Strategy* of

August 1999 that emphasised conflict and development and the need for Japan to henceforth assume a leading role in conflict prevention and post-conflict reconstruction support.[18]

With the 1997 Asian Financial Crisis Japan also forged ahead with a commitment to "human security" in its foreign policy. In his 1988 speech, Obuchi, as Foreign Minister of the Hashimoto Cabinet, describing Japan's intention to cooperate with its Asian neighbours who suffered from economic crises, mentioned health and employment as "human security" concerns and showed an intention to enhance cooperation in this area further by putting priority on social development in Japan's Official Development Assistance (ODA) policy.[19] In July 1998, Obuchi became Prime Minister following Hashimoto's resignation and in December 1998 in a speech in Vietnam he announced that the Japanese government would contribute 500 million yen (4.2 million U.S. dollars) for the establishment of the "Human Security Fund" under the United Nations—the United Nations Trust Fund for Human Security. The fund was established in March 1999.

Since then the Japanese have worked to make "human security" a key term underpinning U.N. operations and defining the role of the organisation in the contemporary world. Prime Minister Mori's speech at the *UN Millennium Summit*, his proposals for multilateral co-operation over the theme of human security led to the 2001 establishment of the UN *Committee on Human Security*, co-chaired by Amartya Sen and Japanese national, Sadako Ogata. The report of this commission, agreed in February 2003, describes human security in the context of conflicts as well as development contending that "empowerment" in addition to "protection" of people would be most important either in conflict and (post conflict) developmental situations. At the G8 Millennium Summit in Kyushu-Okinawa, Koizumi announced "Action from Japan" a far-sighted plan containing measures jointly addressing the issues of "conflict and development". This plan envisioned development assistance that would be delivered rapidly and in concert with NGOs and international organisations; and that would place special emphasis on the perspective of conflict prevention. The ODA Charter revised in 2003 also identified the perspective of 'human security' as a basic principle and the 'consolidation of peace' as one of its priority issues.

By endorsing human security as "the cornerstone of international cooperation in the 21st century," Japan has moved towards strengthening the philosophical foundation as well as establishing an international policy institution through which its financial contributions towards international security are implemented. Moreover, this is in keeping with the more integrated and interventionist approach of the UN itself since the end of the Cold War: an approach that was exemplified by the multi-disciplinary concept of "peace-building" enunciated by UN Secretary-General, Boutros-Ghali, in his "*Agenda for Peace*" and later in the seminal *Brahimi Report*. In the words of Nobumasa Akiyama, "The limited contribution in the security field could be perceived as an obstacle for Japan's quest for a permanent seat on the Security Council. If introduction of the concept of human security enlarges the scope of security-related activities into social and economic dimensions, or at least raises the significance of activities in the social and economic development up to the level of conventional security issues, it would cover up the shortfall of Japan's policy toward collective security and relatively increase the presence of Japan in the United Nations."[20]

To counter criticism that Japan's international economic assistance was 'Asia-centric' Japan started to focus on Africa in the 1990s and has taken the initiative in leading international efforts to support African development. Japan organised the Tokyo International Conference on African Development (TICAD I, II and III) in 1992 1998 and 2003, as well as many related meetings to promote new ideas to help African countries. Japan has contributed more than US$ 12.7 billion in fields such as basic human needs and at the 2000 G8 Okinawa Summit Japan took the initiative to invite to Tokyo three African heads of states—Thabo Mbeki of South Africa, Olusegun Obasanjo of Nigeria and Abdelaziz Bouteflika of Algeria. In 2001 Prime Minister Mori's visit to some African nations was the first by a Japanese prime minister. Throughout the trip Sadako Ogata, the renowned out-going UN Commissioner for Refugees, accompanied the Japanese Prime Minister.

Africa's potentially significant vote in the UN General Assembly in support of Japan's permanent membership in a reformed Security Council has been a significant factor in post-Cold War Japan's African initiative. By taking a leadership role in coordinating development efforts in Africa, Tokyo is able to demonstrate that it is interested in global issues and not totally preoccupied with Asia. Japan's proposal to hold TICAD was initially made at the UN General Assembly in New York and not at the OAU summit in an African capital city. To actively contribute to international peace, in May 1993 Japan also sent about 50 SDF personnel to the UN Operation in Mozambique. The Ministry of Foreign Affairs regarded the dispatch of SDF to Mozambique, one of the poorest African countries with little ties to Japan, as an opportunity to show the international community Japan's initiative in its *kokusai koken* (international contribution) policy, and moreover, to prove itself worthy of a permanent membership of the UN Security Council.[21] The Prime Minister's Official Residence, in particular the then Chief Cabinet Secretary Yohei Kono and Prime Minister Kiichi Miyazawa, decided to send the SDF to Mozambique mainly because they needed a tangible proof of Japanese commitment to international peace in the G7 Summit, which Japan was to host in July 1993.[22] Ogura Kazuo also contends "Japan definitely had in mind the political clout of the African bloc when it called for the Tokyo International Conference on African Development (TICAD) in 1993…On the fringes of the TICAD II meeting, Prime Minister Keizo Obuchi pushed Tokyo's U.N. reform agenda in separate meetings with a number of African leaders."[23]

With the issue of UN reform hotting up again, in April 2005, Prime Minister Junichiro Koizumi announced that Japan would double its official development assistance to Africa in the next three years from US$ 500 million. Tokyo's decision was apparently prompted by concerns that its attempt to become a permanent member of the U.N. Security Council could be jeopardised if it keeps pruning official development assistance (ODA) because of economic weakness and fiscal strains. Japan's ODA budget, once the biggest in the world, has been dwindling steadily since it peaked at US$ 15.3 billion in 19991. Japan is still the world's second-largest aid donor, following the United States. But its ratio of ODA to gross national income has dropped to 0.19 per cent, one of the lowest figures among the developed nations.

Japanese international economic assistance has, therefore, become increasingly involved with aid programmes of an unmistakably political hue, and related to security situations and regional stability, in the form of conflict prevention and aid for post-conflict reconstruction. Japan has adopted a stance of active involvement in reconstruction and peace building in Afghanistan since the end of 2001, and also in the international efforts for reconstruction in Iraq since spring 2003. The link between human security rhetoric and real diplomatic focus is difficult to ignore, more so after the Ministry of Foreign Affairs MOFA, became the central aid coordination ministry after the 2001 administrative reshuffling.

UN Peacekeeping

At the heart of this debate is Japan's obligation under the UN Charter, particularly the dispatch of Japanese personnel to UN peacekeeping missions. According to Article 43 of the UN Charter, all member states must make available to the Security Council, whatever armed forces, assistance and facilities may be needed for the maintenance of international peace and security. Article 9 of Japan's new 'Peace Constitution', on the other hand, stated that:

Aspiring Sincerely to an international Peace based on justice and order, the Japanese people forever renounce war as a sovereign right of the nation and the threat or use of force as a means of settling international disputes.

> In order to accomplish the aim of the preceding paragraph, land, sea, and air forces, as well as other war potential, will never be maintained. The right of belligerency of the state will not be recognised.

As early as April 11, 1952, in the Foreign Policy Committee of the House of Representatives, the Japanese Foreign Minister Okazaki, in response to the question of whether Japan would be obliged to send troops to Korea once it became a member of the United Nations, responded in the negative. Okazaki pointed out that some UN member states were without military forces such as Panama, Costa Rica and Iceland, and said that Japan could perform non-military obligations such as supplying some facilities for UN forces and transportation of military equipments. The Ministry of Foreign Affairs, however, concluded, that it was not prudent to attach an explicit reservation based on Article 9 of the Constitution in the letter for the application to UN membership[24] and Okazaki officially stated in his letter to the UN Secretary General in June 1952 that *"...the Government of Japan hereby accepts the obligation contained in the Charter of the United Nations, and undertakes to honour them, by all means at its disposal from the day when Japan becomes a member of the United Nations."*[25]

The unspoken interpretation of the phrase "by all means at its disposal" was that Japan would fulfill its UN obligations so long as they did not violate the Japanese National Constitution. In 1958 the debate was no longer theoretical as the UN Secretary General asked the Japanese government to send 10 officers of the Japanese Self-Defense Forces as military observers to Lebanon. The Japanese government declined even though Japan at that time was serving as a non-permanent member of the Security Council. In 1961 Ambassador Koto Matsudaira (who had been permanent Representative of Japan to the UN) was reported to have stated, "It is not consistent for Japan to adhere to UN cooperation on the one hand and refuse all participation in the UN armies on the other." Therefore, he insisted that Japan should take a positive step in co-operating with ONUC since it was following a foreign policy centreed on diplomacy through the UN. The suggestion by Matsudaira caused a stormy controversy in the Diet on February 22, 1961 and Matsudaira withdrew his statement.

The Japanese government led by Prime Minister Ikeda tried to suggest that "a dispatch of Japanese forces to UN missions could be constitutional or unconstitutional depending on purpose, mandate, function and organization of the mission. If a UN mission was purely for policing, it could be constitutionally possible to send Japanese forces." Opposition parties, however, strongly objected to this government view. The debate was rekindled in 1966 when the *Tokyo Shimbun* newspaper reported that in the light of Japan having been reelected as a non-permanent member of the UN Security Council in 1965 the Ministry of Foreign Affairs had drafted a United Nations Cooperation Bill, which specifically mentioned personnel, including members of the SDF, as part of Japan's contribution to UN missions. However, the bill did not make much progress within the Government.

The traditional interpretation prevailed again in 1969, in the context of the war in Vietnam. The National Legislation Bureau repeated its 1954 position that Japan has a right to collective self-defense as stipulated in Article 51 of the UN charter, namely '…. the inherent right of individual or collective self-defense if an armed attack occurs….' but its exercise of such right is constrained by Article 9 of the Japanese constitution. Simply put, Japan cannot aid others when they are attacked.

In 1983 the Japanese Government formed a Study Group chaired by former UN Ambassador Shizuo Sato that stated "The commitment of our country to the UN has been apt to be restricted to financial aspects. However, our country should participate in UN peacekeeping operations in terms of the following sections positively and extensively: provision of funds and materials, election supervision, medical assistance, transport and communications activities, police activities, logistic support, and observation and patrol activities."[26] Facing serious criticism from the opposition parties and public, Prime Minister Nakasone publicly dismissed the report, calling it "merely one view put forward by a private study group."[27]

UN peacekeeping operations won the Nobel Peace Prize in 1988 and later in the same year in 1988 Japanese Prime Minster Noboru Takeshita proposed the International Cooperation Initiative identifying five areas in which Japan could play a role on the world stage: active pursuit of diplomatic efforts aimed at strengthening political dialogue and international cooperation; increased contributions for UN-sponsored activities seeking to prevent outbreak of conflicts; active involvement in international efforts to resolve disputes peacefully (such as dispatching civilian personnel to trouble-spots to assist with the supervision of elections or provide transportation, communications, or medical services); strengthened assistance to refugees through both bilateral and multilateral efforts; and vigorous contributions to international cooperative efforts aimed at reconstruction once a conflict is peacefully resolved.[28] Subsequently, Japan, for the first time, dispatched one political officer to the UN Good Office Mission in Afghanistan and Pakistan (UNGOMAP), and another political officer to the UN Iran-Iraq Military Observer Group (UNIIMOG). In the following year, Japan dispatched 27 election supervisors to United Nations Transition Assistance Group (UNTAG) in Namibia. However these were civilians sent under the Ministry of Foreign Affairs Law.

As with the aid policy the peacekeeping issue finally erupted with the Iraqi invasion of Kuwait in August 1990. The Japanese government scrambled to pass legislation establishing a UN Peace Cooperation Corps to provide logistic back up for the multinational forces in the Gulf, only to be defeated by concerted political opposition in the Diet. This Bill envisaged creating a UN Peace Cooperation Corps (UNPCC), which was to consist of non-SDF government employees, private citizens directly subordinate to the Prime Minister, and members temporarily transferred from the SDF. It specified that activities of the corps could include: overseeing cease-fire agreements, monitoring elections, medical activities, disaster relief measures, and transportation, telecommunications, and other logistical support.

Japan's position received immense criticism from the international community. Eventually, in April 1991, the Government sent SDF minesweepers to the Persian Gulf and for the first time SDF activity was described as a contribution to the international community and specifically a contribution in terms of personnel or human resources. According to the Japanese defense white paper, "ensuring safe ship traffic in that sea area at the earliest date possible was called upon by international society. Therefore, the dispatch of the minesweepers was of significance as a measure to contribute to the international community in terms of personnel for peace and humanity".[29]

The lesson learned from the Gulf-war was that Japan risked exclusion from the league of 'big players' in world affairs if it continued to substitute international financial contributions for more direct forms of contribution to international security, including human or physical contributions. The US Ambassador Armacost stated on 13 March 1991 that whether Japanese contingents could be dispatched to Cambodia would be a touchstone of the provision of its peacekeeping commitment in the future.[30] The Foreign Ministry White Paper of 1991 thus announced that personnel contributions were indispensable. According to Prime Minister Miyazawa, Japan's international contribution "should include some 'sweating' or dispatch of personnel to assist UN peacekeeping operations" rather than relying sole on "a lavish scattering around of aid."[31] Gradually, a domestic consensus emerging that Japan must play a more active role in maintaining international peace and security rather than simply contributing money to solve global problems.

On 6 June, 1991, the ruling Liberal Democratic Party created a "Special Study Group on Japan's Role in the International Community" chaired by LDP General Secretary Ichiro Ozawa, which was simply called "the Ozawa Commission." This Commission claimed that the Preamble of the Japanese Constitution has a clear provision for Japan's pursuit of peaceful cooperation with all nations", wherein the dispatch of the SDF to UN forces under Articles 42 and 43 of the UN Charter would be constitutional and strongly recommended Japan's participation in UN peacekeeping operations.

Finally, the second bill, the International Peace Cooperation Bill was presented to the Diet by the Government in September 1991. This Bill differed from the first bill in several aspects. For example, the purpose of this Bill was more clearly specified than the first one as participation in UN peacekeeping operations and humanitarian assistance. This Bill required the approval of the Diet in the case of the SDF's dispatch. Furthermore, this Bill included the so-called "Five Principles" for the participation of Japanese contingents in peacekeeping operations.

1. Agreement on the ceasefire shall have been reached among the parties to the conflicts.
2. The parties to the conflict, including the territorial states, shall have given their consent to deployment of the peacekeeping force and Japan's participation in the force.
3. The peacekeeping force shall strictly maintain impartiality, not favouring any party to the conflict.
4. Should any of the above guideline requirements ceased to satisfy the Government of Japan, she may withdraw its contingent.
5. Use of weapon shall be limited to the minimum necessary to protect the personnel's lives.

The PKO Bill was voted into law in June 1992 and since then the Japanese SDF began to take part in non-combat aspects of peace keeping operations—such as re-building roads and monitoring elections in a number of UN operations, including Cambodia 1992-96, Mozambique in December 1992, Zaire and Tanzania as part of the Rwanda mission in 1994, Golan Heights 1996 and East Timor

1999 representing a shift away from the so-called 'chequebook diplomacy'. In the words of a high-ranking official of MOFA to a journalist, "the participation in Cambodia's PKO alone is not enough for Japan. It is something like graduating from college with minimum requirements. In order to come up to the standard mark in the international community, Japan must participate in at least two UN peace-keeping operations simultaneously."[32]

Importantly, the long-standing political, legal and constitutional barriers to the overseas dispatch of the SDF were "eroded within a discourse centreing on the responsibility of Japan to make an 'international contribution'.[33] The process of policy change that culminated in the passage of the International Peace Cooperation Law of June 1992 was thus clearly precipitated by foreign pressure or *gaiatsu* for greater burden sharing but in contrast, the series of subsequent Japanese government decisions to contribute peacekeepers to UN operations in various parts of the world were driven almost entirely by *naiatsu* or domestic pressure.[34] In the words of a Japanese official, 'power sharing is the other side of the coin of burden sharing.' And as the Ozawa Commission report stated, "...Japan should set the goal of acquiring a permanent seat for itself in the Security Council. To accomplish this, it must first build up a record of contributions in the security system so that it can gain the understanding and support of the U.N. membership."[35]

International Humanitarian Relief Operations

Relief of Rwandan refugees	Refugee relief units	Sep.-Dec. 1994	283 persons
	Airlifting units	Sep.-Dec. 1994	118 persons
Relief of East Timorese displaced persons	Airlifting units	Nov. 1999-Feb. 2000	113 persons
Relief activities of Afghan refugees	Airlifting units	Oct. 2001	138 persons
Relief of Iraqi refugees	Airlifting units	April 2003	56 persons
Relief of Iragi victims	Airlifting units	July-Aug. 2003	104 persons
Sub-Total			**812 persons**

Record of Japan's International Peace Cooperation Activities based on the International Peace Cooperation Law

(*As of March 2005*)

UN Peacekeeping Operations (PKO)			(*Total Numbers*)
United Nations Angola Verification Mission II (UNAVEM II)	Electoral observers	Sep.-Oct. 1992	3 persons
United Nations Transitional Authority in Cambodia (UNTAC)	Military observers	Sep. 1992-Sep. 1993	8 persons × 2
	Ovllian police	Oct. 1992 Jul. 1993	75 persons
	Engineering units	Sep. 1992-Sep. 1993	600 persons × 2
	Electoral observers	May-Jun 1993	41 persons
United Nations observer Mission in El Salvador (ONUSAL)	Electoral observers	Mar/Apr. 1994	15 persons × 2
United Nations Disengagement observer Force (UNDOF)	Staff Officers	Feb. 1996-present	2 persons × 9
	Transport units	Feb. 1996-present	43 persons × 18
United Nations Mission in East Timor (UNAMET)*	Civilian police	July-Sep. 1999	3 persons
United Nations Transitional Administration in East Timor (UNTAET)	Engineer group	Mar.-May 2002	680 persons
	Headquarters personnel	Feb-May 2002	10 persons
United Nations Mission of Support in East Timor (UNMISET)	Engineer group	May 2002-Jun 2004	680 persons × 2 + 522 persons + 405 persons
	Headquarters personnel	May 2002-Jun 2004	10 persons + 7 persons
Sub-Total			**4633 persons**

*UNAMET: UN Political Mission.

Sub-total: 4633 persons

International Election Monitoring Activities

Bosnia and Herzegovina general and regional elections	Elections supervisors and observers	Sep. 1998	30 persons
Bosnia and Herzegovina municipal assembly elections	Polling supervisors	March-April 2000	11 persons
Timor-Leste constituent assembly elections	Electoral observers	Aug.-Sep. 2001	19 persons
Kasavo assembly elections	Electoral observers	Nov. 2001	6 persons
Timor-Leste presidential election	Electoral observers	April 2002	8 persons
Sub-Total			**74 persons**

Total: 5519 persons
(Excl. Liaison and Coordination Personnel))

For the Japanese Foreign Ministry, the issue of Japan's participation in international peacekeeping is inextricably bound up with its ambition to obtain a permanent seat for Japan on the UN Security Council. The Foreign Ministry denies any explicit linkage between peacekeeping and permanent seat issues partly out of fear that such a connection might be counterproductive but "the relationship between peacekeeping and a permanent seat is clearly evident in the Foreign Ministry's eagerness for Japan to sustain the momentum in peacekeeping sufficiently to maintain Japan's international credibility and to deflect international criticism that it is failing to do its part."[36] In 1994, under the leadership of senator William Roth, the US Senate passed two resolutions affirming that the US government should not support Japan's attempt to gain a permanent seat. The Senate's objection was based on uncertainty over Japan's overall commitment to engage fully in UN peacekeeping and peacemaking operations.[37] Therein the Japanese Foreign Minister Yohei Kono in his September 1994 speech to the General Assembly stated "Japan with the endorsement of many countries, is prepared to discharge its responsibilities as a permanent member of the Security Council in accordance with its basic philosophy of not resorting to the use of force prohibited by its constitution." In June 1998, the PKO Law was reviewed in order to meet the demand from the changing climate of international security and of the crisis management system. The amended law stated that weapons for self-defense can be used only under the orders of the commanding officer (rather than at the individual's discretion) and Japanese personnel can participate in humanitarian missions involving the UNHCR even without a cease-fire agreement in place. Gerald Curtis describes this as "situational accommodation", "a desire to assess correctly the trends of the times and make the desired adjustments in order to avoid international isolation and to facilitate international acceptance".[38]

Furthermore, since the September 11 terrorist attacks in the United States Japan has enacted two unprecedented measures in terms of international crisis management, namely, the Anti-terrorism Bill, and a further amendment of the PKO Law. Under these two separate special laws Japan has dispatched Ground Self-Defense Force troops to Iraq on a humanitarian and reconstruction mission and Maritime Self-Defense Force ships to the Arabian Sea to refuel US and other foreign naval vessels involved in military operations in and around Afghanistan. Much of the justification for these measures has been provided by UN resolutions and the Preamble of the Japanese Constitution arguing for international cooperation even though the actual content of the SDF activities has been primarily to support the United States.

Japan as "Normal Country"

The series of attempts, outlined above, by successive governments to widen Japan's engagement with international society in the post-Cold War period are useful indicators of the country's role as a global power. At one end are the efforts to refine the utilisation of economic power with conceptions of comprehensive security, human security and Japan's status as a global civilian power. On the other end are the military measures that have expanded the scope of Japan's use of force revealing it as a proactive military power. For some analysts, Japan's recent actions represent a major incremental leap in its security policy that could take it to the point of no return in terms of breaking with its past traditions.[39] The fact that these measures have been largely legitimised within a broader framework of multilateralism and the United Nations[40] seems to suggest, however, that Japan may be "a step closer" towards realising Ichiro Ozawa's vision of Japan as a "normal country" that had not materialised during the Gulf War.

In his Blueprint for a New Japan Ozawa defined a "normal country" as a nation that "willingly shoulders those responsibilities regarded as natural in the international community" and "cooperates fully with other nations in their efforts to build prosperous and stable lives for their people". A firm supporter of the US-Japan Alliance, however Ozawa argued in favour of the concept of collective security, as opposed to collective defense wherein Japan's use of military force could only be exercised when legitimised by the UN and would place an international constraint on Japan's use of force.[41] Stressing the value of proactively utilising Japan's resources to shape the international order he declared "Japan must align itself further with international society. There is no other way to do this than to participate actively in all activities led by the U.N."[42]

Cautious incrementalism continues to prevail as a strategy within the Japanese policy establishment. Although Article 9 is seen as "problematic" the dominant view is to retain it rather than revise it. According to Christopher Hughes "Article 9 could be read as no longer providing a guide for what Japan should do to contribute to international security and how it should do it, but merely as how it should do it in terms of restrictions on the use of force, whilst the legitimisation for what Japan should do is now provided by the Preamble."[43] This emphasis on reinterpretation rather than revision vis a vis the Constitution stems from the legacy of history and the mistrust with which many neighbouring countries view Japan. Given Japan's history of aggression and colonialism in the region these countries are extremely wary of an enhanced Japanese military role.

The United Nations is therefore for Japan an important conduit through which to seek a global role for itself and accounts for the persistence of the campaign for a permanent seat on the Security Council. According to Prime Minister Junichiro Koizumi, in making the case to the U.N. General Assembly in September 2004, Japan is simply "seeking an honoured place in an international community striving for peace and prosperity."[44] There is a growing body of sentiment that a role within the ambit of the United Nations as the ideal way for Japan to enhance its international standing. As Ueki Yasushiro points out, UN-centrism is a "convenient cover under which Japan can justify its assertive political role and which helps quieten the lingering domestic opposition to Japan getting involved in *real politique*. It also dispels fears of its Asian neighbours about Japan's assertive political behaviour."[45]

Implications for India

On September 21, 1987, Prime Minister Yasuhiro Nakasone addressed the world body, quoting from the poet Henry Wadsworth Longfellow's "The Psalm of Life":

> *Let us, then, be up and doing, With a heart for any fate; Still achieving, still pursuing,*
> *Learn to labour and to wait.*

The spirit of this verse lives on in the heart of the Japanese today. But it has been nearly two decades since Nakasone spoke these words to the world, and Japan continues to wait.

Japan remains unrelenting in the pursuit of one goal: to be a permanent member of the United Nations Security Council. Over the past decade, the Japanese government has spoken out frequently in favour of enlarging the UN Security Council and in recent years Japan has even threatened to reduce its UN financial contribution in an effort to force the issue. The aim, therefore, is not to be taken lightly. Though the U.N. Charter does not allow an elected non-permanent member of the Security Council to succeed itself when the two-year term is completed, Japan has managed to get elected nine times in the past 50 years. Japan's present case essentially consists of two points: first, that the line up of permanent members must accurately reflect the international situation and appropriately represent the international community, and second, that countries with the will and the ability to take on a major role in the maintenance of international peace and security should become permanent members and take part in the decisions of the council. Japan has thus emphasised the results achieved through its international contributions in various areas, such as the consolidation of peace, nation building, human security, and arms reduction and non-proliferation, adding that it will employ the capabilities and experience gained through these efforts to fulfill its responsibilities as a permanent member of the Security Council.

In an adroit diplomatic move, in September 2004, Japan along with India, Brazil and Germany delivered a joint statement launching a united bid for permanent UN Security Council seats after meeting on the sidelines of the United Nations General Assembly in New York. The declaration stated that Germany, Brazil, India and Japan, "based on the firmly shared recognition that they are legitimate candidates for permanent membership in an expanded Security Council, support each other's candidature." A draft framework resolution, announced subsequently, commits the G-4, as the four aspirants call themselves, to seeking six new permanent seats on the Security Council. The Council's size is to be increased from 15 to 25. The new permanent members are to be chosen on the basis of two each from Asia and Africa, one from Latin America/Caribbean, and one from among `West European and Other' states. In addition, the draft calls for increasing the number of non-permanent members by four, up from the present 10, on the basis of one each from Africa, Asia, Latin America/Caribbean, and East Europe.

These events are a radical departure from 1996 when Japan defeated India in a bitterly contested election to become an elected member of the UN Security Council. India's nuclear explosions in May 1998 saw Japan taking an affirmative stand on the issue of proliferation particularly nuclear proliferation. Japan, along with Sweden, Costa Rica and Slovenia, introduced what eventually became UN Security Council Resolution 1172 that strongly deplored the nuclear tests by India and Pakistan, called on the two countries not to assemble or deploy nuclear devices, cease development of ballistic missiles, and unconditionally sign the NPT and CTBT. Japanese Foreign Minister Obuchi said at a press conference that Japan was exploring a leadership role to convene an international conference among "nuclear powers and economic powers" to discuss nuclear problems. He is reported to have commented "The (five) declared nuclear powers and the countries which have a large responsibility in the world should gather to discuss the issue seriously." Similarly the Tokyo Forum Report released in August 1999 said,[46] "India considers the possession of nuclear weapons an attribute of great power status". Seeking to debar India, the report further proposed: "All current and prospective members of the United Nations Security Council should have exemplary non-proliferation credentials."

However, during Foreign Minister Y. Kawaguchi's official visit to India in August 2004, both Governments agreed and announced their mutual support for each other's candidature for the permanent membership of the expanded Security Council. This was followed by Prime Minister J. Koizumi's invitation for a summit-level meeting of the G4, namely Brazil, Germany, India and Japan, to agree upon the pressing need to expand the Security Council membership, both in the permanent and non-permanent seats, as well as mutual support for their respective candidature for permanent membership. The Eight-fold initiative for strengthening Japan-India Global Partnership announced by India and Japan during the Japanese Prime Minister Koizumi's visit to New Delhi in May this year explicitly mentioned cooperation in the United Nations and other international organisations, including cooperation for the early realisation of U.N. reforms, particularly Security Council reform.[47]

So what prompted this change? According to the Japanese Ambassador to India, Yasukuni Enoki, "Japan is convinced that the present time, until the next UN General Assembly, is the most opportune chance for realisation of UN reform. If we miss this chance, such a golden opportunity may never come to us for at least another decade or two. In this sense, it is really—Now or never."[48] In this context it appears that Japan would not like a repeat of the "Declaration on Security Council Reform by the Foreign Ministers of the Non-Aligned Movement" announced on April 8, 1997, in New Delhi during discussion on the Razali recommendations after which the German-Japan initiative for reform ran out of steam. There was a realisation that only through combined efforts is any chance of gaining the support of more than 128 UN member states, the two-thirds of the organisation necessary for a resolution to be adopted. In the words of the Japanese Ambassador, "Japan and India hold the key to this challenge."[49]

The numbers game assumed even greater importance after China's decision to dispense with its customary diplomatic ambiguity on the matter of United Nations reform and come out firmly against

Japan's bid for a permanent seat on the council saying the UN was "not a board of directors" whose composition could be decided by "the financial contribution of its members."[50] During his visit to India in April 2005, China's Prime Minister Wen Jiabao warned Japan that it cannot get a permanent seat on the Security Council until it faces up to its history of aggression and wins its neighbours' trust. "Only a country that respects history, takes responsibility for history and wins over the trust of peoples in Asia and the world at large can take greater responsibilities in the international community," Wen told media persons in New Delhi.[51] Japan hoped to present the five permanent members of the United Nations Security Council (the P-5) with a fait accompli that they must either accept or reject in toto. If China wants to veto Japanese permanent membership, for example, it will have to reject the entire package and run the risk of alienating not just Japan but the other newly elected permanent members as well.

Indian willingness to be part of G4 was similarly a pragmatic strategy of pooling efforts "to enhance effectiveness and credibility" given that the United States has officially, as yet, only backed Japan's candidature. The idea was to also avoid a repeat of the "Declaration on Security Council Reform by the Foreign Ministers of the Non-Aligned Movement" announced on April 8, 1997, in New Delhi during discussion on the Razali recommendations after which the German-Japan initiative for UN reform ran out of steam. The coming together, however, was not without compromises. Despite having campaigned hard and for long against the undemocratic character of the UN Security Council India, went along with the G-4 to postpone the veto for 15 years. The public rhetoric nonwithstanding—several media reports quoted Ryozo Kato, Japan's Ambassador to US, as having said, "The Security Council is not like an aircraft, with first class, business and economy seats."—Japan had all along urged India to have a less rigid position.

Japanese Ambassador to India Yasukuni Enoki, in a briefing to the media prior to Prime Minister Koizumi's visit stated that all aspirants for a Security Council seat should be "realistic and flexible" on the issue of having a "veto power".[52] Again, when asked about Japan's position on veto, Japanese Foreign Minister Machimura during a visit to the United States said "Tokyo would like the new permanent members enjoy same privileges and facilities which the current five—US, Britain, Russia, France and China—enjoy, but the question of veto should not become a hindrance in the reform process including expansion of the 15-member Council."[53] The Japanese side managed to get the Indians to use the words "should have" instead of "shall have" in the paragraph on veto power in the earlier draft resolution.[54] India may find its scope for independent policy further shrinking, rather than expanding as it moves closer to the Security Council's exclusive club.

As events have unfolded it has become even clearer that Japan's endorsement of Indian ambitions at the United Nations is more a matter of strategy rather than principled support. In January 2006 Just one day after India and Japan reaffirmed their commitment to the expansion of the UN Security Council and called for mobilising maximum support to the G-4 grouping formed for the purpose, Japan refrained from joining the other three—India, Brazil and Germany—in resubmitting the July 2005 draft resolution to the UN General Assembly calling for the addition of permanent seats in the Security Council for each of them plus Japan, two African states and four new non-permanent members. Instead, Japan indicated its intention to consult the USA on the best means to secure permanent membership of the United Nations Security Council with reports quoting Japanese Chief Cabinet Secretary Shinzo Abe as saying: "Our country is now pursuing a draft resolution that can get support from more countries and is discussing the matter with the United States of America.

One of Japan's leading newspapers, *Asahi Shimbun*, stated that the foreign ministry had compiled the basic framework for a new draft resolution on expanding the Security Council in a way that is more compatible with the American position on who should be allowed to join. Realising that the U.S. is not likely to agree to Security Council reform as long as there remains the possibility of a nation it does not want on the council becoming a permanent member, the Japanese Foreign Ministry's new plan would increase the Security Council's membership to twenty one. But in a shift from the G-4 proposal, any nation can become a permanent member if it wins the support of at least 128 nations, or two-thirds of the 191 members of the United Nations. The idea is that the increased options would give Washington more leeway in urging other UN members not to vote for nations it deems inappropriate for permanent membership.[55]

It is apparent that Tokyo has decided to sit on the fence for the moment. Japan wants to probe the extent of American support and at the same time keep its options open of joining the other three members of the G-4 if they look likely to succeed. In the words of Japanese foreign ministry official Toshihiro Kitamura: "This time we will first seek to gain support from the USA while simultaneously maintaining support from the G4 group of allies." On balance, Tokyo's tweaking of its UNSC strategy seems to be dictated by robust common sense and putting national interest first while trying to take its friends—old and recently acquired-along. Lessons here for New Delhi, perhaps.

NOTES

1. Akiko Fukushima, *Japanese Foreign Policy: The Emerging Logic of Multilateralism,* (New York, Palgrave, 1999), p. 80.
2. Hisashi Owada, *Gaiko to ha Nani ka* (NHK Shuppan, 1996), pp. 72-3, Quoted in Akiko Fukushima *Japanese Foreign Policy: The Emerging Logic of Multilateralism,* (New York, Palgrave, 1999), p. 81.
3. Robert M. Immerman, "Japan in a Multilateral Dimension" http://www.acdis.uiuc.edu/Research/S&Ps/1993-Su/S&P_VII-4/multilateral_dimension.html
4. Yasushi Akashi, *Kokusairengo: Sono Hikari to Kage* (Iwanami Shinsho, 1985) p. 9, Quoted in Akiko Fukushima *Japanese Foreign Policy: The Emerging Logic of Multilateralism,* (New York, Palgrave, 1999), p. 80.
5. Edward Newman, "Japan and International Organizations", in Inoguchi Takashi and Purnendra Jain ed., *Japanese Foreign Policy Today,* (New York, Palgrave, 2000), p. 51.
6. Reinhard Drifte, "Japan's Quest for a Permanent Seat on the Security Council", *Asia Pacific Review*, Vol. 5, No. 2, 1998. p. 92.
7. *Ibid.*
8. For the historical background of Japan's demand for a permanent UN Security Council seat see, Reinhard Drifte, *Japan's Quest for a Permanent Security Council Seat: A Matter of Pride or Justice?* 2000
9. Alan Dowty, "Japan and the Middle East: Signs of Change?", *Middle East Review of International Affairs,* Vol. 4, No. 2, December 2000, p. 3, http://www.ciaonet.org/olj/meria/meria00_doa01.html
10. Shuzo Kimura, "Japanese Middle East Policy-Impact of the Oil Crisis", *American-Arab Affairs,* No. 17, Summer 1986, pp. 68-69. Quoted in

Alan Dowty, "Japan and the Middle East: Signs of Change?", *Middle East Review of International Affairs,* Vol. 4, No. 2, December 2000 p. 3, http://www.ciaonet.org/olj/meria/meria00_doa01.html

11. Alan Dowty, "Japan and the Middle East: Signs of Change?", *Middle East Review of International Affairs,* Vol. 4, No. 2, December 2000 p. 4, http://www.ciaonet.org/olj/meria/meria00_doa01.html
12. Yasumasa Kuroda, "Japan, the Arab World and Israel," *American-Arab Affairs*, No. 28, Spring 1989, p. 11. Quoted in Alan Dowty, "Japan and the Middle East: Signs of Change?", *Middle East Review of International Affairs,* Vol. 4, No. 2, December 2000 p. 3. http://www.ciaonet.org/olj/meria/meria00_doa01.html
13. Reinhard Drifte, "Japan's Quest for a Permanent Seat on the Security Council", *Asia Pacific Review*, Vol. 5, No. 2, 1998.
14. *Ibid.*
15. See Sueo Sudo *The International Relations of Japan and South East Asia: Forging a New Regionalism,* (London, Routledge, 2002), p. 63.
16. *Ibid.* pp. 63-64.
17. When China conducted nuclear tests in August 1995, Japan imposed a freeze on all grant aid other than for emergencies of a humanitarian nature or for grassroots assistance. Similar action was taken by Japan when India and Pakistan conducted nuclear tests in May 1998.
18. The prototype for this kind of aid for post-conflict reconstruction and peace-building was the Cambodian reconstruction assistance following the establishment of the United Nations Transnational Authority in Cambodia (UNTAC) in 1993 where Japan's tangible involvement in economic support along with significant diplomatic and political activity was path breaking. In December 1999 Japan hosted the East Timor Donors Meeting in Tokyo and announced US$ 130 million aid, the largest amount among donors.
19. Keizo Obuchi, "*Statement by Foreign Minister Keizo Obuchi on Japan and East Asia: Outlook for the New Millennium,*" http://www.mofa.go.jp/announce/1998/5/980504.html
20. Nobumasa Akiyama, "*Human Security at the Crossroad: Human Security in the Japanese Foreign Policy Context*", http://home.hiroshima-u.ac.jp/heiwa/Pub/E19/Chap12.pdf p. 14.
21. Takehiko Ochiai, "*Beyond TICAD Diplomacy: Japan's African Policy and African Initiatives in Conflict Response*", http://jambo.africa.kyoto-u.ac.jp/kiroku/asm_normal/abstracts/pdf/22-1/37-52.pdf p. 5.
22. Takehiko Ochiai, "*Beyond TICAD Diplomacy: Japan's African Policy and African Initiatives in Conflict Response*", http://jambo.africa.kyoto-u.ac.jp/kiroku/asm_normal/abstracts/pdf/22-1/37-52.pdf p. 5.
23. Ogura Kazuo "A New Look on Africa: Reconsidering Japan's Foreign

Policy" *Gaiku Forum,* Fall 2003, http://www.gaikoforum.com/57-64-OGURA.pdf p. 2.

24. Kenpo Chosakai, 'Kenpo Unyo no Jissai ni Kansuru Hokokusho' *Horitsu Jiho*, Vol. 32, No. 14, p. 78. Cited in Akiko Fukushima *Japanese Foreign Policy: The Emerging Logic of Multilateralism,* New York, Palgrave, 1999, p. 56.
25. UNGA A/2140, June 25, 1952
26. Katsumi Ishizuka, "*The Evolution of Japan's Policy Towards UN Peace Operations*" http://www.nottingham.ac.uk/iaps/katsumi%20paper2.pdf p. 6.
27. Henrich L.W., Shibata A. and Soeya Y., *United Nations Peace-keeping Operations: A Guide to Japanese Politics,* Tokyo: UN University Press, 1999, p. 16.
28. Henrich L.W., Shibata A. and Soeya Y. *United Nations Peace-keeping Operations: A Guide to Japanese Politics,* Tokyo: UN University Press, 1999, p. 18.
29. Defense Agency, *Defense of Japan*, 1991, pp. 138-39.
30. Mizuno H., *Kaigai Hi-hahei no Ronri* (The Theory of No Foreign Dispatch), Tokyo: Shinpyouron, 1997, p. 190. Cited in Katsumi Ishizuka "The Evolution of Japan's Policy Towards UN Peace Operations", http://www.nottingham.ac.uk/iaps/katsumi%20paper2.pdf p. 12.
31. *Mainichi Daily News,* October 20, 1991.
32. *Nihon Keizai Shimbun*, 1993. Cited in Takehiko Ochiai "Beyond TICAD Diplomacy: Japan's African Policy and African Initiatives in Conflict Response", http://jambo.africa.kyoto-u.ac.jp/kiroku/asm_normal/abstracts/pdf/22-1/37-52.pdf p. 5.
33. Glenn D. Hook, *Militarization and Demilitarization in Contemporary Japan*, London and New York, Routledge, 1996. p. 98.
34. Aurelia George Mulgan, "*International Peacekeeping and Japan's Response to the Challenge of Collective Security*", p. 4. http://www.pol.adfa.edu.au/resources/int_peacekeeping.pdf.
35. "Japan's Role in the International Community." A draft report prepared by the Special Study Group on Japan's Role in the International Community, LDP. *Japan Echo*. Summer 1992. Vol. 19, No. 2, p. 56.
36. *Ibid.* p. 5
37. Alan Boyd, "India, Japan Still Shooting for Security Council" *Asia Times,* February 6, 2004.
38. Gerald Curtis, *The United States and Japan: Trade and All That*, East Asian Institute, Columbia University, 1992, p. 8.
39. "New Rules of Defense" *Far Eastern Economic Review*, November 1, 2001, p. 20.
40. Christopher Hughes, "*Japan's Security and the War on Terrorism:*

Incrementalism Confirmed or Radical Leap" http://www.ceri-sciences-po.org

41. Christopher Hughes, "*Japan's Security and the War on Terrorism: Incrementalism Confirmed or Radical Leap*", http://www.ceri-sciences-po.org
42. Glen D. Hook, and Gavan McCormack, ed. *Japan's Contested Constitution: Documents and Analysis,* New York: Routledge, 2001, p. 167.
43. Christopher Hughes, "*Japan's Security and the War on Terrorism: Incrementalism Confirmed or Radical Leap*", http://www.ceri-sciences-po.org
44. Edward C. Luck, "Tokyo's Quixotic Quest for Acceptance", *Far Eastern Economic Review,* May 2005.
45. Ueki Yasuhiro, "Japan's UN Diplomacy: Sources of "Passivism and Activism", in Gerald L. Curtis ed. *Japan's Foreign Policy,* New York and London: M.E. Sharpe, 1993, p. 350.
46. Quoted in Brahma Chellany, "Whose Afraid of Disarmament", *The Japan Times International*, August 16-31, 1999. p. 19.
47. http://www.mofa.go.jp/region/asia-paci/india/partner0504.html#eight
48. "Japan and the Reform of the UN Security Council" Lecture at Indian Council for U.N. Relations, on October 5, 2004, by Ambassador of Japan, Yasukuni Enoki. http://www.in.emb-japan.go.jp/Lectures/Lecture28.htm
49. *Ibid.*
50. http://www.chinadaily.com.cn/english/doc/2004-09/22/content_376639.htm
51. http://washingtontimes.com/upi-brea, 31224-1905r.htm
52. John Cherian, "A Strategic Stopover", *Frontline*, Vol. 22, Issue 10, May 7, 2005. http://www.frontlineonnet.com/fl2210/stories/20050520005412300.htm
53. http://www.hindustantimes.com/news/181_1342875,00050004.htm
54. Siddharth Varadarajan, "Security Council reform: A Bridge Too Far?", *The Hindu,* May 28, 2005 http://www.hindu.com/2005/05/28/stories/2005052801191200.htm

5

Japan's Participation in the Global War Against Terrorism

Like most other countries in the world Japan also reacted with horror and Sympathy to the terrorist attacks of September 11, 2001, in the United States. For many Japanese, the attacks revived memories of Japan's own brush with extremism: the Aum Shinrikyo cult's 1995 sarin gas attack on the Tokyo subway system, which killed 12 people and injured more than 5,000. Prime Minister Junichiro Koizumi quickly set the tone for the parliamentary discussion of anti-terrorist measures stating "the September 11 terrorist attacks were a despicable attack not only on the United States but also on humanity as a whole".[1] But how important is terrorism to Japan and how does it perceive it? In *Terrorism Prevention & Preparedness: New Approaches to US-Japan Security Cooperation* Michael Green writes that according to a Japanese legal definition terrorism is wide spread dissemination of fear through violent destructive activities in order to achieve extreme beliefs, yet the meaning of the word terrorism is still up for debate.[2]

Not that Japan is a stranger to the phenomenon of terrorism. See Table 5.1. In Japan anti-government mass mobilisation in the 1950s and 1960s gave way to smaller terrorist attacks staged by extremist groups on both the left and the right and between 1969 and 1989 Japan recorded more than 200 domestic bombings, between 1978 and 1990 about 700 domestic guerilla attacks, using arson and Molotov cocktails.[3] Before September 11, however, the Japanese

Table 5.1: List of Terrorism Incidents Involving Japan prior to September 11

- **Feb. 22, 2001: Bogota, Colombia:** Colombian Rebels kidnapped Japanese businessman for ransom.
- **Oct. 13, 2000: Lombok, Indonesia:** A powerful bomb exploded in Lombok, damaging the offices of a mining company, jointly owned by the United States, Japan, and Indonesia. No one claimed responsibility.
- **Aug. 22, 1999: Bishkek, Kyrgyzstan:** Uzbek militants kidnapped four Japanese geologists, their interpreter, and eight Kyrgyzstani soldiers. The hostages were released in October.
- **Jan. 25, 1999: Sierra Leone:** RUF rebels robbed and kidnapped a Japanese businessman. On 29 January the RUF released the hostage.
- **Sept. 22, 1998: Bogota, Colombia:** Suspected FARC members kidnapped a Japanese businessman from his farm in Bogota.
- **July 20, 1998: Tavildara, Tajikistan:** Unidentified assailants ambushed and killed four members of the United Nations Mission of Observers in the Tavildara area. The victims included a Japanese Civil Affairs officer.
- **Nov. 17, 1997: Luxor, Egypt:** Al-Gama'at al-Islamiyya (IG) gunmen shot and killed 58 tourists and four Egyptians and wounded 26 others at the Hatshepsut Temple in the Valley of the Kings near Luxor. Eight Japanese, were among the dead. Two Japanese were among the wounded.
- **Oct. 1, 1997: Ghaziabad, India:** Three bombs exploded on a passenger train as it approached Ghaziabad killing two persons and injuring 38 others, including one Japanese.
- **Dec. 17, 1996: Lima, Peru:** Twenty-three members of the Tupac Amaru Revolutionary Movement (MRTA) took several hundred people hostage at a party given at the Japanese Ambassador's residence in Lima, Peru. Among the hostages were several U.S. officials, foreign ambassadors and other diplomats, Peruvian Government officials, and Japanese businessmen. The group demanded the release of all MRTA members in prison and safe passage for them and the hostage takers. The terrorists released most of the hostages in December but held 81 Peruvians and Japanese citizens for several months.
- **Jan. 31, 1996: Colombo, Sri Lanka:** Members of the Liberation Tigers of Tamil Eelam (LTTE) rammed an explosives-laden truck into the Central Bank in the heart of downtown Colombo, Sri Lanka, killing 96 civilians and injuring more than 1,400 others. Among the wounded were six Japanese.
- **Nov. 19, 1995: Islamabad, Pakistan:** A suicide bomber drove a vehicle into the Egyptian Embassy compound in Islamabad, Pakistan, killing at least 16 and injuring 60. The Japanese Embassy was among the damaged buildings. Al-Gama'at al-Islamiyya (Islamic Group or IG), Jihad Group, and the International Justice Group claimed responsibility for the bombing.

(*Contd.*)

- **Nov. 15, 1995: Sagamihara, Kanagawa Prefecture, Japan:** Bomb exploded on US military power line in Japan. No group claimed responsibility, but both the Chukaku-Ha and the Kakurokyo-Ha had announced plans to disrupt the APEC summit in Osaka, held from 13 to 19 November.
- **July 13, 1995: Siirt, Turkey:** Kurdish rebels kidnapped, and then released a Japanese tourist in Turkey.
- **March 20, 1995: Tokyo, Japan:** Aum Shinri Kyo cult deposited two containers containing Sarin poison gas in the Tokyo subway system. The incident resulted in 12 persons killed and up to 5000 hospitalized. In terms of casualties created, this is the most serious terrorist incident of 1995.
- **Dec. 11, 1994: Philippines:** The Abu Sayyaf Group (ASG) claimed responsibility for an explosion aboard a Philippine airliner. One Japanese citizen was killed, and at least 10 others were injured.
- **June 27, 1994: Matsumoto Village, Japan:** A group of Aum Shinri Kyo cult members released sarin gas in the village. Seven people were killed and 500 hospitalized.
- **Jan. 11, 1994: Lima, Peru:** Shining Path rebels bombed the Japanese culture centre in Lima.
- **July 7, 1993: Osaka, Japan:** The Chukaku-Ha terrorist group exploded a home-made bomb at the United Nations Technology Centre in Osaka, causing minor damage but no casualties.
- **July 7, 1993: U.S. Air Force in Japan at Camp Zama:** Terrorists fired four homemade projectiles at the headquarters of the U.S. Air Force in Japan at Camp Zama. None of the projectiles exploded and there was little damage.
- **July 1, 1993: U.S. Air Force Base at Yokota, Japan:** A few days before President Clinton's arrival at the base prior to the Group of Seven summit in Tokyo, terrorists fired two home-made rockets at the U.S. Air Force Base at Yokota, causing minimal damage but no casualties.
- **Dec. 28, 1992: Lima, Peru:** Sendero Luminoso guerrillas detonated car bombs at the Japanese and Chinese Embassies in Lima, causing injuries and damaging more than 60 homes and buildings.
- **May 1986: Amsterdam, The Netherlands:** Japanese Red Army (JRA) member Yu Kikumura, 33, was arrested for having a bomb in his luggage at the Schiphol Airport in Amsterdam. He was later deported to Japan.
- **June, 1986: Jakarta, Indonesia:** Indonesian police released photographs of Tsutomu Shirosaki, a JRA member whose fingerprints were found in a hotel room from which crude mortars were fired at the Japanese and US Embassy buildings in Jakarta.
- **May 4, 1986: Japan:** Chukaku-Ha terrorists fired homemade rockets at heads of state arriving for the Tokyo economic summit. There were no casualties.

(*Contd.*)

- **June 23, 1985: Narita, Japan:** A bomb exploded on an Air India flight over the North Atlantic following its departure from Canada, killing all three hundred twenty-nine passengers on board. A second bomb exploded at Narita Airport in Japan, killing two people. Sikh extremists claimed responsibility for both bombings.
- **Sep. 1977: Bombay, India, and Dhaka, Bangladesh, and Algeria:** JRA hijacked a Japan Airlines plane in Bombay and forced it to land in Dhaka, Bangladesh. The Japanese Government agreed to release 9 imprisoned terrorists and to pay US$ 6 million in exchange for 159 hostages. After payment of the ransom and the release of six JRA prisoners, the hijackers were flown to Algeria.
- **Aug. 1975: Kuala Lumpur, Malaysia, and Tripoli, Libya:** Ten members of the JRA took over the US Consulate in Kuala Lumpur, Malaysia, and seized 52 hostages, including the Consul and the Swedish Charge. The terrorists threatened to blow up the building and kill hostages unless seven JRA prisoners in Japan were released and allowed safe passage to the Middle East. Although the Japanese Government was willing to release the prisoners, only five were willing to go; they were flown to Tripoli, Libya, by way of Kuala Lumpur.
- **Feb. 1974: Singapore:** JRA members seized a ferryboat crew and hostages. All hostages were subsequently released.
- **May 30, 1972: Lod Airport, Lod, Israel:** JRA carried out a machine gun and grenade attack at Lod Airport killing 26 people. The attack was made on behalf of the Popular Front for the Liberation of Palestine.
- **March 1970: Tokyo, Japan and Pyongyang, North Korea:** Nine members of the JRA hijacked a Japanese Air Lines (JAL) aircraft with 130 passengers. Initially plotting to fly to Cuba, the group landed and remained in North Korea.

policy establishment had tended to see terrorism not as a security issue but rather as a crisis management problem and treating terrorism as a subset of consequence management for all natural and manmade disaster. The domestic aspect of the anti-terrorist campaign was geared towards effective community policing that relied primarily on cultivating and maintaining close ties between the police and the public that facilitated continuous surveillance. The Japanese police was so effective in its surveillance of left-wing radicals that the leadership of the predecessors of the JRA decided that relocation abroad was preferable to the low odds of operating successfully within Japan.[4]

Even after the sarin attack in Tokyo in 1995 instead of adopting a strong stance against terrorism, most Japanese saw Aum as a bizarre religious cult without any clear ideological or political objectives and the government gave itself more power to monitor and curtail the activities of groups that have been involved in "indiscriminate mass murder" and whose leaders are "holding strong sway over their members. As Naofumi Miyasaka, professor at the National Defense Academy, pointed out in a paper in 2000 the reasons for this were cultural—"the Manichaean belief of peace and war hinders one from considering an in-between [such as terrorism]." This ethos of peace and human rights gives rise to three national ideas on terrorism. First, terrorism is believed to have root causes such as poverty or prejudice, or to be a response to an oppressive government. Second, Japan's anti-terrorism policy is extremely risk-averse: sparing lives is paramount to the Japanese when dealing with a terrorist situation. Third, terrorism remains a taboo subject that is rarely discussed; incidents such as the hijacking of 1999 ANA flight 61 or the 1994 and 1995 sarin gas attacks are seen as actions taken by marginalised individuals and groups to draw attention to social inequalities and are not widely labeled "terrorist" acts.[5]

The *Hojin tokubetsu taisakushitsu* (translated officially as the Anti-terrorism Bureau but better understood as Office of Special measures for Our Citizens Overseas) represented a "case by case" approach to terrorism that was primarily reactive and risk-averse and less willing to respond to terrorism as a global phenomenon. The belief that the government should do everything possible to ensure the safety of Japanese citizens abroad meant that the Japanese government engage in negotiations or pay ransom in cases of high-profile abductions.[6] In 1975, for example, when ten members of the Japanese Red Army (JRA) took over the US Consulate in Kuala Lumpur, Malaysia, and seized 52 hostages, threatening to blow up the building and kill hostages unless seven JRA prisoners in Japan were released and allowed safe passage to the Middle East, five willing prisoners were flown to Tripoli, Libya, by way of Kuala Lumpur. In 1977 when the Japanese Red Army hijacked a Japan Air Lines plane to Dhaka the Japanese Government released nine imprisoned terrorists who were flown to Algeria and paid US$ 6 million in exchange for the one hundred and fifty nine hostages.

The Japanese government adopted the "no concessions" principle in 1996 but Japanese newspapers reported that, contrary to government denials, Japan paid a ransom of between US$ 2-5 million to the Islamic Movement of Uzbekistan to secure the release of four Japanese geologists taken hostage in Kyrgyzstan in 1999.[7] After the Kyrgyzstan attack, the Japanese government continued its aid programmes to the Ferghana Valley — but hired foreign workers to replace the Japanese on the ground. Also in view of the constitutional constraints on the use of military force Japan was unable to deal with crisis like the 1996-97 hostage standoff at the Japanese ambassador's official residence in Peru in a proactive manner. At the time, police in Japan already had formed a special unit trained to deal with terrorists but there is no indication that the government seriously considered dispatching the unit to Lima. In fact, Peru reportedly did not even notify Japanese authorities prior to the successful raid on the ambassador's residence in April 1997 that freed seventy-one hostages.

A second component was to remain neutral regarding international terrorism. The lack of economic prosperity and social stability, were seen as the root causes motivating conflict wherein the Japanese government in pursuit of "comprehensive security," relied primarily upon economic assistance, quiet diplomacy, and diplomatic moderation in its relations with states throughout Asia and the Middle East. Japan was reluctant to engage in organised sanctions against states perceived to be aiding and abetting terrorists for fear that such sanctions could provoke retaliation against Japanese lives or property and interfere with Japanese commercial transactions. Rather, Official Development Assistance (ODA) was often directed to support authoritarian regimes in the belief that these offered the most viable governing structures to support high speed growth, and that they would then steadily evolve into more democratic forms as economic development produced manageable incremental social and political change.[8] The idea being that economic growth held the key to state-building strategies, internal social and political stabilization, and thus ultimately the prevention of conflict domestically and internationally.

Japan's Participation in the Post-September 11 Global War on Terrorism

Consequently, for Japan, beginning in the hours immediately following the 9/11 attacks, the "war on terrorism" led to important policy innovations.[9] A 'Seven Point Plan' for Japanese cooperation was drawn up in response to the September 11 terrorist attacks in the United States, apparently under close direction of the Prime Minister, and announced by September 19, 2001. Its measures included: the provision of logistical support for the U.S. military in the event of a retaliatory strike; strengthened security around U.S. facilities in Japan; the dispatch of Self-Defense Force ships to gather intelligence; US$ 40 million in emergency humanitarian aid to Pakistan and India; and cooperation with other governments to ensure that there is no confusion in the international economy.

The centrepiece of Japan's response was the "Anti-Terrorism Special Measures Law" passed by the Diet on October 29, which, authorised the Self-Defense Forces to implement "Cooperation and Support Activities" including supply, transportation, repair and maintenance, medical services, communications, airport and seaport services and bases, "Search and Rescue Activities" and "Assistance to Affected People" in support of the activities of foreign countries aiming to achieve the purposes of the UN Charter in response to the terrorist attacks of September 11 in the United States.[10] The legislation was subjected to a debate that was almost perfunctory, amounting in total to 62 hours, as compared to 179 hours for the Peacekeeping Organization Cooperation Law of 1992 and 154 hours for the Guidelines legislation of 1999.[11] Effective for two years, the law mandated the prime minister, with Cabinet approval, to draft a Basic Plan regarding the types, areas, and duration of SDF activities and the scale and composition of the troops and equipment to be deployed.

Since then Japan's Self-Defense Forces (SDF) have provided logistical support for the war in Afghanistan, including intelligence collection, supply shipments, and medical and humanitarian relief—marking the first time Japan has lent military support to an international conflict since World War II. Japan began to provide transportation by the Air Self-Defense Force in late November 2001 and to supply fuel in the Indian Ocean in early December, following consultations with the U.S. government on the basic plan. The MSDF dispatched two Fast Combat Support Ships and three Destroyers, and was engaged in refueling U.S. and U.K. ships at sea without charge, with a total of 65 refuelings of approximately 114,000 kiloliters of fuel as of April 21, 2002.[12] As for support by the ASDF, C-130 transport airplanes and other aircraft transported goods such as spare parts between U.S. bases in Japan and the island of Guam with a total of 33 domestic missions and 14 overseas missions as of April 21, 2002.[13]

The cabinet has twice amended the original Basic Plan. The first amendment extended the SDF deployment by one year, and the second amendment added to the activity list the dispatch of a landing (transportation) ship and an additional escort destroyer to transport heavy construction equipment and staff. On December 11, 2002, Japan's vice foreign minister officially offered to transport heavy construction equipment for a 140-men strong Thai army engineering battalion to a port on the Indian Ocean setting a political precedent in transporting the troops of an Asian country and on December 19, Japan moved its 7,250-ton Kirishima battleship, equipped with the high-tech Aegis missile detection system, from Yokosuka to the Indian Ocean. In 2003, the Diet approved a bill to extend the Special Measures Law by two years. In early March 2003, JMSDF ships began refueling Italian, Spanish, French, German, New Zealand, and Dutch warships participating in Operation Enduring Freedom, in addition to the U.S. and British vessels.

Japan has further indicated military support for the United States by passing on July 26, 2003 a Law Concerning Special Measures on Humanitarian and Reconstruction Assistance. This law is designed to enable the dispatch of the Self-Defense Forces to provide logistical support for US and coalition forces engaged in Operation Iraqi Freedom (OIF). On December 18, 2003, Prime Minister Koizumi gave authorisation to send 1,000 non-combat SDF personnel to Iraq to assist reconstruction efforts, the nation's first troop deployment under its own flag rather than the UN's since World War II. The decision was especially bold since terrorists murdered two Japanese diplomats working in Iraq at the end of November 2003. Despite overwhelming opposition in Japan to the US-led war on Iraq, the Koizumi government was one of the Bush administration's firmest backers from the outset and was listed as part of the so-called "coalition of the willing" that formally supported the invasion. Although ground troops were withdrawn in July 2006 this year Japan's lower house of parliament approved a two-year extension of the country's air force transport mission in Iraq.

In addition to the issue of lifting the arms exports ban, the topic of constitutional revision has come to occupy an important place on the security policy agenda in Japan. A civilian panel, advising Prime Minister Koizumi, called in October 2004 for a general revision of the country's post-war security and defense policy in its report *Vision for Future National Security and Defense Capabilities*. The report recommended modernising Japan's military and strategic initiatives and lifting the ban on exporting arms or arms related technology, and suggested that Japan acquire pre-emptive strike capabilities. The panel also strongly advised strengthening the military alliance with the United States identifying the removal of the arms export ban as an important step for this.

After September 11 Japan accelerated its ratification of pending counter-terrorism conventions. Now, having put its stamp on the International Convention for the Suppression of Terrorist Bombings in November 2001 and the International Convention for the Suppression of the Financing of Terrorism in 2002, Japan is a party to all twelve existing conventions related to counter-terrorism, and it is trying to persuade countries that have not yet ratified all the conventions to follow suit. In August 2004, the Legal Issues Working Group (LIWG) was held in Canberra, Australia, and the Law-Enforcement Working Group was held in Bali, Indonesia, as follow-up of the ministerial commitment. Japan has become the coordinator concerning ratification and implementation of international counter-terrorism Conventions and Protocols in the LIWG, and held the Seminar on the Promotion of Accession to the International Convention for the Suppression of the Financing of Terrorism in December 2004. Japan is also actively participating in the negotiations in the U.N. General Assembly's Sixth (Legal) Committee as it undertakes the drafting of a comprehensive convention on international terrorism and an international convention for the suppression of nuclear terrorism.

Japan along with other G-8 countries announced the "Recommendations on Counter-Terrorism" in 2002 and at the Kananaskis summit in June 2002 formalised two documents—"Cooperative G-8 Action on Transport Security" and "G-8 Global Partnership Against the Spread of Weapons and Materials of Mass Destruction". The G-8 leaders further announced the G-8 Action Plan on Building International Political Will and Capacity to Combat

Terrorism at the Evian summit in June 2003. The main thrust of the new G-8 action plan is the creation by donor countries of the Counter-Terrorism Action Group, whose function is to coordinate assistance given to developing countries for the purpose of improving their various counter-terror capabilities. Japan, together with the United States, was the main proponent of this initiative. At the Sea Island Summit in 2004 the, "Secure and Facilitated International Travel Initiative (SAFTI): G8 Action Plan" was adopted. This Action Plan is comprised of projects in the fields of "Document Interoperability through International Standards", "International Information Exchange", "MANPADS Threat Reduction", and "Capacity Building and Collaboration" including aviation security, port security, and document security.

At the regional level Japan hosted the Japan-ASEAN Commemorative Summit in December 2003, and adopted the Japan-ASEAN Plan of Action, which addresses enhanced counter-terrorism measures of both parties. In November 2004, Japan and ASEAN issued "the ASEAN-Japan Joint Declaration for Cooperation in the Fight against International Terrorism". Within APEC, leaders condemned the terrorist attacks of September 11, and agreed to take possible measures to fight against international terrorism ("Leaders' Statement on Fighting Terrorism and Promoting Growth" in October 2002). As a specific forum dealing with counter-terrorism, the Counter-Terrorism Task Force (CTTF) has been established within APEC. In November 2004, the leaders at the summit in Chile adopted the Santiago Declaration that announced their commitment to enhanced counter-terrorism measures including start of issuance of machine-readable travel documents originally proposed by Japan. With respect to ARF, an inter-sessional meeting on counter-terrorism (ISM on CT) has been established that adopted the "Statement on Cooperative Counter-Terrorism Action on Border Security". Japan co-hosted the counter-terrorism Workshop on CT in Tokyo in October 2002, with South Korea and Singapore, in which lessons of the 2002 Japan-Korea FIFA World Cup were shared. In the ARF ministerial meeting in Jakarta, Indonesia, held in July 2004, "ARF Statement on Strengthening Transport Security against International Terrorism" was adopted. An Ambassador in charge of International Counter-Terrorism was appointed in March 2003 who visited various countries such as

India, Pakistan, Indonesia, Malaysia, Philippines and Thailand and held consultations.

Japan is actively involved in international efforts to cut off terrorist financing. Japan participates in anti-terrorist financial frameworks within the United Nations (CTC: Counter-Terrorism Committee), G8 (CTAG: Counter-Terrorism Action Group) and the OECD (FATF: Financial Action Task Force on Money Laundering), and contributes to international effort to eradicate terrorist finance. It has frozen funds and other financial assets of individuals and entities in accordance with UN Security Council Resolutions 1267, 1333, 1373 and 1390. As of January 2005, Japan had cut off access to assets of a total of 450 individuals and entities. Japan concluded the International Convention for the Suppression of the Financing of Terrorism in June 2002 and at the same time enacted domestic legislation that criminalises the financing of terrorism. Further, Japan amended the Foreign Exchange and Foreign Trade Law in 2002 in order to facilitate information exchange among competent ministries and agencies concerning financing of terrorism.

Japan's contribution to attempts to eliminate international terrorism has also come in the form of economic assistance. The Japanese government provided a total of US$ 300 million of bilateral assistance to Pakistan from September 2001 onwards for education, health and poverty reduction. From October 2001 onwards it also discontinued its limited sanctions on India and Pakistan, imposed since May 1998 in response to the nuclear tests on the subcontinent. Japan further pledged a total of US$ 18 million in immediate assistance to Tajikistan and Uzbekistan. In January 2002, it hosted the International Conference on Reconstruction Assistance to Afghanistan, which raised US$ 4.5 billion, including a US$ 500-million pledge from Japan. And it donated US$ 10 million to World Trade Centre relief funds.

Infact, the September 11 terrorist attacks in the United States took place just as Japan's peace-building aid policy was starting to blossom wherein "the Afghan situation presented a means to further expand its programme of human security"[14]. The Japanese government dispatched a fact-finding mission to Afghanistan in March 2002, which concluded that Japan should concentrate its ODA towards Afghanistan not simply in short term humanitarian assistance but also longer term assistance in areas such as the rebuilding of media infrastructure, capacity building in administration; human resource development in education and health, and training for women for reintegration into public life. In February 2002 the Recovery and Employment Afghanistan Programme of UNDP was launched, funded by Japan, and in April the Urgent Rehabilitation Support Programme was begun in Kabul by the Japan International Cooperation Agency. In July 2002 Japan announced its intention to support UN programmes for the disarmament, demobilisation and reintegration (DDR) of former combatants; the training of Afghan civilian police; drug control; and the resettlement of refugees and instituted the Ogata initiative, a programme aimed at filling the gap between relief and development assistance and achieving comprehensive regional development. Japan also sponsored a further conference in Tokyo in February 2003 on the Consolidation of Peace in Afghanistan.

In May 2002, Japanese Prime Minister Koizumi announced that Japan would strengthen its efforts for the "consolidation of peace" and nation building, making this a pillar of Japan's international cooperation. Minister of Foreign Affairs Kawaguchi also emphasised the importance of the "consolidation of peace" concept before her visit to Afghanistan. Japan's ODA related to the "consolidation of peace" has three components: (1) the promotion of peace processes, (2) securing domestic stability and security, and (3) humanitarian and reconstruction assistance. Using this new diplomatic tool, Japan has tried to play an active role in providing humanitarian and reconstruction assistance to several countries, including Afghanistan, Sri Lanka, Aceh in Indonesia, Mindanao in the Philippines, East Timor, and finally, Iraq.[15]

In keeping with Japan's keen perception of the linkages between economics and security the Japanese policy establishment has argued that the root causes of domestic and transnational terrorist phenomena lie in the economic inequalities, societal alienation, human insecurity, and the failure of state apparatuses to provide for the security of their citizens. Japan has contended that the logical response to terrorism should then be the application of economic power which should address not only the humanitarian fall-out from military action, but also address the very root causes of terrorism by engaging in economic stabilisation and state-building programmes. This approach was emphasised particularly by the Japanese government's Advisory Group on International Cooperation for Peace which was established by Prime Minister Koizumi to investigate ways to increase Japan's role in international efforts for the consolidation of peace and nation-building and led to the revision of the ODA Charter in mid-2003, providing Japan's aid policy with an increasingly heavy stress on conflict prevention via the elimination of economic inequalities.

Japanese ODA efforts also include substantial and growing efforts to fuse law-enforcement components into its heavy Official Development Assistance outlays to enhance the capacity of recipient states to respond to or deal with terrorist threats. The Ministry of Foreign Affairs website points out: "In order to deny terrorists a safe haven anywhere in the world, Japan attaches a great importance to capacity building assistance, especially to the countries in Southeast Asia." Correspondingly, Japan has extended capacity building assistance to combat terrorism, mainly to Asian countries, in the following nine areas:

1. immigration control,
2. aviation security,
3. port and maritime security,
4. customs cooperation,
5. export control,
6. law-enforcement cooperation,
7. anti-terrorist financing,
8. counter-CBRN terrorism, and
9. international counter-terrorism conventions and protocols.

Examples of Japan's capacity building assistance include:

- Technical Assistance to introduce computer system identifying finger print, for the purpose of enhancing criminal investigation and counter-terrorism capacity
- Organisation of seminars on Prevention and Crisis Management of Chemical Terrorism as a part of cooperation for SEARCCT (Southeast Asia Regional Centre for Counter-Terrorism) in July 2004 and the Seminar on the Promotion of Accession to the

International Convention for the Suppression of the Financing of Terrorism in December 2004.

- Grant assistance of equipment to strengthen airport and port security in Indonesia. (Aprox. 747 million yen, decided in 2004).
- Contribution to FRTFSI (Fund for Regional Trade and Financial Security Initiative) of Asia Development Bank, which was agreed to be established in the APEC summit in 2003.

Analysing Japan's Counter-terrorism Measures

Memories of the Gulf War, in which Japan's financial contribution was criticised as "too little, too late," weighed heavily on Japanese policy-makers in formulating a response to the September 11 terrorist attacks. They acted with the knowledge that Japan failed to meet its ally's expectations a decade ago and that a similar failure could provide a body blow to an alliance that only weeks earlier had celebrated its 50th anniversary. As Cikako Sekiba points out "There was almost a kind of trauma among Japanese as a result of the reaction to what we did in the Gulf War. It was a very bitter experience, so since then we have been trying to determine what we should do next time. But next time has come."[16] Japanese opinion was united in a determination to avoid a repetition of the 1990-91 Gulf War fiasco in which Japan's unwillingness to contribute troops brought international derision and sharp American criticism.[17] Japanese policy elites were conscious that the response to 9/11 would form a major test of the political credibility of the US-Japan alliance relationship, and an opportunity for Japan to further expand incrementally the potential range of its support for US global and regional military strategy.[18] In this sense, Tokyo's identification of its international responsibilities dovetailed neatly with its responsibilities as an alliance partner of the United States. In the words of Fujiwara Kiichi "Japanese support of American action was essentially based on realpolitik rather than a quest for global justice."[19]

Japan's counter-terrorism measures are therefore designed primarily to increase Japan's role in its alliance with the United States and represent the country's intensified move towards greater security and defense responsibilities—a process referred to as Japan becoming a "normal state". The depth and breadth of defense cooperation between Washington and Tokyo since September 11, 2001 have been unprecedented eliciting widespread praise among American analysts. "We have gone from Japan bashing and Japan passing to Japan surpassing as Tokyo in recent years has generally not only met but exceeded Washington's expectations."[20] The US Deputy Secretary of State Richard Armitage commented, the enactment of the anti-terrorism law and the dispatch of Japan's Self-Defense Forces under that law took place with "remarkable" speed" and that Japan indeed had "shown the flag."[21]

In this endeavor the Japanese government has been undaunted by the possibility of its own citizens becoming a target.[22] At around the same time that revelations were surfacing about the North Korean kidnapping of Japanese civilians, US counter-terror operations in the Philippines and the Bali discotheque bombing in October of 2002 brought the war geographically closer to Japan. This was highlighted when a Toyota auto showroom was bombed in the city of Makassar on the island of Sulawesi in Indonesia in December 2002. Additionally, Imam Samudra, the alleged mastermind of the Bali bombing, purportedly declared on his website that he would exterminate the citizens of the United States and its allies, including Japan.

In October of 2003 Japan received its first overt threat from Al Qaeda when videotape was released on which Osama Bin Laden purportedly promised suicide attacks against the United States and those countries supporting the American occupation of Iraq. That list included Australia, Great Britain, Italy and Japan. This threat was taken to a whole other level in mid-November when Al Qaeda issued a warning against Japan not to send troops to Iraq or it would face terrorist attacks. During the same week, an Al Qaeda operative identified as Abu Mohamed al-Ablaj sent an e-mail to the Arab language weekly Al-Majallah in which he claimed that Tokyo would be "the easiest place to destroy". The threat became manifest with the taking of three hostages (since released) by insurgents in Iraq and the murder of two Japanese diplomats working in Iraq at the end of November 2003. Also, since dispatching about 550 ground troops to Iraq on a humanitarian mission, Japan has been subject to a barrage of criticism in the Arab media. Despite Japan's small commitment of armed forces, some radical elements in Iraq have attempted to put the country in the same league as the United States and the United Kingdom. This development has alarmed many Japanese, especially after hearing the testimony of released South Korean hostages, who described how their Iraqi captors repeatedly chanted, "Kill the Americans, British and Japanese!"[23] The attack on the trains in Madrid, attributed to Al Qaeda, reinforced the reality of terrorist threats against U.S. allies.

The most dramatic implication of Japan's military support to the US-led war against terrorism is that it has significantly extended the perimeter and scope of SDF activities overseas. Under previous legislation enabling Japan-US defense cooperation, geographic guidelines were a major limiting factor; the SDF were to support the US forces only in "areas surrounding Japan". The new anti-terrorism law effectively lifted that geographic limit enabling SDF units to conduct activities outlined above on Japan's territory, the high seas and airspace above and territory of foreign countries whose consent had been obtained. In addition, the anti-terrorism law expanded the functional scope of SDF dispatch allowing the SDF use of weapons to protect not only the lives of individual SDF personnel and their units, but also those who 'have come under their control', which has been read as meaning wounded personnel from US and other forces, and refugees.[24] Furthermore, Japan's anti-terrorism law shed a previous measure requiring the government to seek approval from the Parliament before dispatching troops. Instead, it must seek post-deployment approval within 20 days after the beginning of the operation. "The net importance of Japan's responses to Operation Enduring Freedom (OEF) and Operation Iraqi Freedom (OIF) is that they reflect incremental progress toward an enhanced Japanese security role and serve as foundation blocks for future legislation for overseas dispatches of the Self-Defense Force... Although legislation on OEF and OIF supports are limited in scope and time span, the precedents of deployment set by the maritime, air, and ground self-defense forces will form a fait accompli leading to the writing of a permanent law that generally governs SDF overseas deployment."[25]

Japan has also transformed its security policy in terms of strengthening Japan-U.S. security cooperation in regional security, and smoothing operations of the SDF. Today, unlike the old concept of the United States and Japanese forces acting separately as sword and shield, the vision emerging in both Washington and Tokyo is a more integrated division of labour between Japanese and US military forces. A set of emergency bills, on Japan's response in the case of an armed attack, approved in the House of Councilors and enacted on June 6, 2003, pressed for readjustments in Japan's military policies. The new legislation was the first since the drafting of the Japanese constitution in 1946 to detail specific measures to respond to actual or imminent attacks on Japan. In addition, Prime Minister Koizumi has linked a comprehensive defense policy review to the progress of the U.S. Department of Defense's Global Posture Review. By simultaneously undertaking a National Defense Programme Outline (NDPO) and a bilateral U.S.-Japanese Defense Policy Review Initiative, Tokyo has shown uncharacteristic initiative in alliance policy planning.[26]

The decision that may have the greatest long-term impact on Japan's security strategy is Tokyo's plan to acquire a missile defense system that is interoperable with Washington's.[27] The plan calls for upper and lower BMD systems—the Navy Theater Wide (NTW) system that employs the AEGIS combat system (Japan already has four AEGIS destroyers and is planning to acquire two more) and an upgraded SM-3 as its interceptor missile. Japan will also acquire PAC 3 anti-ballistic missile system for lower-tier protection. The layered approach mirrors U.S. missile defense plans and policies.[28]

Subsequently the report released by the ruling Liberal Democratic Party's Defense Policy Studies Subcommittee in March 2004 contained the most far-reaching recommendations for transforming Japan's defense policy. In discussing the security environment of Northeast Asia, the report emphasised instability caused by North Korean ballistic missile and nuclear weapons development, the Sino-Taiwan issue, and China's naval advance into the East China Sea. In response, the report advocated amending Article 9 of the Constitution to reflect the legitimacy of the SDF, clear recognition of Japan's right to collective self-defense, consolidation of crisis decision-making in the hands of the prime minister, the enactment of a general law to support international peacekeeping operations, and strengthening US-Japan security arrangements to deal with new security threats such as ballistic missiles, terrorism, and the proliferation of biological, chemical and nuclear weapons. The report proposed changing the Basic Defense Force Concept to a "Flexible and Mobile Force

Concept" that would ground Japan's two-fold strategy of effectively responding to various situations related to Japan's territorial defense and playing an active role in achieving international peace and stability.

Seven months later a report by the Council on Security and Defense Capabilities (a private advisory panel to the prime minister referred to as the Araki Commission) adopted many of the ideas expressed in the LDP Defense Policy Studies Subcommittee recommendations, including the central idea of a two-pronged defense strategy that identifies international peace cooperation activities as essential to the defense of Japan. The Araki report also supported revising the ban on weapons exports to allow for the joint development of a missile defense system with the United States and giving consideration to the development of a capability to strike at enemy missile bases in the event of an attack on Japan. With regard to the issue of collective self-defense "the opinion was expressed at this Council that this issue should be settled quickly". The FY 2005 National Defense Programme Outline, released in December 2004, draws upon the central ideas expressed in the two reports.[29] The February 2005 US-Japan Security Consultative Committee meeting made it plain that the alliance is now global in nature and will be increasingly integrated in the future.

Japan's support for US policy is best seen as the necessary price to pay for US attentiveness to Japanese concerns with regard to North Korea.[30] In the words of Yoichiro Sato: "The process of domestic consensus building toward a permanent dispatch law is not driven by a strong sense of mission and international responsibility, but by threats from North Korea and fear of abandonment by the United States."[31] Similarly Takashi Inoguchi writes, "...after 9/11, Japan had to choose between two opposing options: join the United States-led anti-terrorist front or stick to the less coercive action against terrorism sanctioned by the United Nations. While the majority of the Japanese public remains staunchly anti-militarist, the country cannot help but rely on the United States to coercively negotiate with Pyongyang to stop these uncivilized actions."[32]

Initial apprehensions of entrapment in American military strategy, when in January 2002 President Bush's State of the Union Speech promoted North Korea from a regional security threat to one of the three most-wanted global pariahs that forged an "axis of evil", have given way to an understanding that while North Korea's military behaviour may be driven by economic insecurity ultimately its security behaviour can only be moderated through the deterrence of military power. The North Korean regime's disclosure of its secret uranium enrichment programme in October 2002 initiated a new crisis on the Korean Peninsula in which Japan had much to lose but little independent ability to affect the outcome. When the Six-Party Talks to address Korea's nuclear programme commenced in August 2003, Japan depended upon U.S. support to keep its two main concerns—North Korea's No-dong medium-range ballistic missiles and abduction of thirteen Japanese citizens since the 1970s—on the agenda. Today both Washington and Tokyo appear in lock step, with both insisting on an immediate, verifiable halt to Pyongyang's nuclear weapons programmes and ambitions and an immediate full accounting and satisfactory resolution of the abductee issue.[33]

Specifically, Japan has moved away from its traditional position that sanctions against North Korea would require United Nations Security Council approval and is now taking the position that Japan could impose sanctions in cooperation with the United States. Additionally, in June 2003, Japan ordered its customs, immigration, and coast guard to expand safety inspections and searches for illicit contraband on North Korean cargo and passenger ships. According to the Japanese government, more than 70 per cent of the 120 North Korean ships inspected in Japan from January to August 2003 were ordered to halt operations or received safety warnings, compared with a general average of 10 per cent for all countries shipping. The Japanese coast guard's sinking of an alleged North Korean spy ship in December 2001 and Japan's recent pronouncements about its right, under the principle of self-defense, to take preemptive action in the event of an imminent North Korean missile launch provides political support to the U.S. doctrine of preemption while Tokyo's unqualified support in Iraq is sending North Korea a clear message that Tokyo would willingly support Washington in dealing with threats closer to home.

The war on terrorism is also having a significant impact on the primary component of Japan's foreign policy tools—economic aid, in terms prioritizing, i.e., how much aid goes where and to what purpose. In the current climate of economic recession and shrinking aid budgets in response to across the board reductions in government spending and a degree of "aid fatigue" among the public wherein "cumulatively Japan's ODA has fallen by a total of 27 per cent in 1997-2003"[34] it is clear that security interests linked to the 'war on terror' now have a greater priority in Japan. The Japanese policy establishment uses the term "consolidation of peace" rather than "opposition to terrorism" but the goals and priorities are no different and in line with the US-led approach to global security. Kiyokazu Koshida terms these recent changes in Japanese ODA as "militarization of aid". It is a global shift with several significant points: (1) the adoption of a broader definition of terrorism and the introduction of major anti-terrorism legislation; (2) the redefinition of aid and ODA within the framework of geopolitical interests; and (3) the allocation of ODA more on the basis of a selectivity and conditionality that reflects the interests of the donor, particularly under the rhetoric of "opposing terrorism."[35]

Accordingly the new ODA Charter has several significant points from the viewpoint of security: (1) the most significant change is in the objective of aid. Whereas the original Charter sought to help realise sound economic development in developing countries, the new one aims to "contribute to the peace and development of the international community, and thereby to help ensure Japan's own security and prosperity". (2) the four principles of the original Charter remain unchanged but the principle that cautions against military spending by recipient countries is now qualified by the proviso "so as to maintain and strengthen international peace and stability, including the prevention of terrorism". (3) poverty reduction tops the four priority issues but the reason given is that poverty reduction is "essential for eliminating terrorism" and (4) priority issues have a new entrant: peace-building that includes conflict prevention and post-conflict peace restoration.

The impact of these changes is illustrated by the fact that within the official ODA budget funds allocated for peace building and conflict prevention have risen dramatically from 12 billion yen in 2003 to 16.5 billion yen in 2004. The budget for emergency grant aid also jumped from 22 billion yen to 31.6 billion yen in the same period. Meanwhile, Japan cut its total ODA budget from 857.8 billion yen in

2003 to 816.9 billion yen in 2004, with grant aid being most affected.[36] Unlike the past when Japan's ODA policy tacitly supported US interests Japan today is contributing huge amounts of aid for 'peace building' operations. In a sense ODA and Self-Defense Forces operations have become integrated and are, in Prime Minister Koizumi's words, "two wheels of the same cart". Exemplifying this shift is the identification of Afghanistan, Aceh in Indonesia, Mindanao in the Philippines, Sri Lanka and Iraq as priorities for Japanese ODA.[37]

In December 2002, after the launch of US operations in Mindanno Japan announced a support package for peace and security for three programmes: a governance-improvement programme in the autonomous region of Muslim Mindanao received 2.47 billion yen; a human needs programme was given 1.5 billion yen and, most significantly, projects including a peace-building and counter-terrorism programme received 40 billion yen. In addition, in June 2003, Japan and the Philippines agreed to set up an automated fingerprint-identification system under the Mindanao project to fight terrorism, which cost 975 million yen. Japan also attempted to broker in 2002 a cease-fire agreement in Aceh as a means to preserve Indonesia as one unit and its support for the territorial integrity of Indonesia has involved the continued disbursement of large sums of bilateral and multilateral ODA. In December 2002, "the Preparatory Conference on Peace and Reconstruction in Aceh" was held in Tokyo. In this conference Japan provided indirect support for promoting political dialogues between the Government of Indonesia and the Free Aceh Movement (GAM). In May 2003, through the intermediation of the Henry Dunant Centre for Humanitarian Dialogue, the Government of Indonesia and GAM held a meeting in Tokyo for peacefully resolving the conflict. Japan sees the key to tackling terrorism in Indonesia as the strengthening of state capacities, the improvement of economic conditions, and dealing with economic inequalities, poverty and injustice, factors that there were termed in the 2003 Japan-Indonesia Joint Announcement on Fighting International Terrorism as the root causes of terrorism.

The emergence of Japan as a leading player in the negotiations to end nearly 20 years of civil war in Sri Lanka and in the post-war reconstruction plans is underscored by a decision by Tokyo to provide an aid package worth US$ 270 million in February 2003.

"The Tokyo Conference on Reconstruction and Development of Sri Lanka "was held in June 2003. In 2004, the Japanese government committed itself to giving 164 billion yen (US$ 1.5 billion) in grant aid towards the reconstruction of Iraq. This constitutes 70 per cent of total Japanese bilateral grant ODA for 2004 and 40 per cent of its total multilateral grant aid. Japan has absorbed the new security priorities in the context of a shrinking aid budget, cut by 10 per cent in 2002 and 6 per cent in 2003. In late August 2004, Japan's Foreign Minister Yoriko Kawaguchi visited four Central Asian states to build a new framework of regional dialogue christened the "Central Asia Plus Japan" forum.

Notwithstanding constitutional barriers, public acceptance and regional perceptions Japanese policymakers are incrementally promoting a new national security image—that of a proactive Japan that is 'armed, but responsible'. More importantly however it appears Japan is no longer a "reluctant ally" but tightly "locked in" with American global strategy.

Implications for India

No doubt the U.S. led global war on terrorism has facilitated the emergence of a new environment of regular meetings and consultations between India and Japan along with a desire to upgrade relations to a higher multifaceted level. Cooperation against international terrorism is pronounced to be a crucial component of the strategic focus of the 'Global Partnership' that aims at expanding and enriching cooperation between the two countries. On Japan's part however the impulse to be proactive is firmly linked to the United States and arises from the criticism of Japan's tardiness in the Gulf War and from an eagerness of Japanese policy establishment to demonstrate visibly the nation's support for its alliance partner. For India the implications are two-fold. First, Japan like the United States considers Pakistan as a key frontline state whose support is crucial in the war on terror. Secondly, Japan views the security situation in South Asia through the lens of the India-Pakistan dispute over Kashmir and its own role as an 'impartial facilitator' in the normalisation process.

Soon after the September 11 terrorist attacks in the United States, during the Indian Prime Minister's visit to Japan in December 2001 the India-Japan Joint Declaration stated,

> "The two leaders (Indian Prime Minister Vajpayee and Japanese Prime Minister Koizumi) firmly maintained their position that terrorism cannot be justified wherever, whenever and for whatever reason. They also resolutely condemned terrorism in any form. They believed that the fight against global terrorism has to be comprehensive and sustained, with the objective of total elimination of terrorism in all regions. They shared the view that the fight is not only against the perpetrators of terrorist acts, but should encompass those who provide support, sustenance and safe haven."[38]

Addressing an Asian Security conference at New Delhi, in January 2005, the Indian Defense Minister, Pranab Mukherjee identified "shared concerns over maritime and weapons of mass destruction (WMD) terrorism and WMD proliferation" among five areas of strategic convergence between India and Japan.[39] The "Joint Statement on India-Japan Partnership in a New Asian Era" issued during the Japanese Prime Minister Koizumi's visit to India in April 2005 stated,

> "Recognizing the threat posed by terrorism and the importance of the international community working unitedly to counter this menace, the Governments of India and Japan will further consolidate their existing cooperation, both bilaterally and in various international fora. The India-Japan Joint Working Group on Counter-Terrorism will hold its first meeting soon to identify possible future areas of cooperation."[40]

Similarly, the "Joint Statement Towards Japan-India Strategic and Global Partnership" issued during Prime Minister Manmohan Singh's visit to Japan in December 2006 stated,

> The two leaders unequivocally condemn terrorism in all its forms and manifestations and stress that there can be no justification whatsoever for any act of terrorism. They share the view that international community must further intensify efforts and cooperation to fight this scourge. In this context, they confirm that

> the two countries will continue to work together through the Japan-India Joint Working Group on Counter Terrorism. They also call upon all Member States of the UN to work towards the expeditious adoption of a Comprehensive Convention on International Terrorism.

At the same time the events of 11 September 2001 have changed the tone of Japan's relationship with Pakistan. From a real low after the May 1998 nuclear tests on the subcontinent, Pakistan has emerged as an important partner in the international coalition's fight against terrorism in Japanese perceptions. In the words of the Japanese Foreign Minister Kawaguchi "Pakistan's role cannot be replaced by any other country as far as peace and stability in its region and the whole world is concerned. Japan is grateful for this and the great role that Pakistan is playing in fighting nuclear proliferation and terrorism."[41]

Direct ODA from Japan had been a substantial proportion of total development assistance to Pakistan. By 1998, Japanese ODA was nearly one-half of all assistance, and dwarfed all other country donors.[42] Even compared to the international organisations, Japan's assistance (US$ 490m) exceeded the combined aid from the Asian Development Bank (US$ 235m) and World Bank (US$ 170m) in 1998. Empathising with a frontline state[43] soon after the September 11 attack Japan extended approx. 40 million US dollars in the form of refugee assistance and emergency budgetary assistance. In November 2001 Japan decided to discontinue measures (read sanctions) in response to Pakistan's nuclear testing and in April 2005 Japanese Prime Minister Koizumi utilised the occasion of his state visit to Pakistan to announce the resumption of yen loans. The extent of the impact of the Japanese assistance is evident from the fact that in appreciation special postage stamps were issued in Pakistan in 2004.

In September 2006 news reports quoted the newly designated Japanese Ambassador to Pakistan, Seiji Kojima saying "The international community should whole heartedly back President General Pervez Musharraf in his fight against terrorism," and that Japan lauds and supports Pakistan's determination to establish peace in the world.[44] In October 2006 Ambassador Kojima offered to assist

Pakistan in exploring for oil and gas resources, and rapidly thereafter a small delegation from the Japanese trading house Itochu arrived in Islamabad for discussions on energy cooperation. In December, it was announced that the Karachi Circular Railway project would be revived with technical assistance from the Japan External Trade Organization and an US$ 872 million loan from Japanese financial institutions. The same month saw the provision of additional Japanese aid for the Indus Highway Construction Project. In 2007 the momentum in Japan-Pakistan relations has further increased. The "Pakistan-Japan Joint Public and Private Dialogues" were held in Karachi in January, in which a whole host of items were discussed, including issues related to export insurance for Japanese companies, measures against fraud and smuggling, human resources development, and quality control.[45]

The rationale provided by the Japanese government is summarised as "To contribute to consolidating peace and stability in Asia as well as the region by assisting steady development of Pakistan, which is in the process towards moderate and modern Islam and playing a crucial role as a front-line state in fight against terrorism".[46] It is argued that "In broad terms, Pakistan, being the second largest country in South Asia and in the entire Muslim world with a population of 148 million people, requires international cooperation for the following two main reasons. First, Pakistan has been adversely affected by the emerging geopolitical instability in the region since the September 11, 2001 terrorist attacks in the United States. Second, socio-economic structural problems in Pakistan and the region remain at the root of this instability and, therefore, must be addressed."[47] As the Task Force on Foreign Relations for the Prime Minister concluded in its November 2002 report "If Pakistan collapses, it could lead to proliferation of nuclear and missile technologies, and also increased terrorism."[48]

Indeed, in sharp contrast to its own increasingly bellicose attitude towards North Korea Japan has repeatedly urged India to exercise restraint. For example, former Prime Minister Mori's comment "that India should focus on what to do rather than from where it comes from" or Foreign Minister Kawaguchi's statement in 2002 that "While sharing renewed indignation at terrorism, Japan sincerely hopes that India, in light of its responsible position as the major player in the region, and responding to the appeal of the entire international community, will exhaust diplomatic efforts, and work towards de-escalation as well as resumption of dialogue."[49] The threat, in May 2002, that Japan would find it difficult to continue the promised economic aid unless Pakistan puts an end to cross-border terrorism and closes down the terrorist base camps has remained what it was—a threat. Despite Indian defense experts' assertions that the Pakistani nuclear and missile programme was based on technological help from China and North Korea, a link that has now been confirmed by the US Intelligence, Japan has opted to raise its personal concerns quietly in bilateral meetings with Pakistan. Such a view easily finds resonance in society. As Mohammed Badrul Alam in his study of the perceptions of Japanese students on terrorism points out "the perception, possibly, is that the terrorism witnessed in Jammu and Kashmir is domestic in nature. This may imply that India's projections of cross border terrorism have not touched the minds of students in Japan."[50]

Rather, the Japanese policy establishment feels that "Kashmir is a core issue between India and Pakistan which needs immediate resolution" and that "peace could return to the region only by the resolution of the long standing Kashmir conflict."[51] Correspondingly, Japanese commentators feel that the most important task for Japan in the Kashmir dispute is to help create an international framework to ease tensions.[52] In the context of the widely held view that the conflict over Kashmir has global repercussions because India and Pakistan are both nuclear powers they insist that "Japan should make an effective contribution to the resolution of this conflict"[53] and "become a Diplomat for Peace in the region"[54]

NOTES

1. "The Extent of Cooperation", *The Japan Times*, October 2, 2001.
2. http://www.japansociety.org/shop/terrorism_book.pdf
3. Peter J. Katzenstein "*September 11th in Comparative Perspective: The Anti-terrorism Campaigns of Germany and Japan*", http://www.einaudi.cornell.edu/9-11/content/pdf/pkatzenstein.pdf
4. *Ibid.*
5. Naofumi Miyasaka, "Terrorism and Antiterrorism in Japan: Aum Shinrikyo and after" prepared for the Japan Society Roundtable on

Terrorism: Prevention and Preparedness, October 2000. Cited in Robyn Pangi "Consequence Management in the 1995 Sarin Attacks on the Japanese Subway System", http://bcsia.ksg.harvard.edu/BCSIA_content/documents/Consequence_Management_in_the_1995_Sarin_Attacks_on_the_Japanese_Subway_System.pdf
6. David Leheny, "Tokyo Confronts Terror", *Policy Review*, No. 110, December 2001 & January 2002. Available at http://www.hoover.org/publications/policyreview/3462446.html
7. *Ibid.*
8. Akio Watanabe, "Japan's Position on Human Rights in Asia", in Javed S. Maswood, (ed) *Japan and East Asian Regionalism*, London: Routledge, 2001, pp. 68-89.
9. See Paul Midford, "*Japanese Public Opinion and the War on Terrorism: Implications for Japan's Security Strategy*" http://www.eastwestcentrewashington.org/publications/midford.pdf
10. http://www.kantei.go.jp/foreign/policy/2001/anti-terrorism/1116keikaku_e.html
11. Gavan McCormack "Japan's Afghan Expedition", http://www.iwanami.co.jp/jpworld/text/Afghanexpedition01.html
12. Fukushiro Nukaga, "Japan's Emergency Legislation and the War on Terrorism", Heritage Lecture #749, June 10, 2002, http://www.heritage.org/Research/AsiaandthePacific/HL749.cfm
13. *Ibid.*
14. See Emily Perkin "*Japan's Emerging Foreign Aid Activism and the Reconstruction of Afghanistan*".
15. Kiyokazu Koshida, "*Militarization of Japan's ODA*", http://wwwsoc.nii.ac.jp/psaj/05Print/e_newsletter/2005/koshida.pdf
16. Quoted in Doug Struck, "*As Alliances Shift, Japan's Military Role is Widening*", http://www.taiwansecurity.org/WP/2001/WP-092801.html
17. John Miller, "Japan Crosses the Rubicon", *Asia Pacific Security Studies*, Vol. 1, No. 1, January 2002. p. 2.
18. Christopher Hughes, "*Japan, the post-9/11 Security Agenda: Globalization and the Political Economy of Inequality and Insecurity*", CSGR Working Paper No. 127/04, January 2004, http://www2.warwick.ac.uk/fac/soc/csgr/research/workingpapers/2004/wp12704.pdf
19. Fujiwara Kiichi, "*Between Terror and Empire: Japan and the Post-9/11 Empire*", http://www.jfindia.org.in/bulletin/January-March%202005/Jan-March%202005.pdf
20. Ralph A. Cossa and Brad Glosserman, "U.S.-Japan Defense Cooperation: Has Japan Become the Great Britain of Asia, *Issues & Insights,* Vol. 5, No. 3, March 2005. http://www.csis.org/pacfor/issues/v05n03_pdf.pdf

21. Quoted in Kazufumi Hamai and Peter Mauch, "*Defining Japan's Role in the Post-Taliban World Order: Tokyo's Path to Great Power Status*", http://www.japanesestudies.org.uk/discussionpapersHamaiandMauch.html
22. The following details are provide in Joseph Ferguson "Al Qaeda's Threat to Japan: Tokyo's Wake Up Call to the War on Terrorism", *Terrorism Monitor* Vol. 2, Issue 2, January 30, 2004.
23. J. Sean Curtin, "Japan to Polish its Tarnished Middle East Image", *Commentary*, May 6, 2004, http://www.glocom.org/debates/20040506_curtin_japan/
24. Christopher Hughes, "Japan's Security and the War on Terrorism: Incrementalism Confirmed or Radical Leap", http://www.ceri-sciences-po.org
25. Yoichiro Sato, "Japan's Security Policies During OEF and OIF: Incremental Reactions Meet Great Expectations", http://www.apcss.org/Publications/APSSS/Japans%20Security%20Policies%20During%20OEF%20and%20OIF%20Slim%20.pdf
26. Dan Blumenthal "The Revival of the US-Japan Alliance", http://www.fas.org/sgp/crs/row/RL33821.pdf
27. *Ibid.*
28. Foreign Press Centre of Japan, "*Cabinet Approves New National Defense Programme Outline and Midterm Defense Programme*," press release (available at www.fpcj.jp/e/shiryo/jb/0458.html
29. David Fouse, "*Japan's FY 2005 National Defense Programme Outline: New Concepts Old Compromises*", http://www.apcss.org/Publications/APSSS/Japans%20FY2005%20National%20Defense%20Program%20Outline.pdf
30. Gerald L. Curtis, "*For the United States and Japan Multilateralism is the Key*", http://www2.gsb.columbia.edu/japan/pdf/gerald.curtis_mar-apr_2004.pdf
31. Yoichiro Sato, "*Japan's Security Policies During OEF and OIF: Incremental Reactions Meet Great Expectations*", http://www.apcss.org/Publications/APSSS Japans%20Security%20Policies%20During%20OEF%20and%20OIF%20Slim%20.pdf
32. Takashi Inoguchi "The Japanese Decision", *Open Democracy*, August 7, 2003, http://opendemocracy.net/content/articles/PDF/1416.pdf
33. Ralph A. Cossa and Brad Glosserman, "U.S.-Japan Defense Cooperation: Has Japan Become the Great Britain of Asia?, *Issues & Insights,* Vol. 5, No. 3, March 2005., http://www.csis.org/pacfor/issues/v05n03_pdf.pdf
34. Figures from the Ministry of Finance www.mof.go.jp/english cited in Ngaire Woods "*The Shifting Politics of Foreign Aid*", http://

users.ox.ac.uk/~ntwoods/Shifting%20Politics%20of%20Aid%20by%20Woods.pdf

35. Kiyokazu Koshida, "*Militarization of Japan's ODA*", http://wwwsoc.nii.ac.jp/psaj/05Print/e_newsletter/2005/koshida.pdf
36. *Ibid.*
37. American analysts have determined that especially the southern Philippines and Indonesia would be likely arenas for the planning and organisation of further anti-American attacks.
38. http://www.mofa.go.jp/region/asia-paci/india/joint0112.html
39. Cited in B. Raman, "*Indo-Japanese Relations: Hype and Reality*", http://www.observerindia.com/analysis/A448.htm
40. http://meaindia.nic.in/speech/2005/04/29js01.htm
41. http://www.jang.com.pk/thenews/aug2004-daily/12-08-2004/main/main2.htm
42. "*Aid from Tokyo to Islamabad via Washington and Manila*", http://www.parc-jp.org/parc_e/PARCactivities/2004/Pakistan.pdf
43. See Numata Sadaaki "Pakistan: The Challenges of a Frontline State", *Gaiku Forum*, Spring 2003, http://www.gaikoforum.com/P37-47_numata.pdf.
44. See Sarah Kamal "*Japan to Continue Support Pakistan in Its Journey to Progress*", http://pakistantimes.net/2006/07/05/top7.htm
45. See Michael Penn "Japan and Pakistan Move Closer", *Asia Times Online*, February 17, 2007, http://www.atimes.com/atimes/Japan/IB17Dh01.html
46. "*Japan's County Assistance Programme for Pakistan 2005*", available at http://www.pk.emb-japan.go.jp/ECONOMICS/Country%20Assistance%20Programme.htm
47. *Ibid.*
48. "*Basic Strategies for Japan's Foreign Policy in the 21st Century New Era, New Vision, New Diplomacy*", http://www.kantei.go.jp/foreign/policy/2002/1128tf_e.html
49. Statement by Ms. Yoriko Kawaguchi, Minister for Foreign Affairs, on the Tension between India and Pakistan, May 24, 2002, http://www.mofa.go.jp/announce/announce/2002/5/0524.html
50. Mohammed Badrul Alam, "Perceptions of Japanese Students on Terrorism and other Security Problems: Initial Results From a Pilot Study", *Strategic Analysis*, April-June 2003.
51. Remarks made by the Japanese Ambassador in Pakistan, http://www.infopak.gov.pk/news/pidnews/pidnews2004/pid_mar16_2004.htm
52. Purnendra Jain "Japan and South Asia: Between Cooperation and

Confrontation" in Inoguchi Takashi and Purnendra Jain (ed.) *Japanese Foreign Policy Today,* New York: Palgrave, 2000, p. 269.

53. "*Basic Strategies for Japan's Foreign Policy in the 21st Century New Era, New Vision, New Diplomacy*", http://www.kantei.go.jp/foreign/policy/2002/1128tf_e.html
54. South Asian Youth Invitation Programme 2002 "What Japan and South Asia can do Aiming at Peace and SStability in the World", http://www.mofa.go.jp/region/asia-paci/south_asia0210.html

6

Japan's Nuclear Policy

Japan's first major statement to the international community articulating its opposition to nuclear weapons was in 1956, when during a speech at the United Nations, the Japanese Foreign Minister Shigemitsu Mamoru stressed that:

> Whatever may be the nature of the uncertainties and the tensions in which the world is placed today and whatever may be their causes, there should be no problem that cannot be resolved peacefully with the united strength of eighty nations which now constitute our Organization. It would be utter folly for mankind, which today has entered upon the Atomic Age, to pursue a path that leads to its own annihilation.[1]

Since then Japan's non-nuclear policy has come to rest on three institutional pillars.[2] The first is the 1955 Atomic Energy Basic Law that clearly states that "the research, development and utilization of atomic energy shall be limited to peaceful purposes, aimed at ensuring safety and performed independently under democratic management, the results there from shall be made public to contribute to international cooperation."[3] The second pillar consists of the so-called "three no's" that provide that Japan will neither possess, nor manufacture, nor permit entry of nuclear weapons in its territory. These principles were first enunciated by Prime Minister Sato Eisaku in 1968 and subsequently formalized in 1971 through a Diet resolution. The third pillar is the nuclear Non-Proliferation Treaty (NPT) which was signed by Japan in 1970 and which it agreed to extend indefinitely in 1995. Under this treaty Japan is obligated as a non-nuclear weapon state not to produce or acquire nuclear weapons.

In reality, however, the nuclear issue in Japan revolves around three interrelated themes of energy, security and a strong pacifist national sentiment. The result is a "delicate balance between Japan's idealism, as reflected by its pursuit of global disarmament and realism, as reflected by it's dealing with regional security and pursuit of energy security"[4] that plays out in the following way – as the only country to have been attacked with nuclear weapons Japan is a strong advocate of global nuclear disarmament, at the same time Japanese policy makers place great premium on the bilateral security alliance with the United States particularly the extended deterrence provided by the nuclear umbrella, and Japan is a leading proponent of nuclear energy despite repeated accidents in its nuclear plants.

The Nuclear Taboo

No doubt the experiences of Hiroshima and Nagasaki were instrumental in creating the anti-nuclear sentiment among the Japanese people. The two bombs dropped on Japan in August 1945 killed about 140,000 people in Hiroshima and about 70,000 lives were lost in Nagasaki. Many more died in the following years from various illnesses caused by exposure to radiation. The contamination of the Japanese fishing boat *Fukuryu Maru* following the U.S. nuclear test (BRAVO) at the Bikini Atoll in March 1954 and the subsequent concern over radioactive contamination of fish further consolidated public anti-nuclear views in Japan.

The first organized expression of this sentiment was the Suginami Appeal, which fundamentally was a signature campaign in support of elimination of nuclear weapons. Starting in May 1954 in Tokyo's Suginami district it rapidly evolved into a national initiative and in less than two months the appeal had gathered nearly 300,000 signatures.[5] By the time the first World Conference against Atomic and Hydrogen Bombs was held on August 6, 1955, the campaign had obtained 32,000,000 signatures, a number exceeding half of all registered Japanese voters.[6] Subsequently, on the basis of this nationwide petition campaign, a wide range of individuals and groups including political parties, labor unions, religious groups, women's groups, student groups, local governments and so on gathered spontaneously in the cause of banning nuclear bombs and came to be organized under *Gensuikyo* (the Japanese Council Against A & H Bombs) in September 1955.[7] Though *Gensuikyo,* disintegrated into three national centers by the early 1960s the anti-nuclear feelings among the Japanese public have remained. Anti-nuclear sentiments are reinforced and reproduced through educational programs, popular culture and public ceremonies that insure that the experiences of Hiroshima and Nagasaki are not forgotten.[8]

In fact, public anti-nuclear sentiments have remained significant even after the October 2006 North Korean nuclear test. For example, according to a national survey conducted by the Yomiuri Shimbun on November 11, 2006, 80 percent of the respondents favored maintaining the three non-nuclear principles, while only 18 percent supported revising these principles.[9] The survey yielded this result despite the fact that 74 percent of the respondents were not optimistic that the North Korean nuclear problem would be resolved through the six-party talks.[10] Demonstrating the continuing popular opposition in Japan to nuclear weapons is the *Appeal from Hiroshima and Nagasaki for a Total Ban and Elimination of Nuclear Weapons* that began in February 1985 that has succeeded in getting more than 61 million signatures in Japan.[11] Indeed Hiroshima and Nagasaki are the symbolic hubs of Japan's anti-nuclear movement. Thousands of people attend the annual peace ceremonies held in these two cities to commemorate those who died due to the atomic bombings.

There has also been an initiative to persuade local municipalities to sign nuclear-free declarations in line with the Nuclear-Free Kobe Formula, which was established in 1975 in Kobe. With this formula, incoming foreign military ships are mandated to submit a certificate of non-presence of nuclear weapons on board. After World War II, Kobe Port of Hyogo Prefecture was placed under full occupation of U.S. military until 1951 and from 1952 it was used as a base for the U.S. 7th Fleet. The people of Kobe started a movement to oppose the military use of the port and demanded the return of Kobe Port to the citizens and the Kobe City Assembly in 1975 unanimously adopted the "Resolution Concerning the Refusal to Entry of Warships Carrying Nuclear Weapons."

This anti-nuclear sentiment has formed the core of the peace movement in Japan and is central to the public's empathy with the notion of the country as a "peace state". However "unarmed neutrality without nuclear weapons" has never been considered a viable security policy for the country given the security situation in Northeast Asia. Rather Japan's non-nuclear stance is conditional and is primarily premised on the American guarantee of protection. As Yuri Kase points out the importance of the U.S.-Japanese security relationship with regard to Japan's non-nuclear policy cannot be overemphasized.[12] Constraints on Japan's nuclear option derive not only from various legal and policy instruments but also from a more fundamental constraint, and that is the fact that the United States extends its own nuclear deterrent to Japan …it is ultimately the alliance with the United States that makes nuclear weapons unnecessary and means that these ideational and institutional constraints do not have to be tested.[13]

Security Imperatives

Prime Minister Sato who put forward the three non-nuclear principles that led him to win the Nobel Peace Prize himself made it clear that the three principles alone would not be a viable national security policy. Rather he attempted to make them contingent on the continued reliability of the U.S. deterrent, moves towards global disarmament, and the promotion of the peaceful use of nuclear energy. Addressing the Diet in 1968 he declared the "Four Nuclear Policies" which included (1) the Three Non-Nuclear Principles; (2) reliance upon U.S. extended deterrence based upon the U.S.-Japanese Security Treaty of 1960; (3) efforts towards global nuclear disarmament; and (4) promotion of the peaceful use of nuclear energy.[14] This position was reaffirmed in a March 1968 Liberal Democratic Party (LDP) report, which stated "…the LDP supports the three Non-Nuclear Principles under the circumstances where Japan's national security is guaranteed by the other three policies."[15]

The utility of an indigenous nuclear option has been discussed periodically within the Japanese policy establishment. However, it has been consistently acknowledged that the costs far outweigh the benefits – economically, militarily and above all politically.

Particularly the *1968/70 Report* (the first part examined technical and economic issues while the second part reviewed strategic and political issues) has received widespread attention. It was commissioned by Prime Minister Sato and was the first comprehensive analysis of the costs and benefits of Japanese nuclearization.[16] The Japan Defense Agency (JDA) conducted a similar internal review of Japan's nuclear options in 1995 entitled "A Report Considering the Problems of the Proliferation of Weapons of Mass Destruction" that was set against the background of the first North Korean nuclear crisis.[17]

The 1968/70 Report discussed the Chinese nuclear threat, the strategic problems associated with nuclearlization, and the diplomatic and political problems associated with nuclearization. In addressing the Chinese threat the *1968/70 Report* felt that U.S. extended deterrence over Japan and South Korea would constrain China from militarily intervening in East Asia. It further argued that even if Japan developed a small nuclear arsenal, it would remain vulnerable if attached by nuclear weapons. Rather than enhancing Japanese security, nuclearization could alarm even the United States and lead to Japan's diplomatic isolation. The report finally concluded that Japan's status as a non-nuclear weapon state was actually a positive factor for its national security and recommended that Japan promote its security through a multidimensional approach including political and economic efforts, and not through a traditional militaristic, power-based approach.[18]

The 1995 JDA report sought to accomplish three tasks: (1) analyze the impact of the end of the Cold War on the U.S. and Russian nuclear weapons doctrine, (2) examine the threat posed by nuclear proliferation, (3) consider the robustness of the U.S. nuclear umbrella following the end of the Cold War and examine the costs and benefits to Japan developing an independent nuclear deterrent under a range of scenarios. The report also emphasized the continued lack of strategic logic supporting Japanese nuclearization. It noted the costs as including accelerating the disintegration of the NPT, damaging the U.S.-Japan alliance, causing a probable domestic furor, undermining Japanese prosperity that is dependent on trade and incurring huge economic costs related to the infrastructure needed to develop and maintain a nuclear capability. The overall recommendation was, therefore, to develop ways to make sure that the American commitment to Japan remained solid.

Indeed, Japan's policy of strategic dependence on U.S. nuclear deterrence continues to emerge among Japan's senior decision makers as the best option for insuring against nuclear threats.[19] Some key points in this calculation are as follows:[20]

- Japan's possession of nuclear weapons would undermine Japan's national security by triggering an arms in race in Northeast Asia.
- Japan's nuclear option could motivate a number of other countries to pursue nuclear proliferation while only bringing minimal military benefit to Japan.
- Nuclear armament would not be appropriate for Japan as it is inherently vulnerable to a nuclear attack, considering the fact that it is an island country where a large part of its population lives in a limited number of densely populated areas and thus lacks strategic depth.
- Japan is surrounded by seas and does not have sufficient ground for the use of tactical weapons.
- The decision to go nuclear would only weaken Japan's political power internationally and undermine the reputation it has built over past decades.

But most importantly there has been a continuity of shared conclusions that choosing the indigenous nuclear option would not only exacerbate the security dilemma with North Korea or China it would also alienate the United States. As Isiba Shigeru, the former Director General of the JDA stated in 2006, "If we develop nuclear weapons, that would be tentamount to saying we don't trust the nuclear deterrence of the United States…we thereby could make enemies out of both the United States and China, which is the scariest scenario."[21]

Rather than push Japan to reconsider the nuclear option the North Korean nuclear test and China's ongoing military modernization have led Japan to display increasing willingness to share the operational burdens of its security alliance with the United States. Japan is likely to strengthen further its security relationship with the United States and accelerate missile defense programs. Pressure is also building to loosen the current constitutional prohibitions on exercise the right of collective self-defense. For example Japanese policymakers have proposed re-examining constitutional provisions to determine whether it would be possible to shoot down missiles that might be headed towards U.S. naval vessels operating near Japan.[22]

At the same time since the United States is an independent actor the Japanese policy establishment, fearing abandonment, has never ruled out the nuclear option. In May 1957 Prime Minister Kishi Nobusuke stated in the Diet that the constitution would permit the possession of minimally necessary nuclear weapons for self-defense purposes, but Japan forgoes such possession as a matter of policy. Following this line of reasoning the Director of the Cabinet Legislative Bureau while testifying before a House of Councilors Committee in December 1965 held that Japan is able to develop a nuclear capability under the constitution, as long as the weapon type is defined as defensive.[23] In 1970 the Japanese Defense Agency White Paper formalized this interpretation stating "…it would be possible in a legal sense to possess small-yield, tactical, purely defensive nuclear weapons without violating the constitution."[24]

This has become the government's definitive interpretation of the relationship between the constitution and nuclear weapons and has been repeatedly reaffirmed by Japanese government officials, suggesting that if the threat environment changed so that nuclear weapons became minimally necessary for self-defense purposes, such weapons would be permissible. Indeed shortly after China conducted its first nuclear weapons test in 1964 Japanese Prime Minister Sato Eisaku reportedly told the U.S. President Lyndon Johnson during the 1965 Japan–U.S. summit that he personally felt Japan should acquire nuclear weapons if China possessed them.[25] In his words "If the Chicoms (Chinese Communists) had nuclear weapons, the Japanese also should have them."[26]

In a recent example in 2002 Fukuda Yasuo, Chief Cabinet Secretary in the Koizumi Junichiro administration, reconfirmed that the current interpretation of Japan's "Peace Constitution" does not constrain Japan from developing an indigenous nuclear deterrent, although it does place serious limitations on the class of weapon Japan can maintain as part of its arsenal.[27] Fukuda further stirred controversy stating that Japanese citizens might start to favor the acquisition of nuclear weapons if the international security environment should change dramatically.[28]

Also the Japanese policy establishment believes it to be prudent to retain at least a latent capability to exercise the nuclear option. For example as way back as 1969 a Foreign Ministry internal document entitled *"An Outline of Japanese Foreign Policy"* stated that Japan "would maintain a policy of not holding nuclear weapons for the present, but should take care to always maintain the economic and technological potential to manufacture a nuclear device, and not be restrained by others."[29] The six-year gap between the signing of the NPT and its ratification by Japan was another indication of persisting reluctance to narrow the range of policy options. In June 1993, Japanese Foreign Ministry officials once again attempted to resist U.S. pressure for an indefinite extension of the NPT on the grounds that doing so would "tie the hands of future governments if new security threats arise."[30]

Analysts refer to this state of affairs as hedging, a kind of "asymptomatic strategy"[31] that refers to a nuclear armament process through which a nation, without revealing any military intention, proceeds to acquire all nuclear capability except the possession of nuclear warheads. In the words of Christopher Hughes "...the historical record since the mid-1950s demonstrates Japan's position as a threshold, virtual, recessed or hedging nuclear power – that is, a power capable of tipping toward nuclear weapons but choosing to refrain from their possession."[32] And, Japan's relentless pursuit of nuclear energy and space technology has meant that the "choice to go nuclear" has retained its credibility.

Technical Considerations

For Japan, a country deeply constrained by a lack of natural energy resources, the civilian use of nuclear power has been central to the national economic strategy. Japan has, therefore, developed a nuclear program for non-military purposes since the 1950s. Japan started its nuclear research program in 1954, with 230 million yen being budgeted for nuclear energy. The Atomic Energy Basic Law, which strictly limits the use of nuclear technology to peaceful purposes, was introduced in 1955. The law aims to ensure that three principles – democratic methods, independent management, and transparency – are the basis of nuclear research activities, as well as promoting international co-operation. Inauguration of the Atomic Energy Commission in 1956 promoted nuclear power development and utilization and the first commercial reactor began operating in 1966.

Before the oil shocks of the 1970s Japan relied on imported oil for 80 percent of its energy needs. Since then this figure has come down to approximately 50 percent mainly due to the growth in nuclear power.[33] Nuclear energy has been a national strategic priority since 1973. Today, 55 reactors provide some 30 percent of the country's electricity.[34] There are plans to increase this to 37 per cent in 2009 and 41 per cent in 2014.[35] On November 24, 2000, 'Japan's Atomic Energy Commission (AEC) concluded the latest proposal for the Long-Term Programme for Research, Development and Utilization of Nuclear Energy (also known as the Long-Term Programme). The revised plan establishes the issue of safety as paramount, while reaffirming the fact that nuclear power generation will continue to play a major role in the twenty-first century. The Program reconfirms the necessity of nuclear power in Japan despite the criticality accident that occurred at the Tokai Plant in Ibaraki Prefecture.[36] In this context, it has been suggested that a "nuclear quest" is underway to create a complete Japanese fuel cycle and thus virtual independence in all aspects of nuclear power generation.[37]

The Japanese government's current nuclear power stance draws support from the following points[38]:

- The first priority in Japanese energy supply policy is securing the steady supply of energy necessary to support the lives of the people.
- Japan is an island nation that cannot exchange energy supplies with neighboring countries through transmission lines or pipelines, and that it is poor in energy resources and relies on foreign suppliers for most of its energy requirements.
- It is a wise and rational policy for the Japanese government to continue making the fullest possible use of nuclear power generation as one of the mainstays of the nation's energy supply, considering the geographical and resource conditions of Japan,

a nation poor in energy resources, and taking the energy uncertainties of the future into account.

- Nuclear power generation contributes to economic efficiency, supply stability and the environmental acceptability of Japan's energy supply systems.

As the document *Energy in Japan* points out nuclear energy is particularly important for Japan as the key fuel material, uranium, is widely available in politically sound countries making it a highly stable energy source.[39] The development of nuclear power is generally broken down into three developmental phases.[40] In the first period uranium is the major source of nuclear power. In the second phase, the key processes of nuclear fuel recycling – enrichment and reprocessing – are carried out domestically on a commercial basis and the recovered uranium and plutonium from spent fuel are used again as plutonium-uranium mixed oxide (MOX) fuel in light water reactors. In the third and final phase, fast breeder reactors allow for a still more efficient use of uranium resources and account for most electric power generation. Fast breeder reactors produce more plutonium than they originally consume, creating an ever-increasing supply of fuel.

Japan suggests that since even the supplies of uranium for "first use" are limited the focus must be on recovering uranium and plutonium from spent fuel and using it again as plutonium-uranium mixed oxide (MOX) fuel. This serves as an alternative method for supplying fuel for nuclear power generation, and helps improve the stability of that fuel supply. Recycling allows Japan to cut back the consumption of first-use uranium by about half when used in light water reactors (LWRs), and potentially sixty times if it can be used by a fast breeder reactor (FBR).[41] Japan's nuclear fuel cycle policy is, therefore, to reprocess all spent fuel and consume all the extracted plutonium as reactor fuel.

The Guidelines to Nuclear Power Policy adopted by the Japanese Cabinet on October 14, 2005, therefore, continue to clearly emphasize nuclear power as a basic energy resource and affirm that steady development will be pursued.[42] And, that the effective reuse of plutonium, uranium and other recovered constituents will be pursued as a fundamental policy.[43] In May 2006 the ruling Liberal Democratic Party urged the government to accelerate development of fast breeder reactors (FBRs), calling this "a basic national technology".[44] It proposed increased budget, better coordination in moving from R&D to verification and implementation, plus international cooperation. Japan is already playing a leading role in the Generation IV initiative, with focus on sodium-cooled FBRs. In April 2007 the government selected Mitsubishi Heavy Industries (MHI) as the core company to develop a new generation of FBRs.[45] Government ministries, the Japan Atomic Energy Agency (JAEA) and the Federation of Electric Power Companies of Japan all have backed this.

In reality it is not so simple. The main problem is that the MOX and FBR programs in Japan have been delayed. Japan's prototype FBR *Monju* first generated electricity in August 1995 has been shut since December 1995 due to a sodium leak accident. This has resulted in Japan accumulating a large stockpile of separated plutonium. Japan's stockpile of separated totaled 43 tons at the end of 2004.[46] Until recently, British and French companies have done the reprocessing of spent fuel in Europe with wastes being returned to Japan for disposal. This cooperation terminated in 2005. As of July 2006, however, not a single reactor had been loaded with MOX fuel[47] and yet operation of the reprocessing plant at Rokkasho, in Japan started in July 2006. Therefore, it is likely that Japan's stockpile of separated plutonium will increase. It is estimated that once Rokkasho plant goes into full-scale operation Japan's plutonium stockpile will likely grow to more than 70 tons by 2020 from 43 tons in 2005.[48]

Japanese analysts insist that this is only "reactor-grade" nuclear material and cannot be used to build "practical weapons".[49] The argument is that while it is theoretically possible to use reactor grade plutonium for weapons purposes, there is no positive evidence that a meaningful arsenal can be realized through such processes.[50] Further, Japan is a member of the NPT and accepts International Atomic Agency (IAEA) safeguards and inspections on all nuclear materials to assure that any processes are not diverted to military purposes.

Nonetheless the fact remains that "Japan has an advanced nuclear energy program, sophisticated technology, and highly trained civilian nuclear engineers who could be employed in producing nuclear weapons with some adjustments and redirection of Japan's nuclear facilities."[51]

Then there is the issue of Japan's heavy investment in the H-series rockets. In December 2002, the H-2A Launch Vehicle No. 4

was successfully launched from the National Space Development Agency (NASDA) Tanegashima Space Center in Kyushu. It carried the largest satellite ever launched by a Japanese rocket in addition to three smaller satellites and with this Japan's rocket technology has taken a major step forward in establishing its reliability. NASDA developed the H-IIA as the successor to the H-II rocket, which after having five consecutive successful launches was scrapped following failed flights in 1998 and 1999. In addition to carrying the three smaller satellites, the H-IIA put the ADEOS-II, an environmental satellite, into a polar orbit 800 kilometers above the Earth. In March 2003, just a few months after North Korea launched a Taepodong ballistic missile over Japanese territory before crashing into the Pacific Ocean, Japan succeeded in launching two "information gathering satellites". Thus, in terms of technology "it is certain that Japan *could* build a rocket suitable as a ballistic missile, should Japan desire to do so.[52]

Disarmament Dilemma

Japan's basic stance on nuclear disarmament and non-proliferation[53] rests with two fundamental requests:

(i) a request for an effort toward the total elimination of nuclear weapons to improve Japan's security environment as the only country to have ever suffered nuclear devastation, as well as from a long-term perspective, and
(ii) a request not to harm Japan's security while Japan relies on the United States' deterrence, including the nuclear one.

Based on these fundamental requests, on the one hand Japan does rely on the United States' nuclear deterrent against nuclear threats, on the other hand Japan, being the sole country to have suffered nuclear devastation, adopts a realistic and incremental approach to realize a peaceful world free of nuclear weapons through practical disarmament measures to improve Japanese security environment. This clearly comes out in the Japanese Ministry of Foreign Affairs website from which extracts are reproduced below (www.mofa.go.jp/policy/un/disarmament/policy/pamph0603/1-3.pdf).

Japan ratified the Treaty on the Non-Proliferation of Nuclear Weapons (NPT) in June 1976. Upon depositing the instrument of ratification, Japan explicitly stated, "Japan, as the only nation to have suffered atomic bombings, declares anew to the world its fundamental policy of forsaking nuclear armament." At the same time, Japan hoped "as many States as possible will become parties to this Treaty in order to make it truly effective." Furthermore, Japan strongly "urged" the nuclear-weapon states, which have special responsibilities for nuclear disarmament "to take concrete nuclear disarmament measures such as the reduction of nuclear weapons and the realization of a comprehensive nuclear test ban, in accordance with Article VI of this Treaty." Japan made such statements under the belief that "the nuclear-weapon states must rectify this discrimination in the future by totally abolishing their nuclear weapons" since "the NPT permits only the nuclear-weapon states to possess nuclear weapons and allows them a special status."

The basic stance of Japan on nuclear disarmament and non-proliferation and its support for the NPT have remained unchanged since Japan ratified the Treaty. The realization of a world free of nuclear weapons is the essential condition to ensure Japan's national security because Japan renounced its nuclear option by joining the NPT. At the same time, Japan, as the only nation that has suffered atomic bombings, has a humanitarian responsibility to the international community to advocate the total elimination of weapons of mass destruction, in particular nuclear weapons.

Therefore, Japan emphasizes the importance of making diplomatic efforts to implement concrete measures based on a practical and incremental approach so as to achieve its objectives of total elimination of nuclear weapons as early as possible. Instead of arousing negative reactions in nuclear-weapon states by making unrealistic and radical requests that may not be acceptable to them, and thereby causing a stalemate in nuclear disarmament, Japan intends to engage nuclear-weapon states in nuclear disarmament and build up feasible measures one by one, taking into account the undeniable reality that nuclear weapons still exist and that they serve as a deterrent.

Based on those basic stances on nuclear disarmament and non-proliferation, Japan attaches great importance to the NPT as the foundation to achieve the goals of nuclear disarmament and non-proliferation. In addition, Japan also regards the International Atomic

Energy Agency (IAEA) safeguards and the Comprehensive Nuclear-Test-Ban Treaty (CTBT) as major pillars supporting the NPT regime.

The NPT is the most universal disarmament and non-proliferation treaty, ratified by 189 state parties. However, there are states that are not yet parties to the treaty, as well as countries suspected of developing nuclear weapons clandestinely in violation of the treaty (North Korea, etc.). There are three important measures to strengthen the nuclear non-proliferation regime:

- To further enhance the Treaty's universality,
- To strengthen the capability to verity the compliance with the obligations under the Treaty by the State Parties, and
- To take appropriate measures to rectify breaches of the Treaty when they occur.

The IAEA safeguards measures play an important role in verification. By ensuring to prevent nuclear materials and activities for peaceful purposes from being diverted to military ends, it makes nuclear non-proliferation effective through controlling nuclear materials. Triggered by covert nuclear weapon development programs conducted by Iraq and North Korea that had been brought to light during the early 1990s, the importance of strengthening the traditional safeguards systems was recognized. As a result of strenuous work and deliberations, the IAEA adopted a Model Additional Protocol in May 1997. The Additional Protocol is designed with the main aims of further enhancing IAEA's capacity to detect undeclared nuclear activities, by expanding the scope of facilities to be inspected by the IAEA and by granting the IAEA to inspect with shorter advance notice.

Japan concluded the Additional Protocol in December 1999 as the first state possessing nuclear-power reactors for commercial use. However, as of January 2006, only 107 states had signed the Additional Protocol, and only 73 of these countries had placed it into effect. It is an urgent task to universalize the Additional Protocol, so Japan has been vigorously making efforts to this end. Since the latter half of 2004, as a member of the G8, Japan has issued a demarche to non-signatory states of the Additional Protocol and also made a human and financial contribution to various seminars hosted by the IAEA to promote the universalization of the Additional Protocol. While prohibiting non-nuclear-weapon states from developing and acquiring nuclear weapons, the NPT obliges the nuclear-weapon states to make efforts toward disarmament in good faith. Therefore, if nuclear-weapon states only emphasize the nuclear-non-proliferation aspect of the NPT regime and disregard their obligations for nuclear disarmament, it may endanger the credibility of the NPT regime itself, and result in the weakening of the NPT regime.

From this perspective, Japan has been persistently urged the nuclear-weapon states to make progress in nuclear disarmament process. When the indefinite extension of the NPT was decided in 1995, the international community agreed to promote negotiations on the CTBT as one of the nuclear disarmament measures to be implemented by nuclear-weapon states. Japan has been making active diplomatic efforts for the early entry into force of the CTBT since Japan regards the treaty as an effective and practical measure to achieve both nuclear disarmament and non-proliferation. The entry into force of the CTBT still seems far away given the fact that states such as the US, China, India, Pakistan, and North Korea, whose ratifications are required for the entry into force of the Treaty, have not yet signed or ratified it. Nevertheless, fully convinced of the importance of establishing the International Monitoring System, which is a verification measure of the CTBT and to set up a network to monitor nuclear tests around the world, Japan has been making earnest efforts to install monitoring facilities in Japan and to provide technical assistance to other states.

The next significant issue to the CTBT in the multilateral disarmament and non-proliferation negotiations is the adoption of the Fissile Materials Cut-off Treaty (Cut-off Treaty). The Cut-off Treaty, intended to ban the production of fissile material that could be used to produce nuclear weapons, is a concrete measure of nuclear non-proliferation and disarmament. It is an urgent task to activate the Conference on Disarmament for early commencement of negotiations on this Treaty.

It is also of great significance to develop practical international cooperative projects not only to form agreements, but to implement them for nuclear disarmament and non-proliferation. Such demand has been generated in the international environment after the Cold War, and Japan has deployed active efforts for such projects under the policy referred to as "Disarmament in Action." Japan is cooperating within the framework of G8 to ensure the safe control of fissile materials such as plutonium removed from dismantled nuclear weapons of Russia, to dispose such materials so that these materials will not be used again in the manufacture of nuclear weapons, and to prevent the outflow of nuclear scientists from Russia and Ukraine. The dismantlement projects of decommissioned nuclear submarines in Far East Russia (the so-called "Star of Hope") are placed in the context of this type of cooperation. Such cooperation is becoming increasingly important not only to promote nuclear disarmament, but also to minimize the risks of nuclear weapons, fissile materials and related technologies falling into the hands of countries of concern or terrorists.

The resolution proposed by Japan to the UN General Assembly every year since 1994 summarizes and clearly demonstrates the basic stance of Japan on nuclear disarmament and nonproliferation. Japan presented draft resolutions entitled "Nuclear Disarmament with a View to the Ultimate Elimination of Nuclear Weapons" during the period from 1994 and 1999, which was supported by the overwhelming majority of the international community. This idea of "the ultimate elimination of nuclear weapons" was incorporated into the document adopted at the NPT Review Conference in 1995 entitled "Principles and Objectives for Nuclear Non-proliferation and Disarmament." It was quite meaningful that nuclear-weapon states undertook to pursue the objective of "the elimination of nuclear weapons" even though it was qualified by the word "ultimate."

At the NPT Review Conference held in 2000, the Final Document was adopted unanimously. The Final Document mentions "practical steps for the systematic and progressive efforts on nuclear disarmament" that have to be taken up by the international community, which include the early entry into force of the CTBT, and the immediate commencement of negotiations on the Cut-off Treaty with a view to its conclusion within five years. In the Final Document, an "unequivocal undertaking" by the nuclear weapon states to accomplish the total elimination of their nuclear weapons was agreed on. This undertaking marked a step forward ahead of Japan's resolution "Nuclear Disarmament with a View to the Ultimate Elimination of Nuclear Weapons," and it is safe to say that Japan's resolutions laid the groundwork for this progress.

Based on these achievements, Japan submitted a new nuclear disarmament resolution entitled, "A Path to the Total Elimination of Nuclear Weapons," instead of "Resolution on the Nuclear Disarmament with a View to the Ultimate Elimination of Nuclear Weapons" at the United Nations Millennium General Assembly in 2000 this resolution was adopted by an overwhelming majority. This resolution indicated a concrete path based on a practical and incremental approach towards the realization of the total elimination of nuclear weapons, with the goal of "a world free of nuclear weapons." This resolution contained progressive measures in addition to those in the Final Document of the 2000 NPT Review Conference, including further reduction of nuclear weapons with a view to their total elimination, while ensuring an appropriate balance between nuclear disarmament and nuclear non-proliferation.

Since 2001, the US has drastically changed its approach from that of the previous US-Russia nuclear arms control regime. While pursuing unilateral reduction of its nuclear weapons, the US took a passive or negative stance against several multilateral treaties on disarmament and nonproliferation: for example the CTBT. Under such circumstances, Japan has continued to submit the draft resolutions on nuclear disarmament to the UN General Assembly. In 2004, Japan submitted a draft resolution on nuclear disarmament entitled "A Path to the Total Elimination of Nuclear Weapons." This time again Japan was inspired by its consistent stance based on the practical and incremental approach and aimed at bringing about a peaceful and safe world free of nuclear weapons through the accumulation of specific measures for nuclear disarmament.

The draft was prepared with due consideration to the expression of growing concerns over proliferation of weapons of mass destruction and to increasing emphasis on the importance of the compliance with the NPT, thus reflecting shared views emerging from recent developments in the international scene. An overwhelming majority at the UN General Assembly adopted this draft resolution. In light of the failure of the NPT Review Conference in May 2005 and the lack of reference to disarmament and non-proliferation in the UN World Summit Outcome in September of the same year, Japan submitted a new resolution entitled "Renewed determination towards the total elimination of nuclear weapons" which continues to enjoy overwhelming support from the international community (adopted at the UN General Assembly with 168 votes in favour.)

In terms of implications for India, need one say more? India's nuclear explosions in May 1998 saw Japan taking an aggressive stand on the issue of proliferation particularly nuclear proliferation. Japan decided to lift all nuclear-related economic sanctions on India and Pakistan as a measure to help the United States after the terror attacks in September 2001. There has been some talk of nuclear energy cooperation but Japan will wait to see what eventually happens with the Indo-U.S. nuclear deal.

As of now there is no official support by Japan to the deal.

NOTES

1. http://www.mofa.go.jp/policy/un/address5612.html
2. See Michael J. Green and Katsuhisa Furukawa, "New Ambitions, Old Obstacles: Japan and Its Search For an Arms Control Strategy", *Arms Control Today,* July/August 2000.
3. Text available at the website of the *Japan Nuclear Cycle Development Institute,* http://www.jaea.go.jp/jnc/kaihatu/hukaku/english/atomiclaw.htm
4. Katsuhisa Furukawa "Nuclear Option, Arms Control, and Extended Deterrence: In Search of a New Framework for Japan's Nuclear Policy".
5. Anthony Di Filippo, "*The Politics of Japan's Disarmament Initiatives: Where Government Policies and Civil Society Converge and Diverge*".
6. See George Totten and Tamio Kawakami, "Gensuikyo and the Peace Movement in Japan", *Asian Survey,* Vol. 4, May 1964. pp. 833-41.
7. For details see Lawrence S. Wittner, *Resisting the Bomb: A History of the World Nuclear Disarmament Movement, 1954-1970,* California: Stanford University Press, 1997.
8. Mike M. Mochizuki "Japan Tests the Nuclear Taboo".
9. *Yomiuri Shimbun* (Tokyo), November 20, 2006.
10. *Ibid.*
11. The numbers are provided at the *Gensuikyo* website http://www10.plala.or.jp/antiatom/html/e/discription_gensuikyo.htm
12. *Ibid.* p. 65.
13. Katsuhisa Furukawa, "*Nuclear Option, Arms Control and Extended Deterrence: In Search of a New Framework for Japan's Nuclear Policy*".
14. Yuri Kase "The Costs and Benefits of Japan's Nuclearization: An Insight Into the 1968/70 Internal Report", *The Nonproliferation Review,* Summer 2001, p. 59.

15. The *Yomiuri Shimbun*, March 16, 1968 cited in Yuri Kase "The Costs and Benefits of Japan's Nuclearization: An Insight Into the 1968/70 Internal Report", *The Nonproliferation Review,* Summer 2001, p. 60.
16. Comment by one of the four authors of the report. Quoted in Yuri Kase "The Costs and Benefits of Japan's Nuclearization: An Insight Into the 1968/70 Internal Report", *The Nonproliferation Review,* Summer 2001, p. 56.
17. Katsuhisa Furukawa, "*Nuclear Option, Arms Control and Extended Deterrence: In Search of a New Framework for Japan's Nuclear Policy*".
18. These details are from Yuri Kase "The Costs and Benefits of Japan's Nuclearization: An Insight Into the 1968/70 Internal Report", *The Nonproliferation Review,* Summer 2001.
19. Sheila A. Smith, "*Japan's Future Strategic Options and the U.S.-Japan Alliance*".
20. Katsuhisa Furukawa "*Nuclear Option, Arms Control and Extended Deterrence: In Search of a New Framework for Japan's Nuclear Policy*".
21. "National Security Debate Mushrooming Since October 9", *Japan Times Online,* November 25, 2006, http://search.japantimes.co.jp/mail/nn20061125a2.html
22. *Yomiuri Shimbun* (Tokyo) November 4, 2006.
23. Cited in John E. Endicott *Japan's Nuclear Option: Political, Technical and Strategic Factors,* New York: Praeger, 1975, p. 42.
24. Selig S. Harrison (ed.) *Japan's Nuclear Future: The Plutonium Debate and East Asian Security,* Washington D.C.: Carnegie Endowment for International Peace, 1996. p. 12.
25. "Sato Hinted at Japan Nuclear Option", *Japan Times,* May 25, 1998.
26. Declassified U.S. State Department document cited in Masakatsu Ota "Will Japan Keep Renouncing Nuclear Weapons in the Coming Century"? http://www.bsos.umd.edu/pgsd/publications/issbrief 2PGSD.htm
27. Llewelyn Hughes, "*Why Japan Won't Go Nuclear* (Yet), http://web.mit.edu.
28. *Ibid.*
29. See Alan Tonelson"Time for a New U.S.-Japan Security Relationship", *Comparative Strategy,* Vol. 16, No. 1, Jan-March 1997, p. 3. Also Llewelyn Hughes "Why Japan Won't Go Nuclear (Yet)".
30. Andrew Mack "Japan and the Bomb: A Cause For Concern", *Asia Pacific Magazine* No. 3, June 1996, pp. 5-9. Available at http://coombs.anu.edu.au/SpecialProj/APM/TXT/mack-a-03-96.html
31. See George Wuester "Some Conceptional Problems in Nuclear Proliferation", *American Political Science Review* Vol. 66, No. 2, Fall 1997.

32. Christopher W. Hughes "*North Korea's Nuclear Weapons: Implication for the Nuclear Ambitions of Japan, South Korea, and Taiwan*".
33. http://www.enecho.meti.go.jp/topics/energy-in-japan/energy2006Epdf/p56_energy2006E.pdf
34. http://www.world-nuclear.org/info/inf79.html
35. *Ibid.*
36. See http://www.japannuclear.com/nuclearpower/programme/excerpts.html
37. See for example, Michael W. Donnelly "Japan's Nuclear Energy Quest" in Gerald L. Curtis (ed.) *Japan's Foreign Policy After the Colder War*, New York: M.E. Sharpe, 1993, pp. 179-201.
38. http://www.japannuclear.com/nuclearpower/programme/excerpts.html
39. See Energy in Japan (Agency for Natural Resources and Energy, Ministry of Economy, Trade and Industry) 2006. Available at http://www.enecho.meti.go.jp/topics/energy-in-japan/energy2006Epdf/p56_energy2006E.pdf
40. Explained in Mitsuo Kono "The Future of Nuclear Power in Japan", *Japan Review of International Affairs* Fall 1997, pp. 188-203.
41. "Japan's Policy on the Use of Plutonium"—a document put out by the Ministry of Foreign Affairs, Japan, February 1995. Cited in Jeffrey W. Thompson and Benjamin L. Self "Nuclear Energy, Space Launch Vehicles, and Advanced Technology", http://www.stimson.org
42. *Ibid.*
43. *Ibid.*
44. *Ibid.*
45. *Ibid.*
46. http://www.physorg.com/news6316.html
47. Tadahiro Katsuta and Tatsujiro Suzuki ""Japan's Spent Fuel and Plutonium Management Challenges", *Research Report No. 2*, International Panel on Fissile Materials, September 2006. Available at www.fissilematerials.org/ipfm/site_down/ipfmresearchreport02.pdf
48. *Ibid.*
49. See Ryukichi Imai "Can Reactor Grade Plutonium Produce Nuclear Fission Weapons?" http://www.cnfc.or.jp/e/proposal/reports/index.html
50. *Ibid.*
51. Jeffrey W. Thompson and Benjamin L. Self "Nuclear Energy, Space Launch Vehicles, and Advanced Technology"
52. *Ibid.*
53. http://www.mofa.go.jp/policy/un/disarmament/policy/pamph0603/1-3.pdf

7

Future Prospects

According to B. Raman[1], the use of the term strategic generally has two connotations. Firstly, it is a long-term relationship with a common vision and shared interests and concerns and not a tactical, short-term or fire-fighting relationship. Secondly, the national security of the two countries forms an important component of the bilateral relationship. However, the improvement in India-Japan relations in recent years has emerged in tandem with Indo-U.S engagement. This is the thread linking the analysis, in previous pages, of India-Japan cooperation in the five areas that are generally identified as "common concerns". These include: Reform of United Nations, Disarmament, Rise of China, SLOC protection, and Cooperation against International Terrorism. In other words, the vision from Washington linking India, Japan and the United States is guiding Japan's politico-strategic initiatives involving India.

The key points of this trilateral framework are as follows[2]:

- The United States, Japan and India have shared interests in establishing an open and inclusive regional architecture in Asia at a time when a variety of new forums and institutions, such as the East Asia Summit, the six-party talks and the Shanghai Cooperation Organization, are taking shape.
- The three nations should, therefore coordinate closely to ensure

that Asia retains an open regionalism and that the regional agenda in these various forums and institutions advances their shared norms.

- Trilateral cooperation among these three democracies or quadrilateral dialogue with Australia should not be seen as targeted at China but rather as a stabilising factor in broad regional dynamics.

This suggests that if the United States were to loose interest in India the Japanese would also recalibrate their policy. The road ahead for India-Japan relations is economic and this is the arena in which India should continue to direct its energies. No doubt this will not be easy but enhanced economic cooperation between the two countries will develop interdependencies that will be harder to ignore for Japan. There are three reasons for proposing this:

1. Japan continues to be firmly committed to the alliance with the United States as the primary vehicle to advance its security in the international arena.
2. Japan is no longer complacent about the rise of China.
3. There may be some slow downs but the Indian economic growth story is now irreversible.

Indeed there are strong indications that the Japanese are deeply interested in the economic potential of India and want to link the two economies together. Already, from the perspective of India-Japan relations, the most notable initiatives have been in the economic sphere. The Prime Ministers of the two countries in November 2004 set up an India-Japan Joint Study Group to give its recommendations for strengthening economic relations between the two nations. In July 2006 the group released its report recommending that India and Japan should launch inter-governmental negotiations on an Economic Partnership Agreement. In December 2006 the two countries formally agreed to launch negotiations for the conclusion of a Comprehensive Economic Partnership Agreement (CEPA) through a Joint Task Force (JTF) by early 2009. The accord would address trade issues and also promote increased Japanese investment in India as well as cooperation in the South Asian country's banking, insurance and capital markets sector. Japan and India have also signed a memorandum of understanding for construction of the proposed US$ 90-billion Delhi-Mumbai Industrial Corridor. This could turn out to be the single largest investment in India's woefully inadequate infrastructure.[3]

India-Japan trade in FY 2005-2006 reached the figure of USD$ 6.5 billion according to India's Ministry of Commerce website. In this 21.99 per cent increase from the previous year exports from India amounted to approx USD$ 2.5 billion while imports from Japan stood at USD$ 4 billion. As for Foreign Direct Investment (FDI) from Japan, the recently set up Japan Cell within the Commerce Ministry has this information:

- As of September 2006 Japan ranks 3rd & cumulative FDI inflows (1991-2006) from Japan is US$ 2.16 billion (5.85 per cent).
- Top sectors attracting FDI inflows *(from January 2000 to September 2006)* from Japan are Transportation Industry (54.07 per cent), Electrical Equipments (including computer software & electronics) (7.04 per cent), Telecommunications (3.97 per cent), Earth Moving Machinery (3.33 per cent) and Services Sectors (financial & non-financial) (3.25 per cent).
- In terms of technology transfer 852 technical collaborations has been approved for Japan, which accounts for 10.92 per cent of the total collaboration approved from August 1991 to September 2006.
- The highest technical collaboration has been in the Transportation Industry followed by Electrical Equipments (including computer software & electronics) Industry and Chemicals (other than fertilizers).
- As of January 2006, the number of Japanese companies operating in India is 328.

Undoubtedly, these figures are not very impressive when seen in terms of India's share in Japan's total global trade and investment. Japan's trade with India came to US$ 6.7 billion (0.6 per cent of total trade)—US$ 3.5 billion in exports and US$ 3.2 billion in imports. In contrast Japan's trade with China in 2005 came to a total of US$ 189.4 billion (17.0 percent of total trade)—US$ 80.3 billion in exports (13.4 per cent of total exports) and US$ 109.1 billion in imports (21.0% of all exports). In fact China is already Japan's second largest trading partner after the U.S. (17.8 per cent of total trade) and bilateral trade rose 11.5 percent in 2006 compared with the previous year, according to the Japan External Trade Organization (JETRO). Japanese investment in China in 2005 came to US$ 6.58 billion (14.5 per cent of total outward direct investment), and China is the second largest recipient of Japanese direct investment after the U.S. while Japanese investment in India is only US$ 270 million (0.6 per cent of the total).[4]

India-Japan bilateral trade is highly concentrated in a narrow range of products. India's exports dominated by raw materials and minerals, gems and jewellery, marine products, iron ore, garments, tea, spices, chemicals, bulk drugs, computer software, leather goods, etc. India's imports from Japan consist mainly of machinery, chemicals, transport equipment and iron and steel products.

On the other hand Japan is today India's largest bilateral aid donor and India has been the top recipient of yen loans[5] from Japan since March 2004 when Japan signed the Exchange of Notes for extension of Official Development Assistance (ODA) worth more than US$ 1 billion, thus upgrading India as the number one recipient of Japanese ODA, surpassing China, which had been holding that position for many years. Focus Areas of Japan's ODA to India have been as follows:

- Development of economic infrastructure, mainly in the area of power and transportation
- Poverty reduction through agricultural and rural development
- Environmental protection, through afforestation and improvement of quality of water
- Assisting to improve health and medical care

The list of important Japan's ODA projects in recent years includes the following[6]:

Project Name	*Date of Approval*	*Amount (Million Yen)*
Simhadri Thermal Power Station Project (IV)	31-03-2003	5684
Bakreswar Thermal Power Station Units Extension Project	31-03-2003	36771
Ajanta—Ellora Conservation and Tourism Development Project (II)	31-03-2003	7331
Yamuna Action Plan Project (II)	31-03-2003	13333
Delhi Mass Rapid Transport System Project (IV)	31-03-2003	34012
Purulia Pumped Storage Project (II)	31-03-2004	23578
Dhauliganga Hydroelectric Power Plant Construction Project (III)	31-03-2004	13890
Umiam Stage II Hydro Power Station Modernization Project	31-03-2004	1964
Rengali Irrigation Project (II)	31-03-2004	6342
Kurnool Cuddapah Canal Modernization Project (II)	31-03-2004	4773
Bisalpur Jaipur Water Supply Project	31-03-2004	8881
Delhi Mass Rapid Transport System Project (V)	31-03-2004	59296
North Karanpura Super Thermal Power Project (I)	31-03-2005	15916
Rajasthan Minor Irrigation Improvement Project	31-03-2005	11555
Uttar Pradesh Buddhist Circuit Development Project	31-03-2005	9495
Ganga Action Plan Project	31-03-2005	11184
Bangalore Water Supply and Sewerage Project (II-1)	31-03-2005	41997
Delhi Mass Rapid Transport System Project (VI)	31-03-2005	19292
Purulia Pumped Storage Project (III)	31-03-2006	17963
Rural Electrification Project	31-03-2006	20629
Swan River Integrated Watershed Management Project	31-03-2006	3493
Bangalore Water Supply and Sewerage Project (II-2)	31-03-2006	28358
Hussain Sagar Lake and Catchment Area Improvement Project	31-03-2006	7729

(*Contd.*)

Project Name	Date of Approval	Amount (Million Yen)
Kolkata Solid Waste Management Improvement Project	31-03-2006	3584
Visakhapatnam Port Expansion Project (E/S)	31-03-2006	161
Delhi Mass Rapid Transport System Project (Phase2) (I)	31-03-2006	14900
Bangalore Metro Rail Project	31-03-2006	44704

Source: http://www.jbic.go.jp/english/oec/project/yen_loan_list.php

India has called for a shift in the emphasis in India-Japan economic relations to investment from development aid. In the words of the Minister for Commerce and Industry, Kamal Nath[7]:

I am aware of the fact that India is one of the largest ODA recipients from Japan. However, in the changed context of our desire for seeking a new economic partnership, it is important that we shift the emphasis of India-Japan relationship from an ODA-based relationship to an FDI-based partnership. It is no longer aid that India seeks, but trade.

This is certainly the goal but at the same time it is important to understand that Japanese economic cooperation is a holistic system including private and public capital flows. This means that the increases in ODA disbursements are a strong signal of growing Japanese economic focus on India.

It is in the context of declining ODA resources that Japan's aid reorientation has taken place. Japan has revised its ODA Charter in 2003 to clearly state that "The objectives of Japan's ODA are to contribute to the peace and development of the international community, and thereby to help ensure Japan's own security and prosperity." Correspondingly the emphasis is on "strategic, flexible and effective ODA". For example, "Basic Policies for Economic and Fiscal Management and Structural Reforms 2005" that were considered by the Japan Council on Economic and Fiscal Policy, headed by Prime Minister Koizumi, and were then adopted by the Cabinet in June 2005 state that "Japan will continue its efforts toward the goal of providing 0.7 per cent of its Gross National Income for ODA in order to contribute to the Millennium Development Goals, but at the same time the "Basic Policies" require prioritisation of regions and areas, stricter reviews on implementation, and introduction of new effective and efficient approaches.

An important aspect of the ODA focus on "Japan's own security and prosperity" has been the review of Japanese aid to China. The corresponding increases in ODA disbursements to India are indicative of Japan's economic interest in India. The objectives are two fold:

1. steer current Asian integration efforts in Japanese determined directions and
2. diversify trade partners in Asia.

In both cases China certainly is the context and India appears to be the Japanese choice as counterweight. The strategy is to bolster India's economic growth and the mechanism is economic assistance. In the words of Keiichi Iwasaki, "Development assistance to India is thus critical to Japan's policy toward Asia."[8]

As Japan's Country Assistance Programme for India presented in May 2006 points out, "on the basis of Japan's own assisting experience towards East Asia, it is desirable to assist in efficiently strengthening the cause-and-effect linkages in India. Namely, this means

"1. infrastructure building through yen loans and facilitation of trade and the investment climate through human resources development supported by technical cooperation, bringing about
2. economic growth through an increase in private direct investment, leading to
3. economic development and improvement in the standard of living" and
4. "one of the roles that should be played by Japan's ODA is to create a trend in which ODA promotes private sector economic relations, as was seen in the countries of East Asia and South-east Asia".

Indeed the reason for optimism in India-Japan economic relations is the experience of East Asian countries, including China with *"three-into-one"* aid that linked Japanese FDI, trade, and ODA to develop the economy of recipients. For, not only does Japan's ODA have a positive "infrastructure effect" it also has a positive "vanguard effect" on Japanese FDI in terms of recipient country's risks perceived subjectively by Japanese firms, i.e., Japan's ODA works as a "quasi government guarantee".[9] In sum Japanese aid flows have a significant positive impact on private investors, location choice.

The statement released by Nippon Keidanren, Japan's most influential private-sector economic grouping in July 2006 certainly points in this direction.[10] It states

> "India, a demographically young country with a population of over 1 billion, is expected to enjoy strong economic growth on a sustained basis. It has great potentials both as a consumer market and as a manufacturing base, and it is important that Japan strives to strengthen economic ties with India."

A similar sentiment was voiced in the August 2007 proposal "Japan-India Partnership for Sustainable Growth" that was put forward by the Japan-India Business Leaders' Forum.[11] It states

> "The economic relationship between Japan and India is unquestionably destined to evolve into one of the most important strategic relationships of any two countries in Asia and even worldwide."

The Japan Forum on International Relations has also released a set of policy recommendations[12] relating to India entitled *India's Leap Forward and Japan* in September 2007. The opinion expressed is that India, the world's largest democracy, is poised to become an economic giant and therefore this is an opportune time for Japan and India to cooperate in developing a deeper partnership. Importantly this Japanese perspective turns the spotlight inward and suggests concrete steps that Japan needs to take to further relations with India. Key points in the analysis are as follows

- Strengthening Japan-India ties depends on private-sector business activities. The Japan-India relationship can be suitably enhanced only if trade and investment are increased far above their present levels.

- Parallel with the efforts to restructure its global strategies for Asia, Japan should actively participate in the business network now formed by India and the East Asian countries.
- This participation could be achieved, by example, through promotion of further trade and investment between Japanese corporations based in East Asia on the one hand and India on the other, and promotion of further business ties linking Japanese corporations operating in India with East Asian countries.
- Japanese trade missions need to improve their techniques so that their Indian counterparts truly understand the perspective of Japanese corporations, and they should also pursue outcome-oriented, cross-sector dialogue, and then follow up on the results.
- Promising areas for Japanese investment in India include general and industrial machinery, processed foods, everyday items such as sanitary goods and cosmetics, chemical products, pharmaceuticals, retail markets, distribution, real estate, infrastructure, finance, and software development.
- Japanese corporations must invest in fields such as these, and the current pattern of investment — almost exclusively in the transportation equipment sector — must be abandoned if the Japan-India business relationship is to grow.
- Concentrating investment in the Delhi region may end up being a poor strategy, especially because of the rapidly rising cost of land, the difficulty of acquiring industrial land, and Delhi's great distance from ocean harbours.
- A number of states and regions are potentially advantageous investment destinations for certain industries and business models, so investment destinations should be selected after a careful examination of conditions throughout the country.
- Japanese corporations should adapt their business strategies to realities in India.
- Japan's financial sector would benefit most from India's IT expertise. Instead of coddling their affiliated IT companies and client hardware companies, Japanese financial institutions should develop open IT systems and outsource some of their business to Indian software-related companies.
- Increase human interaction, especially by offering more employment opportunities to India's skilled human resources in Japan.

This growing importance of India's economic profile in Japan has important implications for India-Japan relations. Perhaps for the first time strong imperatives have been generated that require Japan to engage with India in a substantial manner. India is fast emerging as a crucial insurance policy in Japan's relations with China. It is necessary that India utilise this opportunity in an effective manner. A relationship based on economic cooperation will better withstand the test of time.

NOTES

1. B. Raman "The Hype Behind India's Japan Ties", http://www.atimes.com/atimes/South_Asia/GF16Df02.html
2. *The United States, Japan and India: Toward New Trilateral Cooperation,* Washington: Report of the Centre for Strategic and International Studies, August 16, 2007.Available at http://www.csis.org/media/csis/pubs/070816_us_j_ireport.pdf
3. C. Raja Mohan "Japan and India: The Making of a New Alliance", http://www.ntu.edu.sg/RSIS/publications/Perspective/RSIS0912007.pdf
4. See Chi Hung KWAN "*Will India Replace China as a Major Recipient of Japanese Investment?—China's Predominance Remains Firm*", http://www.rieti.go.jp/en/china/06112802.html#table1
5. 95 per cent of Japan's ODA to India is in the form of Yen loans.
6. The data is from the Japan Bank for International Cooperation (JBIC) website http://www.jbic.go.jp/english/index.php
7. http://commerce.nic.in/pressrelease/pressrelease_detail.asp?id=1582
8. Keiichi Iwasaki field, "*Dealing Successfully with a Growing Colossus—A Paradigm for Development in India and Assistance from Japan*", http://www.jbic.go.jp/english/oec/post/2006/pdf/em02.pdf
9. See, Hidemi Kimura and Yasuyuki Todo "Is Foreign Aid a Vanguard of FDI? A Gravity-Equation Approach", RIETI Discussion Paper Series 07-E-007, February 2007.
10. http://www.bilaterals.org/article.php3?id_article=5620
11. http://www.keidanren.or.jp/english/policy/2007/070.html
12. http://www.jfir.or.jp/e/pr_e/pdf/29.pdf

Appendix I
India-Japan Fact Sheet

Political Relations

- Japan and India agreed to establish "Japan-India Global Partnership in the 21st Century" when Japanese Prime Minister Mori visited India in August, 2000.
- Indian Prime Minister Vajpayee visited Japan in December, 2001, and both Prime Ministers issued "Japan-India Joint Declaration", which consist of high-level dialogue, exchange in ICT field, joint counter-action against proliferation of WMD and terrorism.
- In April, 2005, Japanese Prime Minister Koizumi visited India and agreed with Indian Prime Minister, Dr. Manmohan Singh, to reinforce the strategic focus of the global partnership between the two countries. They signed Joint Statement "Japan-India Partnership in the New Asian Era: Strategic Orientation of Japan-India Global Partnership"
- Indian Prime Minister Dr. Manmohan Singh visited Japan and had a summit talks with Japanese Prime Minister Abe in December, 2006. The two Prime Ministers decided to establish a Strategic and Global Partnership between the two countries and signed the "Joint Statement towards India-Japan Strategic and Global Partnership".

Security Cooperation

- Both countries have been conducting annual Foreign 0ffice Consultations at the Foreign Secretary level.
- The Security Dialogue between the two countries was set up in 2001 and four rounds of dialogue have been conducted since then.
- High level exchange is continuing between the defense authorities. From Japan, General Massaki, Chief of Staff

(September, 2005), Admiral Saito, Chief of Maritime SDF (February, 2006), General Mori, Chief of Ground SDF (March, 2006), and General Yoshida, Chief of Air SDF (April, 2006) visited India. From India, Admiral Prakash, Chief of Naval Staff, visited Japan in October, 2005. Defense Minister of India, Mr. Pranab Mukherjee, visited Japan in May, 2006, and a Joint Statement was issued to promote defense exchanges.

- Between the coast guards, combined exercises on anti-piracy, search & rescue, etc., have been conducted every year since 2000. Heads of coast guards of both countries visit each other almost every year.
- The two coast guards exchanged a Memorandum on Cooperation at the occasion of commandant Ishikawa's visit to India in November, 2006.
- The first trilateral naval exercise between India, Japan and the United States was held on April 16, 2007 off the western coast of Japan.

Economic Relations

- A Bilateral Trade Agreement signed with Japan in February 1958 governs Indo-Japanese commercial relations. This provides for a 'Most Favoured Nation' treatment to either country in trade matters.
- The first India-Japan IT Summit was held on September 4, 2001 in Tokyo between the Indian Minister for IT Pramod Mahajan and Heizo Takenaka, Minister of State for IT of Japan.
- Current dialogues between the two countries include: MEA-METI dialogue, India-Japan Trade Talks, India-Japan Investment Dialogue, India-Japan Energy Dialogue, and India-Japan Information Technology (IT) Dialogue.
- The Joint Study Group (JSG), composed of government officials and representatives of business and academia from the two countries, held four meetings after July, 2005.
- JSG submitted its report to both Prime Ministers when they met in July, 2006, which includes a recommendation for launching EPA negotiations.
- In December, 2006, the Prime Ministers of the two countries

decided to launch immediate negotiations for the conclusion of a bilateral Economic Partnership Agreement/Comprehensive Economic Partnership Agreement aiming to complete in substance as soon as possible in approximately two years.

- The first round of negotiation was held in New Delhi in January, 2007.
- Japan is among India's top five trading partners. Total Trade between India and Japan was close to US$ 5 billion during 2004-2005.

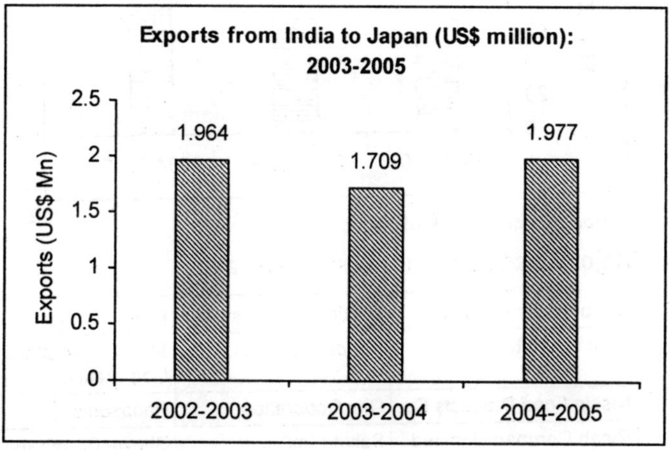

Source: Reserve Bank of India.

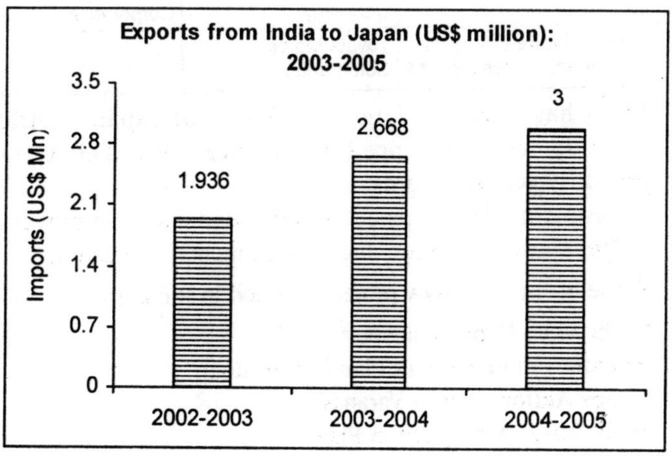

Source: Reserve Bank of India.

- Japanese foreign direct investment into India during 2005-07 has been to the tune of US$ 1.8 billion. Equity investment from Japan into India is also on the rise, touching almost US$ 4.9 billion.

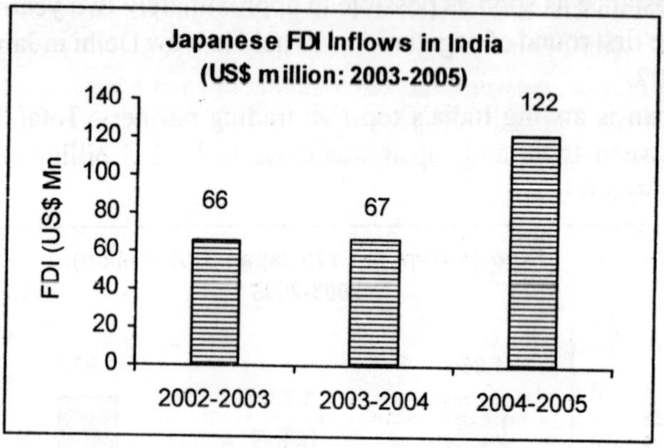

Source: Reserve Bank of India.

- Major Japanese Companies in India are:

Canon India Pvt. Ltd.	Daikin Industries Ltd.	Fujitsu Group
Hitachi Limited	Honda Motor Co. Ltd.	Mitsubishi Materials Corporation
Nissin Food Products Co.	Orix Coporation	Panasonic
Ricoh Company Limited	Sakata Inx	Showa Corporation
Sony Corporation	Stanley Electric Company	Suzuki Motor Corporation
Tokio Marine & Nichido Fire Insurance Co. Ltd	Toyota Motor Corporation	

- India has been the largest recipient of Japan's Official Development Assistance (ODA) since 2003. This ODA is primarily geared towards:

  Infrastructure Development, Poverty Reduction, Improvement of Healthcare Facilities, and Environmental Protection.

  Some of the key ODA projects funded in India are:

  Delhi Mass Rapid Transport
  Irrigation Improvement Plan in Rajasthan
  Ganga Action Plan in Varanasi
  Tamil Nadu Afforestation Plan
  Super Thermar Powe at North Karanpura

Cultural Relations

- In December 2006 a Memorandum between Indian Council for Cultural Relations (ICCR) and the Japan Foundation was signed. The Memorandum will facilitate mutually beneficial cooperation between the ICCR and the Japan Foundation in the areas of art and culture, intellectual exchange, and exchange of information.
- The two governments are observing "Japan-India Exchange Year 2007" both in Japan and in India to commemorate the 50th anniversary of the Cultural Agreement.

Number of Residents

- Number of Japanese nationals residing in India: 2,098 (as of April, 2006)
- Number of Indian nationals residing in Japan: 16,988 (as of December, 2005)

Sources

- Ministry of External Affairs India website http://meaindia.nic.in/
- Ministry of Foreign Affairs Japan website http://www.mofa.go.jp/
- India Brand Equity Fondation website http://www.ibef.org

Appendix II
Joint Statement Towards India-Japan Strategic and Global Partnership
http://meaindia.nic.in/

1. The Prime Minister of India, H.E. Dr. Manmohan Singh, is currently paying an Official Visit to Japan from December 13 to 16, 2006 at the invitation of the Prime Minister of Japan, H.E. Mr. Shinzo Abe. He is accompanied by his spouse, Mrs. Gursharan Kaur and a high-level delegation.
2. Prime Minister Dr. Manmohan Singh was accorded a ceremonial welcome on December 14. Prime Minister Dr. Manmohan Singh and Mrs. Gursharan Kaur had audience with Their Majesties the Emperor and the Empress of Japan. He held extensive talks with Prime Minister Mr. Shinzo Abe of Japan, who also hosted a Banquet in honour of the visiting dignitary. He addressed a Joint Session of the Diet on December 14. Mr. Taro Aso, Minister for Foreign Affairs, Mr. Koji Omi, Minister for Finance and Mr. Akira Amari, Minister for Economy, Trade and Industry called on the Prime Minister of India. Mr. Yoshiro Mori, former Prime Minister and President of Indo-Japanese Association and Dr. Taro Nakayama, President of Japan-Indo Parliamentarians' Friendship League also called on the Prime Minister of India. The two Prime Ministers unveiled the Joint Logo and launched the India-Japan Friendship Year 2007, to be organised in both countries, and attended the inaugural event of the Festival of India in Japan on December 14. Prime Minister Dr. Manmohan Singh also addressed the business organisations of Japan at a luncheon meeting. Prime Minister Mr. Shinzo Abe received representatives of the Indian business delegation who accompanied Prime Minister Dr. Manmohan Singh. Mr. Yasuhisa Shiozaki, Chief Cabinet Secretary and Mr. Akihiro

Ota, Chief Representative of New Komeito will call on the Prime Minister of India on December 16.

3. The two leaders recall the impressive development of India-Japan relations in recent years, noting in particular the establishment of a Global Partnership in 2000 during Prime Minister Mr. Yoshiro Mori's visit to India and the decision taken last year during Prime Minister Mr. Junichiro Koizumi's visit to India to reinforce the strategic orientation of the partnership. They also note with satisfaction the all-round progress made towards the implementation of the Joint Statement on the "India-Japan Partnership in a New Asian Era: Strategic Orientation of the India-Japan Global Partnership" and the "Eight-fold Initiative for Strengthening India-Japan Global Partnership", signed between the Prime Ministers of the two countries on April 29, 2005 in New Delhi, and reaffirm the principles and understandings embodied in these documents.

Strategic and Global Partnership

4. The two Prime Ministers recall that India and Japan share ancient bonds and a proud civilisational heritage. The current context of India-Japan relations is rooted in their similar perceptions of the evolving environment in the region and the world at large. It is driven by converging long-term political, economic and strategic interests, aspirations and concerns and underpinned by a common commitment to democracy, open society, human rights, rule of law and free market economy. It is based on deep respect for each other's contributions in promoting peace, stability and development in Asia and beyond, unencumbered by any historical differences.
5. The two leaders affirm that India and Japan are natural partners as the largest and most developed democracies of Asia, with a mutual stake in each other's progress and prosperity. Indeed, a strong, prosperous and dynamic India is in the interest of Japan, and likewise, a strong, prosperous and dynamic Japan is in the interest of India. They have responsibility for, and are capable of, responding to global and regional challenges, and they must play an active role in the promotion of peace and stability in

Asia and world at large. Recognising that Asia is emerging as the leading growth centre of an increasingly interdependent global economy, the two countries are also keen to pursue a comprehensive economic partnership in the region and nurture sustainable economic growth, social peace and political tolerance in open and cooperative regional frameworks.

6. Given their shared determination to raise bilateral relations to a higher level, the two leaders decide to establish a Strategic and Global Partnership between India and Japan. This will impart stronger political, economic and strategic dimensions to bilateral relations, serve long-term interests of both countries, enhance all-round cooperation and contribute to greater regional peace and stability.
7. The Strategic and Global Partnership will involve closer political and diplomatic coordination on bilateral, regional, multilateral and global issues, comprehensive economic engagement, stronger defence relations, greater technological cooperation as well as working towards a quantum increase in cultural ties, educational linkages and people-to-people contacts. This partnership will enable both countries to harness the vast potential of bilateral relations, drawing upon complementarities and each other's intrinsic strengths, and also work together to address regional and global challenges.

Political, Defence and Security Cooperation

8. The two leaders welcome the important contribution made to bilateral cooperation by various existing dialogue mechanisms. With a view to sustaining and giving high-level guidance to the continued growth and development of bilateral relations, the two leaders confirm their intention to hold annual Summit-level meetings in respective capitals as well as on the sidelines of multilateral events. The Prime Minister of Japan will visit India in 2007 for the next bilateral Summit at the invitation of the Prime Minister of India. The two leaders encourage the continuation and enhancement of regular exchanges between members of their respective Cabinets in charge of Foreign, Defence, Finance, Trade and Industry, Agriculture, Information

and Communications Technology, Science and Technology, Tourism and Civil Aviation portfolios. They also endorse the institutionalisation of Strategic Dialogue at the Foreign Ministers level as well as a regular Policy Dialogue between the National Security Advisor of India and his Japanese counterpart.

9. The two leaders endorse the continuation and enhancement of consultations between the Ministry of External Affairs of India and the Ministry of Foreign Affairs of Japan, including the Foreign Office Consultations (Foreign Secretary-level Talks), to advance the shared agenda of the relationship. The Indian side welcomes the Japanese plan to establish a consular post in Bangalore.
10. The two leaders welcome the Joint Statement issued following talks between the Defence Minister of India and the Minister of State for Defense of Japan in May, 2006 and reiterate their commitment to enhance defence cooperation to achieve the common goal of promoting the security, stability and prosperity in Asia and in the world at large as well as in tackling regional and global security challenges. They urge their concerned agencies to develop an annual calendar of cooperation and exchanges relating to defence and security and to progressively enhance cooperative activities, including high-level exchanges and consultation between services. The two leaders appreciate the recent developments in service-to-service cooperation, including cooperation in UNDOF. The two sides will also undertake a goodwill exercise between the Japan Maritime Self-Defense Force and the Indian Navy in 2007.
11. Recognising that India and Japan have large Exclusive Economic Zones and maritime interests, the two leaders confirm their intention to work closely to enhance cooperation in capacity building, technical assistance and information sharing between their respective agencies and undertake anti-piracy measures. They share the view that India and Japan must cooperate closely to ensure the safety and security of international maritime traffic that are vital for their economic well-being as well as that of the region.

12. The two leaders endorse regular exchanges between the two coast guards through meetings of heads of coast guards, mutual visits of coast guard ships and holding of combined exercises. In this context, the signing of a Memorandum on Cooperation between the coast guards was welcomed. They also welcome the coming into force of the Regional Cooperation Agreement on Combating Piracy and Armed Robbery against Ships in Asia (ReCAAP) and reaffirm their intention to enhance cooperation in respect of anti-piracy countermeasures under its framework.
13. The two leaders unequivocally condemn terrorism in all its forms and manifestations and stress that there can be no justification whatsoever for any act of terrorism. They share the view that international community must further intensify efforts and cooperation to fight this scourge. In this context, they confirm that the two countries will continue to work together through the India-Japan Joint Working Group on Counter Terrorism. They also call upon all Member States of the UN to work towards the expeditious adoption of a Comprehensive Convention on International Terrorism.

Comprehensive Economic Partnership

14. The two leaders welcome the report of the India-Japan Joint Study Group, which has made a series of recommendations covering trade in goods, trade in services, investment flows, role of Japan's Official Development Assistance (ODA) in promoting economic partnership and other areas of economic cooperation, and direct that those recommendations be implemented expeditiously. Convinced that comprehensive economic engagement between the two countries must be a core element of their strategic partnership and also recognising that closer economic integration between India and Japan will contribute to further growth and stability in the broader Asian region, the two Prime Ministers have decided to launch immediate negotiations for the conclusion of a bilateral Economic Partnership Agreement/Comprehensive Economic Partnership Agreement (EPA/CEPA), on the basis of the recommendations submitted by the Joint Study Group. They

note with satisfaction that a Joint Ministerial Statement, constituting a Joint Task Force to undertake the inter-governmental negotiations on the EPA/CEPA, has been signed during the visit. It will be the endeavour of the Joint Task Force to expedite these negotiations aiming to complete them in substance as soon as possible in approximately two years.

15. The two leaders welcome recent positive developments in bilateral economic relations and direct that the potential of economic partnership must be fully realised.
16. The Indian side expresses its appreciation for the fact that India is presently the largest recipient of Japan's ODA. The Japanese side affirms that India will continue to be a priority country for its ODA. The two leaders confirm that Japan's ODA will continue to support India's efforts at accelerated economic and social development as well as to further strengthen India-Japan partnership. They direct their concerned agencies to intensify cooperation under the ODA, particularly in priority sectors such as infrastructure, environment, social development and human resource development.
17. In order to widen and deepen economic engagement even as an EPA/CEPA is negotiated, the two leaders announce an "India-Japan Special Economic Partnership Initiative" (SEPI). This initiative will promote enhancement of investment from Japan to India and help develop India's infrastructure and manufacturing capacity, taking full advantage of the ample availability of skill and human resources and the public-private partnership policy initiative of the Government of India. The SEPI will, inter alia, consist of the following:

    A. *Development of Infrastructure and Promotion of Manufacturing, Trade and Investment*:

    - Further cooperation in realising the Dedicated Multi-modal High Axle Load Freight Corridors with computerised control on Mumbai-Delhi and Delhi-Howrah routes. The two leaders note with satisfaction that the Japan International Cooperation Agency (JICA) has submitted its Interim Report of the Feasibility Study on the Project and that the Final Report will be ready by October 2007. The two sides will consult on the ways and means to realise the Project, utilising Japan's Special Terms for Economic Partnership (STEP) Scheme and with the inputs of Japanese technology and expertise. The two sides will also examine the possibility of using Japanese technology in locomotives and signalling and electrical equipment, and in construction in railway sector;

- Promotion of "Delhi-Mumbai Industrial Corridor", supported by Multi-modal Dedicated Freight Corridor between Delhi and Mumbai. This will include cooperation in development of one or two sea ports on the west coast and industrial estates and Special Economic Zones with high quality physical and social infrastructure, and other initiatives, through collaboration between private and governmental sectors of the two countries, with the objective of developing the requisite infrastructure and facilitating investment. The two governments will further discuss how to facilitate its development, including the formulation of a master plan;
- Cooperation in the setting up of a multi-product Special Economic Zone/Cluster in India to locate investments from Japan, with facilities for manufacturing and processing industries, hotels and recreational units, and educational and training centres. It will be an integrated conglomeration based on industrial needs and global best practices. The Government of India will facilitate the establishment of the Zone/Cluster;
- Efforts by the Government of Japan to encourage investment by Japanese companies in India, including through assistance in development of infrastructure relating to Special Economic Zones and industrial estates;
- Assistance by Japan External Trade Organization (JETRO) to Japanese small and medium enterprises

to set up operations in India, with its Business Support Centre in India acting as an incubator;

- Support by JETRO for the rural business and industrialisation initiatives of the Government of India, under its "One Village One Product" programme, initially through the implementation of a pilot project; and
- Promotion of participation of Japanese companies in the power sector in India, including through the initiative of the Ministry of Economy, Trade and Industry of Japan on the establishment of a 'Task Force on Indian Power Sector'. Projects proposed by the Indian side for the participation of Japanese companies include, inter alia, 4000 MW Coastal Ultra Mega Power Project at Chayyur, Tamil Nadu and 3000 MW Lohit Hydroelectric Project in Arunachal Pradesh.

B. *Human Resource Development for Promotion of Manufacturing*:

- Cooperation within the framework of Japan-assisted 'Visionary Leaders for Manufacturing' (VLFM) programme, under which Japanese manufacturing management and skills will be transferred to senior managers of Indian manufacturing industry;
- Continued involvement of Japanese private sector in training and quality control and utilisation of training programmes of the Government of Japan; and
- Collaboration towards the development of the Indian Institute of Information Technology for Design and Manufacturing, Jabalpur and exchanges between technological institutes of the two countries.

18. The Policy Dialogue between the Ministry of Commerce and Industry of India and the Ministry of Economy, Trade and Industry of Japan, to be upgraded to the Ministerial level, will advance the relevant elements of the agenda of the SEPI. An MOU on Delhi-Mumbai Industrial Corridor was signed between

Minister of Commerce and Industry of India and Minister of Economy, Trade and Industry of Japan.

19. The two leaders welcome enhanced cooperation in the financial sector, including through Japanese participation in India's capital markets, banking and insurance. They also welcome the collaboration through cooperation agreement between the Government of India and the Japan Bank for International Cooperation (JBIC). They take note of the business cooperation agreement between JBIC and the ICICI Bank as a useful model to enable companies of India or Japan to raise funds in local currency in either country. The Ministries of Finance of the two countries will further exchange views on the development of regional financial and capital markets.
20. The two leaders welcome major investment projects from Japan to India, including by Suzuki Motor Corporation, Honda Motor Co. Ltd., Nissan Motor Co. Ltd. and Mitsui & Co. Ltd., among others. The two sides will cooperate to facilitate the following projects:
    - Development and setting up of integrated logistic platforms with rail-connected Inland Container Depot (ICD) and specialised warehouses based on Free Trade & Warehousing Zone (FTWZ) framework; and
    - Setting up of new capacities in India by Japanese auto and auto-parts companies.
21. Emphasising the major role of the private sector in strengthening economic engagement, the two leaders announce the setting up of a Business Leaders' Forum, comprising ten business leaders from each country. This Forum will have the mandate to develop a roadmap for enhanced partnership and cooperation between the two countries at the business level and generate ideas for furthering the goals of the SEPI and taking forward the negotiations on the EPA/CEPA. The two leaders express the hope that this Forum will provide inputs to them for promoting a comprehensive economic engagement between India and Japan. The two leaders will also designate senior representatives to guide the Business Leaders' Forum.
22. The Japanese side welcomes Indian investments in Japan. The two sides will coordinate to facilitate their location and activities

in the country. Recognising the competitive advantage of India in software development and IT-enabled services, the two sides will also work together to facilitate the functioning of Indian companies in this field in Japan.

23. The two sides will continue cooperation in the field of urban development, including water supply, sanitation and construction of urban transportation systems in Indian cities along the lines of Delhi Metro, which is a shining example of India-Japan partnership. The two countries will coordinate to launch a Working Group in the field of water environment, urban development and urban transportation.

24. The two leaders welcome the outcomes of meetings of Working Groups set up under the India-Japan Information and Communication Technology Forum, which include field trials in India for introduction of Japanese wide-band wireless technology i-Burst for field trials in India, joint research on Natural Language Processing by National Institute of Information and Communications Technology (NICT) of Japan and Centre for Development of Advanced Computing (CDAC) of India, and exchange of researchers, software experts and other technical personnel. The two leaders urge their Ministries concerned to pursue actively the identified areas of cooperation. The Japanese side will give consideration to the request for assistance in setting up a National Gigabit Backbone Network in India.

25. The two sides are determined to tackle global energy security issues jointly and direct that the dialogue between their governments be strengthened. They also welcome the Joint Statement regarding cooperation in the hydrocarbon sector signed between the Minister of Petroleum and Natural Gas of India and Minister of Economy, Trade and Industry of Japan in September 2005, the signing of five MOUs and the progress made under them.

26. Recognising the critical importance of securing the energy needs of both countries, the two leaders share the desire to enhance the level and scope of cooperation in the energy sector. They endorse the setting up of an India-Japan Energy Dialogue, co-chaired by Deputy Chairman, Planning Commission of India

and the Minister of the Ministry of Economy, Trade and Industry of Japan, to promote cooperation in the energy sector in a comprehensive manner. The areas covered will include oil and natural gas, coal, electric power, renewable energy sources, energy efficiency and other relevant sectors. The existing forum between The Energy Resources Institute (TERI) of India and New Energy and Industrial Development Organisation (NEDO) of Japan, which was successfully convened for the first time in December 2006, will provide inputs to the Energy Dialogue.

27. The two sides will expand cooperation in energy efficiency through exchange of experts, capacity building and technical cooperation.
28. Recognising the respective strengths of India and Japan in high technology and knowledge economy and the potential benefits of fostering cooperation and also noting the importance of promoting the objectives of non-proliferation, the two leaders decide to launch a consultation mechanism to facilitate bilateral high technology trade and address matters relating to respective export control systems of the two countries.
29. Recognising the importance of intellectual property for economic development, the two leaders confirm that their governments will continue to cooperate in capacity building activities in this area, including in developing human resources.

Science and Technology Initiative

30. The two leaders believe that cooperation in science and technology, including in frontier areas of research and development, constitutes a key element of the strategic partnership between the two countries. The two leaders welcome the holding of the 7th Joint Committee on Science and Technology in November 2005 as well as the India-Japan Science and Technology Initiative Meeting in October 2006. Taking note of the outcome of intensive bilateral consultations in recent months, including the above meetings as well as consultations at the level of the Ministers in charge of Science and Technology, they approve the launching of the following joint projects under the Science and Technology Initiative:

- Joint R&D Programme in areas such as nano-technology, life science and information and communication technology;
- Development of Open Access Database of the available ongoing and prospective research undertaken individually and through joint collaboration in their respective academic, public and industrial institutions; and
- Collaboration in the area of scientific deep sea drilling.

31. The two leaders recognise the importance of strengthening mutually beneficial research collaboration between the relevant organisations of the two countries. In this context, they welcome the signing of the following documents: (i) MOU on cooperation in science and technology between the Department of Science & Technology (DST) of India and RIKEN; and (ii) MOU on scientific cooperation programme between DST and Japan Science and Technology Agency (JST), (in addition to the existing MOU between DST and Japan Society for the Promotion of Science (JSPS) on Core University Programme). The two leaders also welcome the collaboration between the National Institute of Advanced Industrial Science and Technology (AIST) of Japan and Indian research institutions, particularly the Council of Scientific and Industrial Research, DST, Department of Biotechnology and Jawaharlal Nehru Centre for Advanced Scientific Research in advanced industrial science and technology fields, including nano-technology and materials, energy and environment (clean coal and biomass resources), life sciences and information and communication technology.
32. The two leaders note with satisfaction the mutually beneficial cooperation between the Indian Space Research Organisation (ISRO) and the Japan Aerospace Exploration Agency (JAXA) in peaceful uses of outer space. The two leaders reaffirm their keenness to cooperate in such fields as space science, including lunar missions and X-ray astronomy, satellite remote sensing, satellite communication, and disaster management support. They also recognise the importance of capacity building and promotion of regional cooperation in space applications in the Asia Pacific region. In this context, the Japanese side appreciates

the ISRO's decision to participate in the disaster management support system "Sentinel Asia".

33. The two leaders welcome the signing of the agreement on ITER, in which they are partners.

People-to-People Exchanges

34. The two leaders believe that in order to substantiate the India-Japan strategic partnership there must be a quantum increase in cultural, academic and people-to-people exchanges. Such contacts will also build upon the goodwill that exists in the two countries in respect of each other and help raise the profile of India in Japan and of Japan in India. With this larger policy objective in mind, the two leaders endorse a number of initiatives to qualitatively upgrade such contacts.

35. Recognising the important role played by the youth of both countries in fostering closer people-to-people ties, the two leaders launch an 'Investing in the Future Initiative', the main elements of which will, inter alia, consist of the following:
   - The Japanese side will expand the Also programme, announced in January 2006, with the support of the Indian side, with the objective of sponsoring visits of five thousand persons between India and Japan over the next three years in such fields as Japanese language, technology and youth interaction;
   - The Indian side welcomes the designation of India as a target country for the Japan Exchange and Teaching Programme. Exchanges under this programme will be stepped up;
   - The Governments of India and Japan will work together to promote Japanese language studies in India, with a target of 30,000 learners at different levels by the year 2010. The Japanese side welcomes the introduction of Japanese language as an optional foreign language in the secondary school curriculum in India;
   - The two sides will continue promotion of Japanese language in India through Japan Overseas Cooperation Volunteers programme; and

- The Japanese side will assist the Indian side in setting up of Japanese language teaching cells in seven Indian Institutes of Technology and establishing centres of Japanese studies at selected institutions and universities in India.

36. The two leaders welcome the signing of a Memorandum on the development of the Indian Institute of Information Technology for Design and Manufacturing at Jabalpur, with Japanese assistance. The two sides will also make every effort to collaborate towards the development of an Indian Institute of Technology.
37. The two leaders designate the Year 2007 as the "India-Japan Tourism Exchange Year" and direct the Ministries concerned to carry out various activities to promote tourism exchanges. They welcome a Joint Document on expansion of tourism exchanges between the two countries. The Indian side expressed its appreciation for Japanese assistance in development of tourism-related infrastructure, including the Buddhist pilgrimage circuit in India. The two sides will enhance their ongoing cooperation in development of infrastructure at Buddhist sites in India.
38. Noting that civil aviation links between the two countries are a key element for fostering closer economic and people-to-people contacts, the two leaders welcome the positive outcome of bilateral civil aviation talks and direct their respective authorities to expeditiously implement the agreed measures to expand air links commensurate with the requirements of growing economic relations and enhanced tourist flows. The Indian side invites Japanese participation in the development of airports in India through public-private partnership and also under the ODA. The Japanese side will give serious consideration to the idea.
39. Recalling the important role of Nalanda in the ancient period as a leading international university contributing to Buddhist and secular studies, the two sides will explore the idea of re-development of Nalanda as a major centre of learning with the establishment of an international university on the basis of regional cooperation.

40. The two leaders welcome the signing of an MOU on cooperation between the Indian Council for Cultural Relations and the Japan Foundation.
41. The two Prime Ministers welcome the understandings on Sister Province/State relationship reached between Delhi State and Fukuoka Prefecture and Maharashtra State and Okayama Prefecture and encourage further expansion of such twinning arrangements to enhance people-to-people relations and closer economic ties.
42. The two leaders direct the concerned authorities to implement at the earliest the arrangement on the waiver of visas for holders of Diplomatic Passports. They also direct that the simplification of visa procedures to facilitate two-way travel be undertaken as soon as possible.

Regional and Multilateral Cooperation

43. The two leaders confirm their intention to continue to work closely in the East Asia Summit (EAS) framework. While acknowledging the ASEAN as the driving force in the process of creating this new regional architecture, they reaffirm the need for all sixteen EAS countries to fully participate in and actively contribute to the objective of closer cooperation and community building in the region. In this regard, they stress the importance of the development of a roadmap and modalities for the progressive realisation of an East Asian community in the EAS framework.
44. The two leaders reaffirm the need to further promote regional economic integration and, in this context, recall their respective proposals for a Pan Asian Free Trade Area and for a Comprehensive Economic Partnership in East Asia. They decide to cooperate with each other in studies that will take forward these proposals. It is also decided that the two sides will cooperate towards the establishment of the Economic Research Institute for ASEAN and East Asia, which will conduct research, analyse as well as develop policy recommendations to advance the regional economic integration.
45. The two leaders note that the initiative by the G-4 for reforming

the Security Council has brought the issue to the attention of the international community. They further reaffirm the determination to strengthen cooperation and coordination between India and Japan for comprehensive reform of the United Nations, including the expansion of the UN Security Council in both permanent and non-permanent categories to reflect contemporary realities of the world.

46. The two leaders share the view on the usefulness of having dialogue among India, Japan and other like-minded countries in the Asia-Pacific region on themes of mutual interest. The two governments will consult on the modalities.
47. The two sides reiterate their commitment to disarmament and non-proliferation objectives, and their determination to work as partners against proliferation. While expressing their respective positions on the approaches towards the shared goal of achieving a world free of nuclear weapons, they reaffirm that they will continue to promote commonalities and identify areas of convergence for mutual cooperation between them in a constructive manner, contributing to the advancement of overall bilateral relations. In this context, they welcome the First Joint Secretary/Director General level Annual Dialogue on Disarmament and Non-Proliferation, held in New Delhi in May 2006, and confirm that the Second Round of the Dialogue will be held in Tokyo in 2007.
48. The two leaders express serious concern regarding the threat of proliferation of weapons of mass destruction and their delivery systems, which confront the region and the wider world. They reaffirm that India and Japan need to work in a concerted manner to effectively counter these dangers, which imperil their peaceful societies.
49. The two leaders discussed recent events on the Korean Peninsula and shared grave concerns on the nuclear test conducted by DPRK, which has greatly complicated the security situation in the region and highlighted the true extent of clandestine proliferation. The two leaders stress the importance of fully implementing the UN Security Council resolution 1718 and confirm that they will promote practical cooperation towards this end. They welcome the recent progress towards the

resumption of the Six-Party Talks for the denuclearisation of the Korean peninsula, an objective DPRK has also endorsed. They urge that the abduction issue be resolved at the earliest as a humanitarian concern.

50. The two leaders share the view that nuclear energy can play an important role as a safe, sustainable and non-polluting source of energy in meeting the rising global demands for energy, and that international civil nuclear energy cooperation should be enhanced through constructive approaches under appropriate IAEA safeguards. The two sides will continue to discuss the international civil nuclear cooperation framework with respect to India.
51. The two sides will establish Inter-Governmental Consultations on Environment and Climate Change. They will also promote cooperation in Asia-Pacific Partnership on Clean Development and Climate.
52. Recognising that it is a matter of priority for both countries to also strengthen the ability to mitigate damages caused by natural disasters like earthquakes, tsunami and cyclones, the two sides confirm that they will promote mutual cooperation, including through Asian Disaster Reduction Centre, in the field of disaster management in line with the Hyogo Framework of Action.
53. The two Prime Ministers note with satisfaction that India has become a Member of ASEM and Japan an Observer in SAARC. Both countries resolve to work in close consultation in these forums. The Indian side looks forward to Japan's attendance as an Observer at the 14th SAARC Summit in New Delhi in April 2007.
54. The two leaders reaffirm their shared recognition of the importance of strengthening the multilateral trading system. The two countries will make their utmost efforts towards the early conclusion of the WTO Doha Round negotiations as responsible members of the G-6.

Conclusion

55. The two leaders express their conviction that Prime Minister Dr. Manmohan Singh's highly successful Official Visit to Japan

and the decision of the two countries to establish a Strategic and Global Partnership has opened a new chapter in friendly and cooperative relations between them.

56. Prime Minister Dr. Manmohan Singh has extended an invitation to Their Majesties the Emperor and Empress to pay a State Visit to India.
57. Prime Minister Dr. Manmohan Singh thanks the Government and the people of Japan for the warm hospitality accorded to him and his delegation. He has extended a cordial invitation to Prime Minister Mr. Shinzo Abe to pay a return visit to India at a mutually convenient date in 2007. The invitation was accepted with pleasure, with dates to be decided through diplomatic channels.

(Manmohan Singh)	(Shinzo Abe)
Prime Minister of Republic of India	Prime Minister of Japan

Tokyo, December 15, 2006

Appendix III
Joint Statement India-Japan Partnership in a New Asian Era: Strategic Orientation of India-Japan Global Partnership

1. H.E. Mr. Junichiro Koizumi, the Prime Minister of Japan, is currently paying an official visit to India from April 28 to 30, 2005, at the invitation of H.E. Dr. Manmohan Singh, Prime Minister of the Republic of India. The two leaders held in-depth discussions on April 29, during which they covered the entire gamut of bilateral relations as well as regional and international issues of mutual interest. The discussions focussed in particular on adding greater substance to bilateral relations and on measures to further deepen the India-Japan Global Partnership, taking into account the steady development in bilateral relations and the far-reaching changes in the international situation, in particular the new surge of change taking place in Asia.
2. The two leaders recalled that their meeting was taking place in the fifth anniversary year of "India-Japan Global Partnership". Observing that spiritual affinities, enduring cultural contacts, shared commitment to the ideals of democracy, tolerance, pluralism and open society, and a high degree of commonality of political, economic and strategic interests provided a strong basis for a long-term partnership, the two leaders noted the increasing salience of the India-Japan Global Partnership and decided to strengthen it through an Eight-fold Initiative.

The New Asian Era

3. The two leaders reccgnise that the current international situation, characterised by inter-dependence and the advent of globalisation, offers fresh opportunities to both India and Japan for enhanced engagement for mutual benefit. In this context, they expressed

happiness at the rapid transformation taking place in Asia and their confidence in the bright future that lies ahead. A new surge of change, creativity and vitality is transforming Asia, aided by the strengthening of economic linkages, that include bilateral and regional arrangements, initiatives for greater regional integration as well as multilateral trade liberalisation. Asia is now truly emerging as the leading growth centre of the global economy and exerting an ever-greater influence in the global affairs.

4. The two leaders are deeply aware that these developments will shape the future contours of Asian economies and politics. They also share the recognition that peace, stability and development in Asia is indispensable for world peace and development and the future of the world is intimately linked to the future of Asia. The two leaders recognise the need for concerted efforts among Asian countries to translate the positive developments into an 'Arc of Advantage and Prosperity' involving growth, prosperity, stability and closer integration in Asia. They are also aware of the responsibility that the two countries shoulder in this new emerging Asian era and are committed to closely working towards that end.

Common Vision of Partnership

5. India and Japan share a global vision of peace, stability and shared prosperity, based on sustainable development. Shared democratic values and commitment to human rights, pluralism, open society, and the rule of law underpin the global partnership between the two countries. The global partnership between India and Japan reflects a broad convergence of their long-term political, economic and strategic interests, aspirations, objectives and concerns. Japan and India view each other as partners that have responsibility for, and are capable of, responding to global and regional challenges in keeping with their global partnership. A strong, prosperous and dynamic India is, therefore, in the interest of Japan and vice versa. In the above context and in view of the current international situation, the two leaders decided to reinforce the strategic focus of the global partnership between India and Japan.

Expanding Cooperation: New Strategic Focus of Global Partnership

6. As partners in the new Asian era and with this new strategic orientation of their partnership, India and Japan, as two responsible and major players in Asia, and as nations sharing common values and principles, will expand their traditional bilateral cooperation to cooperation in Asia and beyond. With this new focus, India and Japan will be partners in peace, with a common interest in and complementary responsibility for promoting the security, stability and prosperity of Asia as well as in advancing international peace and equitable development.
7. The renewed partnership between India and Japan will feature the following three layers of cooperation:
   - Bilaterally, the two countries will further strengthen their cooperation and pursue an all round and comprehensive development of bilateral relations with a particular and urgent focus on strengthening economic ties through full utilisation of the existing and potential complementarities in their economies;
   - Regionally, the two countries will strive to develop closer dialogue and collaboration to secure peace, stability, and prosperity in Asia, promote democracy and development, and explore a new architecture for closer regional cooperation in Asia; and
   - Globally, the two countries will strengthen cooperation in diverse areas such as environment, energy, disarmament, non-proliferation and security, taking advantage of, and further building on, their strategic convergences.

Eight-fold Initiative for Strengthening India-Japan Global Partnership

8. In order to realise the full potential of their global partnership, the two leaders decided on an Eight-fold Initiative and decided to make their utmost effort to implement this Initiative, which comprises of measures for cooperation in eight key areas of

interaction, namely: (i) enhanced and upgraded dialogue architecture, including strengthening of the momentum of high-level exchanges, launching of a High Level Strategic Dialogue and full utilisation of the existing dialogue mechanisms; (ii) comprehensive economic engagement, through expansion of trade in goods and services, investment flows and other areas of economic cooperation, and exploration of a Japan-India economic partnership agreement; (iii) enhanced security dialogue and cooperation; (iv) Science and Technology Initiative; (v) cultural and academic initiatives and strengthening of people-to-people contacts to raise the visibility and profile of one country in the other; (vi) cooperation in ushering a new Asian era; (vii) cooperation in the United Nations and other international organisations, including cooperation for the early realisation of U.N. reforms, particularly Security Council reform; and (viii) cooperation in responding to global challenges and opportunities. The details of the Eight-fold Initiative are attached herewith.

9. H.E. Prime Minister Koizumi thanked the Government and the people of India for their warm hospitality and extended a cordial invitation to Prime Minister Manmohan Singh to visit Japan at a mutually convenient time. Prime Minister Manmohan Singh accepted the invitation with appreciation. The dates of the visit will be decided through diplomatic channels.

Prime Minister of Japan Prime Minister of the Republic of India

New Delhi, April 29, 2005

Eight-fold Initiative for Strengthening Japan-India Global Partnership

In order to realise the full potential of their global partnership for peace and prosperity, the Prime Minister of India and the Prime Minister of Japan decided on the following Eight-fold Initiative:

1. *One, Enhanced Dialogue and Exchanges*: The two leaders recognise the importance of regular dialogue and exchanges in increasing mutual understanding. They note with satisfaction

in this context that their meeting was the third one between them in a period of one year. They decided to hold annual Prime Minister level meetings, alternately in the two capitals or elsewhere, taking advantage of opportunities at regional and multilateral meetings. They also confirm their intention to promote regular ministerial level exchanges, including those between their Foreign, Defence, Trade, Finance and ICT Ministers. A High Level Strategic Dialogue will also be launched between the two countries. The two sides will fully utilise their existing dialogue mechanisms, and launch an oil and natural gas cooperation dialogue between the Ministry of Petroleum and Natural Gas of India and the Ministry of Economy, Trade and Industry (METI) of Japan.

2. *Two, Comprehensive Economic Engagement*: The two sides will take several measures for broadening and deepening economic and trade cooperation between India and Japan based on the complementarities of the two economies, and decided to work towards quantum increase of the trade volume as well as for diversifying trade.
3. The two leaders directed the India-Japan Joint Study Group (JSG), which is to be launched by June 2005, to submit its report within a year, focusing on measures required for a comprehensive expansion of trade in goods, trade in services, investment flows and other areas of economic relations between the two countries. The JSG will also consider the feasibility of the two countries moving towards a liberalised and upgraded framework for economic engagement, including an India-Japan economic partnership agreement. The Policy Dialogue, which was recently launched between the Ministry of Commerce and Industry of India and METI, will be utilised to identify and implement on a priority basis measures required to remove impediments and facilitate closer economic relations. The JSG comprising of government ministries, business leaders and academics, may take into account inputs provided by this Policy Dialogue.
4. The Governments of India and Japan will make a special effort, in collaboration with the private sector, to encourage higher levels of investment by Japanese companies in India. They will

strengthen technical cooperation to improve the competitiveness of Indian manufacturing industries. The Government of Japan is also prepared to provide every possible support to International Engineering & Technology Fair organised by Confederation of Indian Industry in 2007, exploring the possibility to be a partner country. The Joint Task Force on ICT and the ICT Forum will be utilised to develop a roadmap for increased ICT cooperation, taking into consideration the potential for synergising the advantages of both countries in this field, including the idea of an IT databank.

5. The Government of India highly appreciates the fact that India is the largest recipient of the Japanese Official Development Assistance. The Government of India also notes with appreciation that the Japanese side has committed yen loans of JY 134.5 billion for eight projects in FY 2004, including North Karanpura Super Thermal Power, Delhi Metro and Ganga Action Plan for water purification (Varanasi). It is confirmed that the ODA will continue to be utilised to support India's efforts at accelerated economic development, particularly in priority sectors like infrastructure, including transportation and power, and environment. The Governments of India and Japan agree in principle to resume the Japan Overseas Cooperation Volunteers (JOCVs) scheme in India.
6. Keeping in view the renewed focus of the global partnership and the goal of bringing about a quantum increase in the level of economic engagement, the two sides shared the view that Japan's Special Terms for Economic Partnership (STEP) Scheme could be one of the effective means for carrying out large-scale priority projects in infrastructure sector in India. The two sides confirmed their intention to examine the feasibility of proposals for dedicated multimodal high-axle load freight corridors with computerised train control system on Mumbai-Delhi and Delhi-Howrah routes utilising STEP Scheme and with the inputs of Japanese technology and expertise.
7. The two Governments will work for improved connectivity between the two countries, including through civil aviation links and shipping links. Negotiations to revise the existing tax treaty will be concluded at the earliest possible date.

8. *Three, Enhanced Security Dialogue and Cooperation*: The two leaders recognise the important roles India and Japan play in tackling regional as well as global security challenges. They reaffirm their desire to further develop dialogue and exchanges between the two countries in the security and defence fields, including through full utilisation of the Comprehensive Security Dialogue, Defence Policy Dialogue and Military-to-Military Talks. Service-to-Service exchanges between defence establishments of the two countries will also be strengthened. Recognising the importance of ensuring the safety and security of international maritime traffic, the two leaders directed the coast guards and related agencies of both countries to work together on a sustained basis, including the annual Indian Coast Guard—Japan Coast Guard talks, joint exercises against piracy as well as cooperation through means of information sharing and technical assistance. The Indian Coast Guard and the Japan Coast Guard will commence efforts to establish a framework of effective cooperation. The two leaders, in view of the importance of maritime security, also instructed Indian Navy and the Maritime Self-Defence Force of Japan to enhance their cooperation, including through exchange of views, friendship visits and other similar activities.
9. *Four, Science and Technology Initiative*: India and Japan, as two countries seeking to transform into knowledge-based societies, recognise the importance of science and technology cooperation. The two sides note in particular the areas of their respective strength, and will work together to exploit the enormous potential for cooperation in this field, including in the area of high-technology. They will work together to launch a new Science and Technology Initiative, which will explore possible substantial cooperation in areas such as modern biology, biotechnology and health care, agriculture, hydrocarbon fuels, nano-science and technology, environment, information and communication technology, robotics, alternative sources of energy, etc. The Governments of India and Japan will reinvigorate the India-Japan Joint Committee on Science and Technology Cooperation, the next meeting of which will be held later in 2005, and which will discuss the modalities and

implementation of this new Science and Technology Initiative. The two Governments will also step up cooperation in high technology, including by exploring ways and means to expand high tech trade.

10. *Five, Cultural and Academic Initiatives and Strengthening of People-to-people Contacts:* The two leaders share the view that greater interaction between the peoples, particularly among the youth, provides a stronger basis for the relationship between the two countries. They also recognise the importance of raising the profile of India in Japan and of Japan in India. They firmly believe that cultural and academic initiatives and stronger people-to-people contacts will create the right environment for the leaders of tomorrow to carry forward the vision of the global partnership, and will build upon the goodwill that exists in the two countries in respect of each other.
11. Accordingly, the Governments of India and Japan will work together to promote Japanese language studies in India, with a target of 30,000 learners at different levels in the next five years, and through measures including the introduction of Japanese language as an optional foreign language in Indian secondary school curriculum. In this regard, the Government of Japan welcomes and encourages the Government of India's initiative to establish Centres of Japanese Studies at Indian universities and institutions where Japanese language is being taught and to set up Japanese language teaching cells in seven Indian Institutes of Technology.
12. The Governments of India and Japan will encourage people-to-people exchanges especially among the younger generation, including through student exchange and the Japan Exchange and Teaching Programme, continue promoting cultural and academic exchanges, which will be regularly reviewed and reinforced through the Mixed Cultural Commissions; develop institutional links between the The Indian Council of Cultural Relations and the Japan Foundation and; establish a Japan Cultural Centre of the Japan Foundation in New Delhi and an Indian Cultural Centre in Tokyo; develop tourism related infrastructure including the Buddhist pilgrimage circuit in India with Japanese assistance; enhance two-way tourism and in this

regard, the Japanese Government will dispatch a study mission to India in 2005. The Governments of India and Japan will also introduce a new academic exchange programme involving ten designated educational institutions on either side. The two sides will also make every effort to collaborate towards the development of an Indian Institute of Technology as well as the Indian Institute of Information Technology for Design and Manufacturing, Jabalpur. The two Governments will also hold a Festival of India in Japan and a Festival of Japan in India in 2007/08 to commemorate the 50th anniversary of the Cultural Agreement between India and Japan.

13. *Six, Cooperation in Ushering a New Asian Era*: The two leaders realise and appreciate the importance of the respective roles and responsibilities of their countries in promoting peace, security and prosperity in Asia. Towards this end, they intend to realise an East Asian Community and work together to promote the vision of an Asian Economic Community as an 'Arc of Advantage and Prosperity'. The Japanese side conveyed its decision to support India's membership in the East Asia Summit and the Indian side expressed its appreciation for the Japanese support. The Governments of India and Japan will also cooperate in combating transnational organised crimes, and work together for disaster mitigation, including earthquake, cyclone and tsunami.

14. *Seven, Cooperation in UN and Other International organisations*: The two leaders acknowledge the vital importance of the role of the United Nations in world peace, stability, and prosperity, and reaffirm their intention to work together for the early realisation of U.N. reforms, particularly Security Council reform. They also stress the importance of revitalisation of the General Assembly, as it represents the general will of all Member States, as well as the importance of enhancing the efficiency of the U.N. agencies and organs in the social and economic fields in order to effectively address urgent challenges. In this connection, they stress the importance of taking a decision on Security Council reform before the Summit in September 2005, as the Secretary-General recommended. They note with satisfaction the on-going cooperation between

India and Japan, including in the G-4 setting, to bring about reform of the U.N. Security Council, by expanding the membership of both permanent and non-permanent categories, to make the U.N. more representative, more credible and more effective. They reiterate their support for each other's candidature, based on the firmly shared recognition that India and Japan are legitimate candidates for permanent membership in an expanded Security Council. They also stress the importance of moving the process forward through consultation with a wide range of like-minded countries, and decide to strengthen their cooperation for this.

15. The Governments of India and Japan will also expand and enrich their cooperation in other international organisations, including in the WTO. The two Governments will work together to achieve the objectives enshrined in the Doha Work Programme of August 1, 2004. As key players in global economic management, the two Governments support an open, fair, equitable and transparent rule-based multilateral trade system and intend to work together to preserve stability and growth in the global economy.
16. *Eight, Responding to International Challenges*: Recognising the threat posed by terrorism and the importance of the international community working unitedly to counter this menace, the Governments of India and Japan will further consolidate their existing cooperation, both bilaterally and in various international fora. The India-Japan Joint Working Group on Counter-Terrorism will hold its first meeting soon to identify possible future areas of cooperation.
17. The Governments of India and Japan will also work as partners against proliferation. While expressing their respective positions on the approaches towards the shared goal of achieving a world free of nuclear weapons, the two Governments affirm that they will seek to promote commonalities and identify areas of convergence for mutual cooperation between them in a constructive manner, contributing to the advancement of overall bilateral relations.
18. The two Governments will also strengthen their energy and environmental cooperation, including on sustainable

development and environmentally sound technologies. In doing so, they will ensure increased focus on energy security, energy efficiency, conservation, and pollution-free fuels. They will also cooperate in the hydrocarbons sector in the areas such as exploration and production, and downstream projects including in third countries as well as on improving Asian oil markets and increasing investments in Asian energy infrastructure.

Index